POETRY OF THIS AGE

By the same author

Criticism

ROBERT BROWNING
A HISTORY OF WESTERN LITERATURE

Anthologies

COMIC AND CURIOUS VERSE
MORE COMIC AND CURIOUS VERSE
YET MORE COMIC AND CURIOUS VERSE
THE PENGUIN BOOK OF SPANISH VERSE

Translations

SELECTED POEMS OF BORIS PASTERNAK
DON QUIXOTE
PÉREZ GALDÓS: TORMENT
EIGHT TALES OF HOFFMAN
THE CONFESSIONS OF JEAN-JACQUES ROUSSEAU
RABELAIS: GARGANTUA AND PANTAGRUEL
THE LIFE OF ST. TERESA, BY HERSELF
MONTAIGNE: ESSAYS

J. M. COHEN

Poetry of This Age

1908–1958

HUTCHINSON OF LONDON

HUTCHINSON & CO. (*Publishers*) LTD.
178–202 Great Portland Street, London, W.1

London Melbourne Sydney
Auckland Bombay Toronto
Johannesburg New York

First published 1960
Second Impression November 1960

*This book has been set in Times type
face. It has been printed in Great Britain on
Antique Wove paper by Taylor Garnett
Evans & Co. Ltd., Watford, Herts, and
bound by them*

for

RACHEL LEVY

CONTENTS

PREFACE

As an introduction to modern poetry this book takes plenty of risks. In the first place its choice of poets is of course personal. I have chosen about three dozen as the greatest number that a small book like this can treat at all adequately. This of course does not mean that these seem to me the only significant poets of the last fifty years. They are, however, in my opinion the most important; and if I have left out others whose work my readers may consider equally attractive, it is rather from lack of space than lack of interest. I have taken care not to clutter up my text with lists of near-inclusions. Anyone who begins to explore the work of those I have chosen will quickly widen his reading to include some of those whom I have omitted.

I have moreover limited myself to the six principal languages of Europe and America. I think that the best poetry of the last fifty years has in fact been written in these. But since they are the only modern languages I can read in the original, this limitation has been forced upon me. It is impossible to come to any firm conclusions about a poet known only from translations.

My quotations are given in the original with a simple prose rendering at the foot of the page. This will enable anyone with the slightest knowledge of the poet's language to catch something of his rhythms and verbal patterns, which would be lost in even the best verse translation. I have had to make an exception, however, in the case of Russian, where English versions have to do duty for the originals. I trust that sufficient of Blok's and Pasternak's original quality will come over to give some understanding and some enjoyment to those without Russian.

Some passages and judgements are taken from articles contributed over the last eight years to the *Times Literary Supplement*. I am grateful to the Editor and to the Times Publishing Company for permission to make fresh use of them. I am grateful also to Miss Rachel Levy and to my son Mark for reading my first typescript and giving many valuable suggestions which have been incorporated in the second draft.

J.M.C.
October 1958

9

A*

I

Le Frisson Nouveau

'Vous dotez le ciel de l'art d'on ne sait quel rayon macabre', wrote Victor Hugo in a letter congratulating Baudelaire on *Les Fleurs du Mal* of 1857, 'vous créez un frisson nouveau'.[1] Hugo had himself for fifty years endeavoured to arouse new thrills, and the supernatural was a device that had been exploited not only by himself and his generation, but by writers as far back as the middle of the eighteenth century. Swedenborg had described his experiences on the borders of the unknown, and the Gothick novelists, in their endeavour to provide 'pleasing thrills'—to use Horace Walpole's words—had set the ghosts walking through many a deserted manor long before Baudelaire began to write of a new kind of strangeness, which he did not attempt to make 'pleasing'.

Baudelaire, indeed, provided a new thrill, which shocked and horrified a Paris used to ghost stories and literary dabblings in the occult. For where E. T. A. Hoffmann and others had described the external marvels and perils which a man might meet and over which he might triumph, Baudelaire presented his own mind and heart as a ghostly limbo from which there was no escape into another and more comfortable world. He in fact *internalized* the supernatural, substituting the thrill of psychological complexity for the outworn devices of hauntings and psychic appearances.

The romantic poet—Shelley, Hugo, Byron—saw himself as a hero, the successor to Prometheus or Hercules. Though society rejected him, he believed that he had been chosen to bring it great benefits, to acquaint it with the powers of inspiration, and even to perform the labours of political leader and prophet. Whatever his

[1] You have thrown an indescribable and eerie light into the artistic sky. You are creating a new thrill.

11

doubts about the external world, he unhesitatingly believed in himself as a figure of undivided purpose, capable of decisive criticism and action.

Baudelaire too was to some extent his own hero. He was, at the same time a surgeon performing an autopsy upon himself, but not upon society. For the subject of his poetry was invariably himself, not as a single hero but as a divided man. One of the most revealing of his self-dissections is to be found in 'La Voix', not otherwise one of the more important poems in *Les Fleurs du Mal*. The division is immediately stated by the conflicting voices that speak to the child brought up on the dust and ashes of the classical past:

> Mon berceau s'adossait à la bibliothèque,
> Babel sombre, où roman, science, fabliau,
> Tout, la centre latine et la poussière grecque,
> Se mêlaient. J'étais haut comme un in-folio.
> Deux voix me parlaient. L'une, insidieuse et ferme,
> Disait: 'La Terre est un gâteau plein de douceur;
> Je puis (et ton plaisir serait alors sans terme!)
> Te faire un appétit d'une égale grosseur.'
> Et l'autre; 'Viens! oh! viens voyager dans les rêves,
> Au delà du possible, au delà du connu!'[1]

The poet has no doubt which voice to follow. Even boundless pleasure and equally boundless appetite to enjoy it are less attractive than a life of dreams. Byron would have accepted the sweet cake and consumed it with a chosen companion among the Greek Isles; Hugo would have feasted upon it with his family and friends, interrupting his pleasure at times to vituperate against some favourite enemy; Shelley would have rejected it for some quintessential nectar on which the spirits feed. But Baudelaire prefers a voyage of discovery beyond the frontiers of possibility and knowledge. And this journey is not an outward exploration of nature or society, but a descent into the depths of his own heart. It is from this moment of choice, he says, that he dates his 'wound' and his 'evil destiny':

---

[1] My cradle backed on the library, a dark Babel in which romance, science and story, everything, the ashes of Rome and the dust of Greece, were mixed. I was the size of a folio. Two voices addressed me. The first, insidious and assured, said: 'Earth is a cake full of sweetness. I can (and your pleasure would then be boundless!) give you an appetite of the same size'. And the other said: 'Come, oh come and travel in dream, beyond the possible, beyond the known!'

> C'est d'alors
> Que date ce qu'on peut, hélas, nommer ma plaie
> Et ma fatalité. Derrière les décors
> De l'existence immense, au plus noir de l'abîme,
> Je vois distinctement des mondes singuliers,
> Et de ma clairvoyance extatique victime,
> Je traîne des serpents qui mordent mes souliers[1]

The poem's imagery is ill-assorted; the 'wound' is a clinical comparison that will be repeated by many modern poets down to W. H. Auden, who in his early poetry addresses it ironically as a pampered and rather tiresome friend, and to Eliot's 'wounded surgeon' in 'East Coker'. But the Bacchante's snakes seem to have crept down from the library shelves behind the infant's cradle. The modern poet will prove not an ecstatic victim but a perplexed interpreter of his rare moments of clairvoyance.

Baudelaire carries his claim further, and compares himself to the prophets who, like him, loved the desert and the sea-shore, thus calling up associations with the Desert Fathers. But with clairvoyance and prophecy goes also a certain naivety. So deep is this vision that often the poet confuses fact with illusion, and with his eyes on the sky stumbles as he walks. His voice, however, comforts him with the assurance that this too brings a benefit:

> Garde tes songes;
> Les sages n'en ont pas d'aussi beaux que les fous.'[2]

Clairvoyant, prophet, fool, and dreamer, Baudelaire is, nevertheless, no dweller in artificial paradises; these would be as tasteless to him as the cloying cake of worldly pleasure. The two themes that occur most constantly in his poetry are those of the voyage over unknown seas, and the search among childhood memories for some secret innocence, long ago forgotten:

> le vert paradis des amours enfantines,
> Les courses, les chansons, les baisers, les bouquets,
> Les violons vibrants derrière les collines,
> Avec les brocs de vin, le soir, dans les bosquets.[3]

Here once more the despised library has given the poet his imagery. For this is the classical Arcadia, the shepherds' Sicily

---

[1] It is from then that there dates what can, alas, be called my wound and my evil destiny. Behind the backcloth of vast existence, in the blackest of the pit, I clearly see strange worlds, and as the ecstatic victim of my own clairvoyance, I drag snakes behind me that bite at my shoes.

[2] Preserve your dreams; fools have more beautiful dreams than the wise.

[3] The green paradise of childish loves, the races, the songs, the kisses. the bunches of flowers, the violins thrumming behind the hills, and jugs of wine at evening in the woods.

of Theocritus, the *Déjeuner sur l'herbe*, recalled by Baudelaire's contemporary Edouard Manet. In Manet's picture the theme of innocence is treated more simply; the naked and the clothed sit unselfconsciously side by side. But into Baudelaire's vision enters the same division as in his other poems. For his is not only the green paradise of childish lovers; it is also, paradoxically,

L'innocent paradis plein de plaisirs furtifs.[1]

Poets of the past, Shelley, Wordsworth, Hugo, had looked back on childhood as an age when intimations of the spiritual world were clear and direct. Among lesser writers there had grown up a sentimentality that led to the later mawkishnesses of *Peter Pan*. But Baudelaire remembered not only the innocent picnics of his childhood, but also the premature intimations of adulthood that accompanied them.

Doubt and contradiction pervade not only the memories of the new writer who purveys *le frisson nouveau*, and his own view of himself. They also affect his attitude to the act of poetic creation. Gautier, an elder contemporary of Baudelaire, saw the ideal poem as one of ever increasing clarity. The more difficult the material, the greater the need of craftsmanship. To him, a man of uncomplicated attitudes, complex thought, such as Baudelaire's, would have provided a special challenge to clarity. For only perfection of utterance could possess eternity:

Oui, l'œuvre sort plus belle
D'une forme au travail
   Rebelle,
Vers, marbre, onyx, émail.

Point de contraintes fausses!
Mais que pour marcher droit
   Tu chausses,
Muse, un cothurne étroit.

Fi du rhythme commode,
Comme un soulier trop grand,
   Du mode
Que tout pied quitte et prend![2]

[1] The innocent paradise full of furtive pleasures.

[2] Yes, the work of art emerges more beautiful from a form which resists working, verse, marble, onyx, enamel.
No false constraints! But to walk straight, Muse, put on a narrow buskin.
Shame on the easy rhythm, like a shoe that is too large, of a kind that every foot can put on and take off.

Baudelaire aimed at no such formal perfection, and hardly any poets since his day have attempted to conform to Gautier's ideal. The tendency has been to make the line conform to the thought, and reproduce the turns, obscurities and contradictions of a complex argument in language as broken and baffling. Licence for this predominant difficulty, which has robbed modern poetry of so many readers, was given by Paul Verlaine, a disciple of Baudelaire, whose defence of his own not very difficult style was conceived as an answer to Gautier's call for formal perfection. Its scorn for rhyme—though Verlaine was a master of rhyme—its praise of imprecision, and its assault on rhetoric, provide a theoretical justification for much modern poetry which deliberately matches imprecision of thought with imprecision of language and, in its swift colloquial changes of mood and stress, seeks to represent a mind reaching out towards experiences for which satisfactory words hardly exist. These lines of Verlaine apply more fittingly to the intricacies of Rilke, Eliot or the Italian, Eugenio Montale, than to his own poetry of simple nuance:

> Il faut aussi que tu n'ailles point
> Choisir tes mots sans quelque méprise:
> Rien de plus cher que la chanson grise
> Où l' Indécis au Précis se joint. . . .
>
> Prends l'éloquence et tords lui son cou!
> Tu feras bien, en train d'énergie,
> De rendre un peu la Rime assagie.
> Si l'on n'y veille, elle ira jusqu'ou?[1]

Baudelaire himself made no break with the formal conventions; many of his lines recall lines of equal psychological subtlety in Racine. His scorn for antiquity was greatly overstated. It was in his choice of moments from the past, in his greater sympathy for Rome's decadence than for her prime, that he differed from the poets of previous centuries. As one of the first of the self-styled Decadents, he felt a special affinity with the Empire in its decadence, since he suspected that he too was living towards the end of a cycle of civilization.

---

[1] Also you must be a little scornful in choosing your words: there is nothing more precious than the grey song where indecision is joined with precision. . . . Take eloquence and wring its neck! You will do well while you are about it to give Rhyme a little correction. To what lengths will it go if we do not watch it?

Despite the decline of classical reading and the more extensive knowledge of history and science that have changed our culture in the last hundred years, the attitude of the modern poet to the Greco-Latin inheritance has certainly not been one of neglect. The ancient myths and the literature of Greece and Rome continue to provide them with subjects, since they set out the archetypal situations which each poet has felt compelled to reinterpret in terms of his own fresh insights. Rilke's *Sonnets to Orpheus*, Yeats's variations on Sophoclean themes, Pound's Greek and Latin reconstructions, Valéry's refinements on Greek philosophical thought, are examples that readily come to mind. It is in their choice among the ancient masters that poets since Baudelaire have differed from those of the eighteenth and early nineteenth centuries. They no longer think of the classical ideal as one of faultless perfection; a grinning Tanagra figurine seems to them to represent the Greek spirit more perfectly than a Laocoon in the formal agony of his battle with the serpents.

One of the last French poets to accept the older classical values, and to remain unaffected by the modern division of mind and purpose, José-Maria de Hérédia, wrote sonnets of a technical perfection that conformed to Gautier's ideal, in each of which he drew, as on a medal, some scene to typify an aspect of the ancient past. It is noteworthy that he came to this past almost as a stranger, having been born in Cuba. His sonnet 'Antoine et Cléopatre' presents, therefore, an outsider's view of a historical moment seen as a picture, into which feeling and movement hardly enter before the last line:

Tous deux ils regardaient, de la haute terrasse,
L'Egypte s'endormir sous un ciel étouffant
Et le Fleuve, à travers le Delta noir qu'il fend,
Vers Bubaste ou Saïs rouler son onde grasse.

Et le Romain sentait sous la lourde cuirasse,
Soldat captif berçant le sommeil d'un enfant,
Ployer et défaillir sur son cœur triomphant
Le corps voluptueux que son étreinte embrasse.

Tournant son tête pâle entre ses cheveux bruns
Vers lui qu'enivraient d'invincibles parfums,
Elle tendit sa bouche et ses prunelles claires;

Et sur elle courbé, l'ardent Impérator

Vit dans les larges yeux étoilés de points d'or
Toute une mer immense où fuyaient des galères.[1]

The poet seems to stand aside from his subject. The classical
names, the Latinate conventionality of the adjectives, the
deliberate introduction of the ancient word Imperator, all remove
the poem from its own century into a past so remote that even the
prophecy of its last line hardly brings it nearer to the present day.
Shakespeare's Cleopatra, by contrast, requires no archaeological
substantiation; she is contemporary and timeless; the gods are
introduced only to be eclipsed:

> The barge she sat in, like a burnish'd throne,
> Burn'd on the water; the poop was beaten gold,
> Purple the sails, and so perfumèd that
> The winds were love-sick with them, the oars were silver,
> Which to the tune of flutes kept stroke, and made
> The water which they beat to follow faster,
> As amorous of their strokes. For her own person,
> It beggar'd all description; she did lie
> In her pavilion — cloth-of-gold of tissue —
> O'er-picturing that Venus where we see
> The fancy outwork nature: on each side her
> Stood pretty-dimpled boys, like smiling Cupids,
> With divers-coloured fans, whose wind did seem
> To glow the delicate cheeks, which they did cool,
> And what they undid did.

While the Hérédia sonnet is lifted out of realism by the
sudden widening of the panorama and the hint of magical
divination in its conclusion, Enobarbus's speech attains the same
effect from the beginning by the use of luxuriant metaphor.
These are respectively the Classical and the Baroque way of
arousing that thrill which Hugo admired in Baudelaire. The
modern poet, however, in building up a similar scene, presents it
on two levels at once. True to the division which he has recognized in his own mind, he is painter and commentator at once;

[1] From the high terrace, they both watched Egypt sleeping beneath a stifling sky,
and the river rolling its oily waves towards Bubastis or Sais, through the black Delta
that it divides.
    And beneath his heavy armour, the Roman, a captive soldier cradling a child's
slumber, felt the voluptuous body grasped in his embrace yielding and fainting on his
triumphant heart.
    Turning her head, pale amid her dark hair, towards him who was maddened by
irresistible perfumes, she offered her mouth and her clear eyes.
    And bent over her, the passionate Imperator saw in her wide eyes, starred with
golden specks, a whole vast sea on which galleys were in flight.

the scene is presented, and with it, as an ironic frame, a statement of the context in which he sees it. The second section of T. S. Eliot's 'Waste Land' begins with a reference to Enobarbus's opening.

> The Chair she sat in, like a burnished throne,
> Glowed on the marble.

This, like the recital of place-names in Hérédia's first lines, suggests the timeless majesty of the scene. Virgil produced a similar effect by writing lines that recalled passages from Homer. But Eliot is not describing heroic actions; he is presenting a modern situation of uncertainty, contradiction and doubt. Therefore, ironically, he introduces references to a number of poets of the past, building his scene out of acknowledged borrowings from Milton, Virgil and Ovid. But where Hérédia and Virgil are certain of their respectful attitude to the past, Eliot uses legend as a comment on actuality, and the patter of the everyday pub and street-corner as a method of casting disrespect on the present. He portrays a kept woman's luxury in terms of Cleopatra's barge, and introduces only the representation of a classical scene in a tapestry on her wall, to hint at a different set of values that cannot make its voice heard at the present day:

> Above the antique mantel was displayed
> As though a window gave upon the sylvan scene
> The change of Philomel, by the barbarous king
> So rudely forced; yet there the nightingale
> Filled all the desert with inviolable voice
> And still she cried, and still the world pursues,
> 'Jug Jug' to dirty ears.

The strength of the poem lies in its contrasts and parallels. This is the same world as that in which Ovid wrote the tale of Philomel, but it is also the world of a perplexed woman who lives in luxury and can understand nothing:

> My nerves are bad to-night. Yes, bad. Stay with me.
> Speak to me. Why do you never speak. Speak.

Contrast and parallel also heighten the effect of Lorca's poems about the feud between the Gipsies and the Civil Guard, sordid squabbles that are raised to poetry by their primæval quality. For similar bands have fought similar knife-battles in

Andalusia ever since the Punic wars, and the judge who rides down to count the dead and record the event is so timeless a figure that he cannot remember what parties it is that have been fighting:

El juez, con guardia civil,
por los olivares viene.
Sangre resbalada gime
muda canción de serpiente.
—Señores guardias civiles:
aqui pasó lode siempre.
Han muerto cuatro romanos
y cinco cartagineses.[1]

This Lorca passage illustrates another deliberate confusion in modern poetry: the substitution of one kind of sense perception for another. The spilt blood becomes audible, thus suggesting the groans of the dying men, which are not otherwise heard; and the red trickle on the ground is described not by its colour but by its imaginary silent song, by its failure in fact to make any sound at all. This exchange between aural and visual impressions is a sign of the exhaustion of language. Had Lorca described the blood of the dying men as red, and its trickle as snakelike, he would have been repeating a conventional effect, and would have failed to strike the reader's imagination. A similar device or conceit, was used in the seventeenth century, especially in Spain, by poets trying to rival the hyperbole of the great masters of the Renaissance. This is one of the features of the Gongoristic style. Thus the minor poet Gabriel Bocángel compares a trumpet's sound over the sea to the flight of an invisible metal bird.

Clearly in a poetry concerned with comment rather than description, the mind, which co-ordinates the findings of the senses, can be permitted to draw on all four indiscriminately, and to jumble their messages. Some modern poets—Edith Sitwell and Wallace Stevens in particular—have attempted to develop the idea of *correspondances*, first put forward by Baudelaire, and to make sound alone suggest associations and feelings. Rimbaud, in his sonnet 'Voyelles', drew up a list of supposed universal relationships between colour and sound:

A noir, E blanc, I rouge, U vert, O bleu[2]

[1] The judge comes with the civil guard through the olive plantations. . . . Slippery blood groans its silent snake's song—Gentlemen of the civil guard, this is the same old story. Four Romans have been killed and five Carthaginians.

[2] A black, E white, I red, U green, O blue

and concluded by assigning to the long O of the Greeks a mystical significance like that attributed by the Hindus to the divine syllable AUM:

> O, suprême clairon plein de strideurs étranges,
> Silences traversés des Mondes et des Anges:
> —O l'Omega, rayon violet de Ses Yeux![1]

More recent poets, however, have resorted to this confusion of the senses only sporadically using it as a means of avoiding a stock association between noun and adjective or in order to administer a special shock to the reader.

The poet's divided mind, his political disillusion, his claim to clairvoyance, his changed attitude to the past, his different ideal of artistic perfection, and the confusion of his senses all contribute to the *frisson nouveau*, which poetry has continued to arouse in its readers from Baudelaire's time to that of Eugenio Montale, Dylan Thomas, and even younger poets of the present decade. But two even more revolutionary changes have occurred since Baudelaire's time, which have carried modern poetry far beyond the point at which Hugo saw it when he so generously welcomed *Les Fleurs du Mal*. In the century since 1857, the poet's attitude both to language and to time have fundamentally altered.

Baudelaire's poetry, as has been noted, was both formally and in its vocabulary completely traditional. Even his prose poems, *Le Spleen de Paris*, do not advance beyond the stage of lyrical prose already reached by de Quincey and Poe and by sundry minor writers of prose poems in France. It was principally in England that the demand was heard for a poetic diction close to that of popular speech. Wordsworth had advocated it, but failed to find it. Byron had often found it, but failed to advocate it. Tennyson and Arnold had returned to the grand style, and Browning, anxious though he was to extend the resources of his medium, was fatally hampered by his addiction to the Elizabethan blank verse line. Even when he is most inventive, his verse follows the rhythms of literature, not of speech.

The one example of a poet who had broken with the forms, the rhythms and the language of tradition was Walt Whitman,

[1] O, highest trumpet, full of strange stridencies, silences crossed by Worlds and Angels: O Omega, violet beam of His Eyes!

whose freedoms greatly attracted various minor French poets of
the generation that followed Baudelaire. But his style could not
be aped. Though it acted as an encouragement to the inventors of
vers-libre, which has been the predominant measure of modern
poetry, Whitman's example could only have been followed by a
poet sufficiently convinced of his message to let it dictate its
own rhetoric.

> Ages, precedents, have long been accumulating undirected
> materials,
> America brings builders, and brings its own styles.
> The immortal poets of Asia and Europe have done their work and
> pass'd to other spheres,
> A work remains, the work of surpassing all they have done.

A new poetry that saw itself to be at the end of an epoch
could not use a voice of such confidence, Whitman was too little
concerned with half-lights and contradictions, too insensitive to
the details of poetic texture to be a fit model for the new poets of
France, which had been humbled and depressed by the war of
1870, or of a Europe moving towards an epoch of disastrous
wars and revolutions. Only two twentieth-century poets owe any
considerable debt to Whitman, Vladimir Mayakovsky and
Pablo Neruda, and both, as Communists, have believed themselves to be, like Whitman, heralds of a new age.

The new poetic language and rhythms owe far more to the
lesser French poet of the 'eighties, Jules Laforgue, than to
Browning or Whitman. Laforgue, a sensitive ironist with an ear
for folk-song, music-hall patter and the new slang of the cities,
perfected in his last poems the subtly cadenced line that Eliot
took over from him for 'Prufrock', and that was adapted also by
such French poets as Guillaume Apollinaire a year or two earlier.

Laforgue's is the strength of a sound compromise. Neither
rhyme nor rhythm is abandoned. But the rhyme is no longer part
of a regular scheme, and sometimes yields to assonance or
alliteration. The pattern of sound, in fact, is applied evenly to a
whole passage rather than at certain fixed points in it: and this
practice has been developed by subsequent poets as various as
Neruda and Dylan Thomas. But this tendency has been greatly
strengthened in England by the influence of Gerard Manley
Hopkins and of the alliterative Anglo-Saxon and Middle English

verse from which he developed his techniques. Laforgue's strictly cadenced *vers-libre*, however, with its train of allusions and broken rhythms, still appears as original and contemporary as it did when it was written. No innovators have succeeded in making his magnificent poem on the coming of winter appear less exciting.

Allons, allons, et hallali!
C'est l'Hiver bien connu qui s'amène;
Oh! les tournants des grandes routes,
Et sans petit Chaperon Rouge qui chemine!...
Oh! leurs ornières des chars de l'autre mois,
Montant en don quichottesques rails
Vers les patrouilles des nuées en déroute
Que le vent malmène vers les transatlantiques bercails!
Accélerons, accélerons, c'est la saison bien connue, cette fois.
Et le vent, cette nuit, il en a fait de belles!
Ô dégats, ô nids, ô modestes jardinets!
Mon coeur et mon sommeil: ô échos des cognées!... [1]

It is the same sound of axes as in the last act of *The Cherry Orchard*. Laforgue is a poet of endings and memories. He looks back to childhood with the same divided feelings as Baudelaire. He remembers a freshness of vision, but with it the boredom of a recurrent refrain, the constant repetition of tuneless scales practised behind closed shutters on hot Sunday evenings. His prevailing mood is ironic, his habitual gesture a shrug and a wry smile. Yet philosophically, he is a courageous poet, able to accept the nothingness of much that is generally accepted as reality, and yet to pursue some ultimate meaning behind that blank façade.

Laforgue's vision of time is of some cyclic repetition in which the same events, recalling the same incidents from literature, fairy tale or childhood, return and return, bringing ever increasing boredom. The panorama of time has closed in on the modern poet. There is for him only the moment of intense experience; all the rest is memory or foreboding. A sonnet by Edwin Muir crystallizes a situation that owes something of its intensity to

[1] Forward, forward, and away! It is the usual winter coming on. O bends in the high roads, without Little Red Riding Hood walking there!... Oh their ruts of last year's carts, climbing like quixotic rails towards the retreating cloud patrols, that are harried by the wind towards transatlantic folds! Hurry, hurry, this time it is the familiar season, and tonight the wind has done some fine work! O destruction! O nests, O modest gardens! My heart and my slumber: O echoes of axes!...

familiarity with the new physics of relativity, but more to the modern poet's inability to believe, as Hugo or Tennyson believed, in a possible betterment of human conditions by means of man-guided progress. Muir describes man's situation as one in which—to quote the title of his poem—'There is Nothing there but Faith':

> Nothing, it seemed, between them and the grave.
> No, as I looked, there was nothing anywhere.
> You'd think no ground could be so flat and bare:
> No little ridge or hump or bush to brave
> The horizon. Yet they called that land their land,
> Without a single thought drank in that air
> As simple and equivocal as despair.
> This, this was what I could not understand.
> The reason was, there was nothing there but faith.
> Faith made the whole, yes all they could see or hear
> Or touch or think, and arched its break of day
> Within them and around them every way.
> They looked: all was transfigured far and near,
> And the great world rolled between them and death.

The landscape and the situation echo those of Browning's 'Childe Roland to the Dark Tower came'. Yet here the incidents of the knight's journey, the hideous scapegoat horse, the brothers who had been overthrown in the same ordeal, even the hint of a spectral adversary, are absent. What remains is a timeless moment in the experience of a nameless *they*, in which the possession of faith turned defeat into victory. This is the moment that most concerns contemporary religious poets. They do not treat of belief and disbelief as Browning did in 'Christmas Eve' and 'Easter Day', but of the sudden presence or absence of faith or vision. T. S. Eliot's glimpse of a hidden reality in 'Ash Wednesday', which foreshadows a similar moment in the rose garden in 'Burnt Norton', may seem to express a positive and unshakable faith acquired in an instant:

> The silent sister veiled in white and blue
> Between the yews, behind the garden god,
> Whose flute is breathless, bent her head and signed
>   but spoke no word.

Yet a line or two later comes the return to the unenlightened level of common living:

> And after this our exile.

In the same way the departure of just such a vision leads the Spanish poet Miguel de Unamuno to ask his despairing question at the end of his poem 'Hermosura':

> La noche cae, despierto,
> me vuelve la congoja,
> la espléndida vision se ha derretido,
> vuelvo a ser hombre.
> Y ahora dime, Senor, dime al oído:
> tanta hermosura
> ¿ matará nuestra muerte?[1]

Neither poet is concerned with dogma, or with questions of belief and disbelief. What matters to both is the glimpse of the 'still point of the turning world', the central experience of the mystic. To Eliot it brings assurance, followed by a resigned return to the common level of living, while Unamuno's moment of insight only plunges him deeper into the anxious questionings of the divided man. But the preoccupation of both is with the mystical approach, whereas that of the nineteenth-century poet was with institutional religion.

The *frisson nouveau* has thus brought not only a new way of feeling, a new attitude of the poet to himself, but also a new attitude to religious truth. Though many contemporary religious poets belong in name to the Roman Church, their standpoint as poets is essentially a Protestant one. What most preoccupies them is the individual's experience of God outside time, and without reference to theology or creed.

---

[1] Night falls, I awake, my anxiety returns, the splendid vision has melted away, I am a man once more. And now tell me, Lord, tell me in my ear: Can all this beauty abolish our death?

2

Different kinds of failure

Were there a Muse of modern poetry—and perhaps one of those many-faced stony figures with enigmatic features in Picasso's *Atelier du Peintre* may serve for one—she must many times have repeated those despairing lines in 'East Coker', in which T. S. Eliot states his difficulties of expression. For these are difficulties which he shares with most of the poets of his age:

> So here I am, in the middle way, having had twenty years—
> Twenty years largely wasted, the years of *l'entre deux guerres*—
> Trying to learn to use words, and every attempt
> Is a wholly new start, and a different kind of failure
> Because one has only learnt to get the better of words
> For the thing one no longer has to say, or the way in which
> One is no longer disposed to say it. And so each venture
> Is a new beginning, a raid on the inarticulate
> With shabby equipment always deteriorating
> In the general mess of imprecision of feeling.

Eliot's verdict on his achievement is an excessively severe one. Every poet since Baudelaire has been conscious that the equipment he has inherited from the great poets of the past is shabby, if not worn out. But, as has been pointed out in the last chapter, new measures have been invented and new resources of vocabulary explored by the poets of the last hundred years. It is not so much that the equipment has deteriorated, but that the demands upon it are very much greater than those made by Wordsworth and Keats, Hugo, Tennyson and Heine. For the poetry of the divided man needs to be psychologically far subtler than that of the outward-looking poets of the past. We have returned to a situation roughly parallel to that of the seventeenth century when only the exceptional insight can be translated into a poem, and when the enthusiasms, the aspirations and the regrets, that

25

were the material of the sixteenth century and of the nineteenth century, fail to convince either poet or reader. Hence the unequal race which Eliot describes between technical ingenuity and an increased insight into the complexities of experience. The last fifty years of European poetry have seen several 'raids on the inarticulate', attempts like that of the surrealists to tap inspiration at a deeper source than the waking consciousness can comprehend. But on the whole modern poets have probably kept up with the increasing demand on their powers of expression. It is the reader, whose taste has been trained on the far less complex styles of the nineteenth-century giants, who has been left behind. Yet none of the greater modern poets is more difficult than Shakespeare or Donne, whose lines also abound in secondary meanings, allusions and paradoxes; and certainly the situation has not deteriorated in the present century. For both Mallarmé and Rimbaud wrote poems from which it is more difficult to extract a simple statement than from Eliot, Apollinaire or Dylan Thomas.

The failure to communicate, of which Eliot complains, is only a partial one. Intellectually we may be unable to trace the logical development of such a poem as Thomas's 'A Winter's Tale', but the rhythms and the imagery have a logic of their own which supplies its own solution; Thomas has 'got the better of words' in his own way.

The age of anxiety, of analysis, unease and catastrophe, which first found full expression in *Les Fleurs du Mal*, can from the standpoint of poetry be divided into two halves: the first covering that half-century during which the modern movement was confined to France, and the second, beginning around 1908, when the poets of other countries began to adapt the new styles to their own needs. It is the last fifty years of experiment and expansion that this book is designed to cover.

That the age of anxiety should first strike France is not surprising. Politically the country's decline began with the Terror, the Napoleonic adventure, and the exhaustion that followed Waterloo. A culture and a ruling class had been overthrown, and the dictatorship of taste now rested with a small and hectic urban society, whose standards were chiefly those of fashion. In the last century new styles have been almost as frequent in Paris, the centre of France's poetry as well as of her *haute couture*, as new hats and waist-lines. But other kingdoms were threatened by decay, war and revolution, in particular those like Austria and Russia, which were unable to adapt a torpid society to an increasing need for guided change. France's nineteenth-century decline was hastened by her failure to industrialize at the same rate as Britain, Germany and the United States; Austria and Russia met with break-up and revolution because they failed to industrialize at all.

One of the principal themes of the modern poet has therefore been the break-up of a society from which he has felt himself increasingly alien. Priding himself ever since Baudelaire's day on his clairvoyant powers, he began even before the turn of the century to prophesy the age of wars and revolutions that was to come. Hugo von Hofmannsthal, for example, gave warning in a handful of poems, all written before he was twenty-five, of the approaching end of the Austro-Hungarian Empire and of its culture, whose last great representative he was. Not only did he foresee the coming proletarian revolution; he saw and felt the cause of the growing rift between the rulers and the ruled. In his poem 'Manche freilich . . . ' (Many, it is true . . .) he described society as a ship in which the shadows of the toiling sailors fall across the seats of the sibyls and queens, where they sat aloft on the prow:

Doch ein Schatten fällt von jenen Leben
In die anderen Leben hinüber,
Und die leichten sind an die schweren
Wie an Luft und Erde gebunden:

Ganz vergessner Völker Müdigkeiten
Kann ich nicht abtun von meinen Lidern,
Noch weghalten von der erschrockenen Seele
Stummes Niederfallen ferner Sterne.[1]

Hofmannsthal's vision of a failure in mutual responsibility between leaders and led, and his compassion for the completely forgotten make him a rare poet in a decade when such depth of vision was hard to find. Ten years later, after the abortive Russian revolution of 1905, the poet Alexander Blok, whose

---

[1] But a shadow falls from those lives over the other lives, and the light are bound to the heavy as much as to air and earth. I cannot shake from my eyelids the weariness of completely forgotten people, nor protect my terrified soul from the silent falling of distant stars.

sympathies were with the rebels and who both feared and welcomed the approaching disaster of 1917, uttered an even more despairing prophecy. In his majestic sequence of 1908, 'On the Field of Kulikovo'—the site of an ancient battle between the Russians and the Tartars—this greatest Russian poet of the century tells of a clash of weapons still to be heard, that tells not only of past wars but of even more terrible wars to come:

> No more the heart may live at peace,
> The clouds have gathered, and arms weigh
> Heavy for battle. Fate has brought
> Your hour. It has begun now. Pray!

In approximately the same year Thomas Hardy was writing—or perhaps rewriting, for many of the pieces in *Times Laughing-stocks* were in fact first drafted many years before—a poem in which he offered even less hope for man than Blok, since for Hardy there was no God who would listen to human prayer. The Universe, he says, in 'Before Life and After', was a better place before man appeared, and will be so again when he has departed:

> A time there was—as one may guess
> And as, indeed, earth's testimonies tell—
> Before the birth of consciousness,
>   When all went well.
>
> None suffered sickness, love, or loss,
> None knew regret, starved hope, or heart-burnings;
>   None cared whatever crash or cross
>   Brought wrack to things.
>
> If something ceased, no tongue bewailed,
> If something winced and waned, no heart was wrung;
>   If brightness dimmed, and dark prevailed,
>   No sense was stung.
>
> But the disease of feeling germed,
> And primal rightness took the tinct of wrong;
>   Ere nescience shall be reaffirmed
>   How long, how long?

This completely despairing view of man's future overstates the prevailing pessimism. No poet of the next fifty years was to write off the whole human experiment as conclusively as Hardy, as a mere prank of the malign gods. Complete rejection of the world is as foreign to modern poetry as complete acceptance. Both gestures are too final and determined for one who sees himself not as a unified man, but as an assemblage of contradictory characteristics.

Nevertheless the years between the wars brought more poetic prophecies of catastrophe, sometimes as explicit as Yeats's 'The Second Coming', which speaks of the end of an epoch, and of the signs that a new revelation is at hand. The first part of the poem states the confusion of values that followed the Kaiser's war and the Irish disorder, and the second, drawing a parallel between Christ's coming and this promised revelation, stresses the impersonal cruelty of the age to follow:

> somewhere in sands of the desert
> A shape with lion body and the head of a man,
> A gaze blank and pitiless as the sun
> Is moving its slow thighs, while all about it
> Reel shadows of the indignant desert birds.

It is difficult to be certain that Yeats saw in this new sign any hope for present-day man, or whether he believed that this 'vast image out of *Spiritus Mundi*' portended an entirely fresh civilization born out of long centuries of barbarism. Yeats, like Blok, and Hardy, saw history as a chronicle of heroisms and disasters; escape from the wheel of recurrent lives was possible, according to his theories, only if man were content to withdraw from outward activities, and to recapture the simplicity of the Saint, the Beggar and the Fool.

Yeats's was a personal mythology, built from elements of Hinduism, Neo-platonism and Astrology. How far from Christian thought he was is evident from the implied comparison in 'The Second Coming' between the child Christ and the lionman. The Gospel story had seemingly only astrological significances for him; at the beginning of the Christian era the earth moved out of Capricorn into Aquarius, and now at the end of this century it will go into Pisces.

In the past, particularly in the seventeenth century, also a period of cruel wars, the hopelessness of man's position in historical time was seen by the poet in simple Christian terms. There was no belief in the perfectibility of human society, and the disaster that Blok, Yeats and Hardy placed in the near

historical future was seen in every minute of a man's life which
drew him imperceptibly nearer to death. All worldly events had
their parallels in the life of the human mind; Donne in his sickness sees his spirit as both Adam and Christ, and his body as the
world:

> Is the Pacifique Sea my home? Or are
> The Easterne riches? Is *Jerusalem?*
> *Anyan*, and *Magellan*, and *Gibraltare*,
> All streights, and none but streights, are ways to them,
> Whether where *Japhet* dwelt, or *Cham*, or *Sem*.

> We think that *Paradise* and *Calvarie*,
> *Christ's* Crosse, and *Adams* tree stood in one place;
> Looke Lord, and finde both *Adams* met in me;
> As the first *Adams* sweat surrounds my face,
> May the last *Adams* blood my soul embrace.

This reading of legend as a symbolic story that can be shown
to correspond to the events of a man's life was foreign to Yeats
and to Hardy, though perhaps not entirely so to Blok. It is
nevertheless an important constituent in modern poetry. The
term Symbolist, applied to the first generation of French poets
after Baudelaire, and rather more loosely to the first modern
poets in other countries, suggests this very idea: that the poet can
best express the drama of his intuitions, his feelings and uncertainties in the form of a symbolic legend. He uses an old myth or
invents a new one as a means of revealing perceptions for which
he cannot find direct language. Symbolism is a method of oblique
statement suitable to an age that finds its truths only in rare
moments of intense vision: it is half way to parable.

It is the longing for these moments of vision that has brought
poetry back to one of its oldest themes, the theme of travel or
search. Baudelaire restates it in the spirit of Donne. For 'Le
Voyage' is a symbolist poem, and the journey that it describes is a
journey through the mind in search of an imprecise state which
the poet called *le repos*, and which he could find little hope of
attaining:

> Singulière fortune, où le but se déplace,
> Et, n'étant nulle part, peut être n'importe où!
> Où l' Homme, dont jamais l'espérance n'est lasse,
> Pour trouver le repos court toujours comme un fou![1]

[1] What a curious destiny, that the goal is always shifting and, since it is nowhere, can
be anywhere; that man, whose hopes never tire, ever runs like a madman in search of
rest.

True virtue lay, as Baudelaire saw it, not in discovery, for the goal would never come nearer, but in the incidents of the voyage itself. The real traveller sets out only for the joy of going:

> Mais les vrais voyageurs sont ceux-là qui partent seuls
> Pour partir; cœurs légers, semblables aux ballons,
> De leur fatalité jamais ils ne s'écartent,
> Et, sans savoir pourquoi, disent toujours: Allons![1]

Not all modern poets have felt the journey to be quite so fruitless. Both Yeats and Rilke, for instance, believed that they had discovered at least some aspects of the truth they were seeking. Rilke saw deeply into the processes of poetic creation, and, using them as an analogy, divined something of a greater creative process working throughout the Universe. Yeats, by pursuing his Neoplatonic and theosophical ideas, came to distinguish between the ceaseless movement of things that are subject to Time, and the fire which lies behind them and consumes them:

> Flames that no faggot feeds, nor steel has lit,
> Nor storm disturbs, flames begotten of flame,
> Where blood-begotten spirits come
> And all complexities of fury leave,
> Dying into a dance,
> An agony of trance,
> An agony of flame that cannot singe a sleeve.

Eliot, on the other hand, accepts a traditional picture of reality, that of the Anglican creed, and in setting out on his voyage seeks only to confirm his beliefs. For him the incidents of the voyage are all-important, as they were to Baudelaire. For in the 'Four Quartets' at least, he is in no doubt as to what he will find. But the journey itself is difficult. For is the searcher who reaches his destination that same man who set out?

> Fare forward, travellers! not escaping from the past
> Into different lives, or into any future;
> You are not the same people who left the station
> Or who will arrive at any terminus.

[1] But the true travellers are those only who set out for the sake of setting out; with hearts light as balloons, they never shun their fate, but always say, Let's be off! without knowing why.

The truth exists, in Eliot's belief, but can only be reflected by the idiosyncratic mirror of a defective sensibility. There being no accepted world-picture, like that of Platonism or mediæval Catholicism, by which the poet can rectify the imperfections of his partial vision, the poem, even of a believing poet, must always remain an approximation to something more perfect that will never be written.

A general world-picture, common to poet and reader, serves other purposes than that of self-correction. It provides a common stock of references on which the poet can draw for his imagery. The obscurities of Marino and Góngora, of Donne and La Ceppède, in the seventeenth century can be resolved more easily than those of Mallarmé and his successors, because even their most complicated images are drawn from the Bible, from the science and discoveries of their time, or from classical mythology. The contemporary poet, on the other hand, elaborates his metaphors either out of incidents from his own experience, or from his casual reading, which will certainly be unfamiliar to his audience. William Empson's 'Bacchus', which covers three and a half pages of his *Collected Poems* requires, despite the expectation aroused by its classical title, more than six pages of notes at the end of the volume; and it is not very clear even so. Nor is much light thrown on the 'Waste Land' by the list of references and sources which follows it. The poet now says that he only added them to fill up space. Several detailed expositions of the poem have been published, which differ amongst themselves not only in detail but in fundamental viewpoint. A dictionary of mythology and a concordance to the Bible were all the source books a Victorian poetry reader required.

The noble equipment has indeed deteriorated even as our stock of universally accepted ideas has diminished. But at the same time the poet's responsibility for making true statements has enormously increased. With the decay of religion, the narrow specialization of science and philosophy, and the contraction of the practical man's vision to social, personal and economic issues, many men, discontented with the general account of life and its possibilities offered to them, have turned to the imaginative artist for an answer to questions which in former generations would have seemed beyond his scope.

The poet, therefore, willing or unwilling, has been forced to assume an office not really his, though it was claimed for him by Shelley and usurped by Baudelaire and Mallarmé. He not only prophesies but prescribes laws, sometimes successfully as in the cases of Yeats and Rilke just mentioned, but sometimes, as in that of Rilke's German contemporary Stefan George, grandiosely and disastrously.

George did not look deeply into his own heart or into any philosophy, but described the whole outer world in the image of his own dream. His vast inflation of the ego, indeed, goes counter to the whole spirit of modern poetry, just as Rilke's subordination of the outer man to the inner creator makes him one of his truest and greatest representatives. For once a man recognizes the divisions in his own personality, once he accepts the state of anxiety and doubt in which he must pass his days, once he comprehends the rarity of those few creative moments by which he lives, his claim to authority will be a modest one.

Yeats, Rilke, George and Blok found mature expression in a decade of mediocre poetry. In France there were no successors to Baudelaire, Mallarmé, Rimbaud and Laforgue, only minor poets who echoed Verlaine's weak line with its undertone of tears. A few attempts to revert to classical subjects proved vain. The most original minds squandered themselves on such elaborate music-hall skits as *Ubu Roi*. It was a time when the most promising writers failed to develop. The Belgian Émile Verhaeren, potentially the greatest, having once portrayed the horrors of urbanism in *Les Villes Tentaculaires* (Cities with Tentacles) repeated his effects in ever more disorderly lines choked with increasingly banal imagery, without finding any but the most rhetorical answers to the age's persistent questions.

In Italy, d'Annunzio made a poetry of steel and blood and raw sensuality which, though it seemed to welcome war, was just as much out of tune with the war of artillery and poison gas that actually came as the work of his more peaceable contemporaries; and the Scot John Davidson, who had appeared, if only on the strength of a single poem, 'Thirty Bob a Week', likely to be capable of a poetry not entirely built up of tags from the past, soon gave little hope that he would ever redeem his promise of the 'nineties.

A cycle appeared to be running out in bombast, preciosity or smug provincialism. The most appealing poets were those who,

B

like Francis Jammes, deliberately constricted their vision to their own region and their favourite books. Ranging thoughts were deliberately called home:

> J'ai bien réfléchi, l'année avant, dans ma chambre,
> pendant que la neige lourde tombait dehors.
> J'ai réfléchi pour rien. A présent comme alors
> je fume une pipe en bois avec un bout d'ambre.
>
> Ma vieille commode en chêne sent toujours bon.
> Mais moi j'étais bête parce que tant de choses
> ne pouvaient pas changer et que c'est une pose
> de vouloir chasser les choses que nous savons.[1]

Better this than the grandiose emptiness of Francis Thompson at his most banal, loud with echoes of all the poets who had gone before him:

> In a little peace, in a little peace,
> Thou dost rebate thy rigid purposes
> Of imposed beings, and relenting, mend'st
> Too much, with naught. The westering Phœbus' horse
> Paws i' the lucent dust as when he shocked
> The East with rising.

In such poetry, built up of reminiscences from Shakespeare, Shelley, Coleridge and Patmore, or in the even flatter pastiche of Stephen Phillips and William Watson, the commonplaces of the Renaissance tradition received their final twist of bathos; the motifs of heroism and romantic love, of rejoicing with the rebirth of Nature in Spring and grief at her death in Autumn, of the relation between a god that could be drawn in man's image and a man who faced the world in the confidence that he was captain of his own soul, were no longer capable of inspiring even passably good poems. First the poet and then the sensitive public had come to realize that there was a hollowness at the heart of things. The first reaction to this discovery was the so-called 'Decadent' movement of the 'nineties, but it was impossible to make a new poetry only out of tears. Moreover the emptiness

---

[1] I certainly reflected last year, in my room while the heavy snow was falling outside. I reflected to no purpose. Now as then, I smoke a wooden pipe with an amber mouth-piece.
My old oak chest still smells good. But I was stupid because so many things are unchangeable, and it is a pose to want to drive away the things we know.

that the poets of the 'nineties were trying to express had been far
better described by Baudelaire forty years before:

> J'ai vu parfois, au fond d'un théâtre banal
>> Qu'enflammait l'orchestre sonore,
> Une fée allumer dans un ciel infernal
>> Une miraculeuse aurore;
> J'ai vu parfois au fond d'un théâtre banal
>
> Un être qui n'était que lumière, or et gaze,
>> Terrasser l' énorme Satan;
> Mais mon cœur, que jamais ne visite l'extase,
>> Est un théâtre où l'attend
> Toujours, toujours en vain, l'Etre aux ailes de gaze![1]

All modern poetry, whatever its programme, has been conscious that this Being is most often absent from the poet's heart,
has been aware that the theatre of his soul is frequently empty,
and has suspected that it is perhaps inhabited by ghosts. Each
poet has sought to call on to the stage some significant forms
capable of flooring the giant Satan of self-doubt, self-disgust,
indifference or horror that possesses modern man, standing
always between him and that ecstasy which, like Baudelaire, he so
much desires; and each, in so far as he is a true poet, has to some
extent succeeded in his purpose.

---

[1] I have sometimes seen at the back of a cheap theatre ablaze with the din of an
orchestra, a fairy lighting a miraculous dawn. I have sometimes seen at the back of a
cheap theatre a fairy all light, gold and gauze, floor the giant Satan. But my heart,
which is never visited by ecstasy, is a theatre where the audience waits always, always in
vain, for the Being with gauze wings!

3

George, Rilke, Valéry

THE Decadent movement was a speedy destroyer of poets. Of
the new talents that emerged in the little magazines of the
'nineties, drink, drugs, tuberculosis, suicide, journalism, the
writing of commercial fiction and the madhouse, took approximately equal proportions. Those who survived as poets, therefore,
were compelled by the turn of the century to look for new beliefs
on which to base their lives and poetry.

In these years there were two advancing ideas abroad that
offered something to replace a dying religious faith, a dying self-
confidence, and a short-lived aestheticism which had failed to
provide a substitute for either. These were Socialism and
Theosophy. Neither in its orthodox form offered much food to
the poet; both demanded unimaginative acceptance and advocacy.
Both, however, in their opposite ways, influenced—if only by
reaction—the principal poets of the new era. The Russian
Alexander Blok was captivated by each in turn; W. B. Yeats was
much influenced by Theosophy's founder Madame Blavatsky,
whom he frequently visited, and put together his own version of
the doctrine; Stefan George, though hostile not only to Socialism
but to any form of levelling, was nevertheless as utopian in
his idiosyncratic ideas as William Morris himself, and Rilke,
the most independent of the four, while making no approach to
Theosophy, was as much attracted as Yeats to Neo-Platonism,
the aspect of the new creed most attractive to creative artists.

The European Symbolist movement, of whom these are the
principal representatives, began in the mood of autumn, setting
dreams above reality, and advocating the poet's withdrawal from
a world too sordid for him to come to terms with. Walking in the
Strand, Yeats watched the dancing balls of a shooting booth,
aloft on their jets of water, and was transported to the solitude

36

of a distant Irish lake; Rilke, in Paris, lived a life of fantasy, described in his *Notebooks*, dwelling in memory among the great works of art that he had seen in other lands, or wandering in imagination with the Russian pilgrims he had once visited, from village to village across the illimitable plain; and George succumbed to that most German of idiosyncrasies: the invention of an imaginary culture in which the artist receives due honour, and life is lived with the licensed simplicity of a fictitious primæval era.

Autumn and withdrawal, however, were to yield to warmer moods. In time each of these poets felt himself impelled to return to the world, to interpret it, and to invent symbols that would set forth the deepest meanings of life as the symbols of religion had done in the past, and still did for believers. None of the four was a believer, and each had therefore to start from fundamentals, to speak of life and death, love and art, as if they had never been spoken of before, to put themselves and their own prejudices aside, and lay themselves open to vision. In this task Yeats and Rilke triumphantly succeeded, but George failed, and Blok was so deflected by political events that it is doubtful whether he should be considered as primarily a Symbolist at all. For the purposes of this book, indeed, he seems to take a more natural place among the poets of war and revolution, whose brief emergence hardly checked the smooth development of this last major movement in European poetry.

The growth of European Symbolism was slow. The major achievement of Yeats and Rilke covers at least fifteen years, during which time at least one other important movement was born and died.

Stefan George (1868-1933) was, at the outset, the most European of German poets since Goethe. A Rhinelander by birth, he thought of his native province, the only part of Germany to have been thoroughly Romanized, as the essential link between the Latin and Teutonic cultures. Widely read in the poetry of half a dozen languages, he made excellent translations from Dante, Rossetti, Baudelaire and many of his contemporaries. Not satisfied with the tongues he knew, he invented others, romantic and high-sounding, and adapted for himself a hieratic German full of obsolete and invented words. Furthermore, he printed his poems in special type with his own punctuation.

George was, throughout his life, an aesthete who believed

that every facet of living should be subordinated to an ideal. Everything must be artificial; man's hand must bring the world of nature under control. Of his mission as a poet, and the prophet of a new way of life, he was never in doubt. His over-riding wish was to form a small circle of intimates devoted to the making of poetry—and to the cult of himself. But the recruitment of his followers presented difficulties. George could recognize first-class talent but found that those who possessed it—von Hofmannsthal, for instance, and the Dutch poet Albert Verwey—preferred to pursue their own ways. The George circle was con-sequently made up rather of admirers than of original minds. The price of admission being the virtual surrender of independ-ence, the influence of the circle was small, and younger men, when they emerged in the years just before the war, reacted against George even though they were prepared to learn some-thing from his technical innovations. To them he seemed just as far removed from reality as the complacent middle-class national-ists he so despised.

Despite George's large aesthetic claims his best poems were short autumnal lyrics influenced by Verlaine rather than by the major Symbolists with whom he ranked himself. *Das Jahr der Seele* (The Year of the Soul) his second principal collection (1897) has little to say of any month before the harvest time. Its finest pieces have a melancholy music that is, however, far more subtle than that of our *Yellow Book* poets, with whom he can here best be compared:

> Wir schreiten auf und ab im reichen flitter
> Des buchenganges beinah bis zum tore
> Und sehen aussen in dem feld vom gitter
> Den mandelbaum zum zweitenmal in flore.[1]

This is not a wild but a cultivated landscape. Every detail testifies to man's formative hand. The beech avenue has, of course, been planted, and its leaves, fallen or still on the trees, suggest the most artificial of comparisons, with the tinsel of pantomime. Outside the gate, moreover, set up to exclude undisciplined nature, the almond—a tree strange to the German landscape—has been forced by human cultivation to bloom twice in the year. Not only nature, but society is shut out of this

---

[1] We stride up and down in the rich tinsel of the beech avenue, almost to the gate, and look out through the bars into the field at the almond flowering for a second time.

formal park. The initial *we* conceals not two persons but one. 'Seldom,' says George in his introduction to the second edition of this book, 'have thou and I been so much the same person as here.' Verlaine, conversing also in a deserted park, at least called up the ghost of a dead lover. But here it is the poet and his creation, or merely two shadows of himself who in the poem's second quatrain link arms in dream, and in the third listen to the thud of the ripe fruit falling on the ground. The poem is neither a love nor a nature lyric; its autumn mood is chosen only because it chimes with the mood prevailing in George's heart. Autumn is the time of farewells, of death and decay; and George sees himself living in the autumn of poetry, when all has already been said.

In this last poem the poet presents himself as passive. In another of his best nature pieces, however, taken from his next collection of two years later *Der Teppich des Lebens* (The Carpet of Life), he presents himself as an active figure, of whom he speaks in the third person as the 'Friend of the Meadows'. This 'Friend', while ostensibly a kind of guardian of the harvest, in fact symbolizes George as a very conscious creator, lopping a shoot here, setting up a stake there, and testing the ripeness of the grain on his tongue. This piece opens like his poem of the autumn parkland with a purposeful stride. Instead of ending in dream and reflection, however, it tells of continuous activities:

> Er schöpft und gieszt mit einem kürbis napfe
> Er beugt sich oft die quecken auszuharken
> Und üppig blühen unter seinem stapfe
> Und reifend schwellen um ihn die gemarken.[1]

George pictures himself as a conscious artist working in the spirit of Gautier, and consciously planning every detail. Nothing could be further from him than those depths of experience which dictated their own form to Rilke and to Yeats. Yet George was in all his best poems guided by emotions that ran counter to his intellectual intentions. It was this contradiction in him that made the work of his middle life on the whole unsatisfying.

In George's next book, written after a long interval *Der siebente Ring* (The Seventh Ring) (1907), something far more

---

[1] He draws water and pours it from a gourd. He often bends down to root out the couch grass, and beneath his tread the region yields luxuriant bloom, swelling as it ripens around him.

ambitious was attempted; the poet set out a whole mythology and plan for a new world on the basis of his own peculiar experience. Early in the century he had known and conceived an attachment for a youth called Maximin, in whom he—and he alone—detected the greatest promise, but who died at the age of sixteen without fulfilling it. Stealing his symbolism from Christianity, which he had rejected, George cast Maximin for the part of the dead God who had assumed flesh, and saw in himself another aspect of the same figure, the Suffering Servant. The two figures are in fact as intimately connected as the two strollers in the beech avenue; there is no Maximin, only a youthful shadow of the poet.

In the prologue to *Der Teppich des Lebens*, George had written of a message delivered to him by an angel, whose voice was, significantly, almost like his own, concerning 'the beautiful life'. Now he prepared in the name of the new god and the new teaching to preach this message to his people. Formerly George had not been narrowly nationalist, but now his message was for the Germans alone. Indeed it was a typically German message, of the kind that Heine had so mercilessly mocked when it was delivered by von Platen some three quarters of a century earlier. For what George preached was a homosexual amalgam of the German hero cult and the ancient Greek worship of the body.

The first group of poems *Der siebente Ring* castigate the modern age, which they compare with the glorious past. The medium is a splendid but somewhat hollow blank verse, in which George celebrates the greatness of Rome and the Middle Ages, casting himself in turn for the part of Dante, Goethe and Nietzsche, the world's neglected poets and prophets, and addressing his contemporaries in terms of grandiose superiority.

The best of the poems in the new book are those in which he remembers his affection for the dead boy. These retain some of the Verlainean charm of George's early work. Those however in which Maximin is proclaimed a god ape the Psalms and the Lutheran hymnbook by turns:

Du wächst über uns
    In deiner unnahbaren glorie:
Schon wurdest du eins
    mit dem Wort das von oben uns sprach.[1]

[1] You grow above us in your unapproachable glory. Already you have become one with the Word that spoke to us from on high.

This third piece in the series, 'On the Life and Death of Maximin' makes no concessions to poetry; it is an ecstatic address in which grandiose statement is made to pass as evidence of emotion. The fourth piece in the same series fails in another way by dropping into a banal jog-trot:

Du schon geweiht für die ruhe des siebten
Warst unsrem tag ein entfernter genoss . .

Nur dieses zeichen verblieb den geliebten
Dass unsrer erde nicht ganz dich verdross:[1]

This attempt of George's to found a new myth which would replace the dying religions failed to inspire him to great poetry. Only a few 'Lieder', which are closer to runic incantations than to songs, rescue this book from complete banality. Whether the mystical experience that these songs apparently claim is genuine or not, they are lit by flashes of genuine beauty. It is, however, akin in spirit to the autumnal beauty that George had achieved in the years before he received his revelation:

Kreuz der strasse . .
Wir sind am end.
Abend sank schon . .
Dies ist das end.
Kurzes wallen
Wen macht es müd?
Mir zu lang schon . .
Der schmerz macht müd. . . .[2]

The lines are briefer than those of his earlier poems, and the pronoun *we* seems to speak for more than two shadows in a park, or the poet and his remembered friend. Yet the crossroads and the sunset belong essentially to the private landscape of Stefan George. He is not speaking of humanity but of himself.

The prophetic poetry of George's next book, *Der Stern des Bundes* (The Star of Alliance) (1914), is more objective. It is directed against the evils of the age: the false belief in progress, the prevailing materialism, and the lack of heroic spirit. No small-scale political morals are drawn, and no individuals or specific crimes attacked. Appearing on the eve of the Kaiser's

[1] Already hallowed for the rest of the seventh (sphere), you were a distant companion to our day; only this sign remained to your lover that our earth did not entirely repel you.

[2] Crossroads. We have come to the end. Evening has already fallen. This is the end. A short pilgrimage. Whom does it tire? Grief has tired me for too long already.

B*

war, the book was accepted by some as a call to battle. Many young men carried it in their haversacks in the first delirious advance to the Marne. It had been written with no such patriotic purpose, however, but rather in furtherance of the Maximin cult to which it frequently refers. There is little poetry in the book— the poorest that George wrote—and this little is in George's familiar autumn mood:

> Durch die gärten lispeln zitternd
> Grau und gold des späten tags.
> Irr-gestalt wischt sich versonnen
> Sommerfäden aus der stirne
> Wehmut flötet.[1]

It is easier for George to celebrate the world's decline than to adumbrate new laws. There is only the harshest intellectual theory behind such injunctions as

> Mit den frauen fremder ordnung
> Sollt ihr nicht den leib beflecken
> Harret! lasset pfau bei affe. . . .[2]

These were rules for a society which could never be born. Even the small George circle itself was split by quarrels. The outer world, moreover, did not wait for its revelation, nor interpret in the sense that George would have desired the new book's final chorus:

> Gottes pfad ist uns geweitet
> Gottes land ist uns bestimmt
> Gottes krieg ist uns entzündet[3]

This address to the chosen disciples chimed with the mood of Autumn 1914, but corresponded to nothing later than the check before Paris. Ypres, the Somme, Verdun, the long Russian campaigns, were better interpreted by younger poets who took part in them, and many of whom fell in the service of an Imperialism to which they did not subscribe.

The defeat of 1918, the fall of the Imperial house, and the

---

[1] Through the gardens tremblingly whispers the grey and gold of the late day. The will-o'-the-wisp dreamily brushes summer's threads from its forehead; sorrow plays its flute.

[2] You must not soil your bodies with women of a different class. Be patient! leave peacocks with apes!

[3] God's path opens before us, God's land is reserved for us, God's war is kindled for us.

apparent victory of democracy, were blows that, while destroying
George's immediate hopes, raised him to fresh prophecy and a
renewal of poetic inspiration. His last collection, *Das Neue Reich*
(The New Empire) (1928), contains poems written during and
after the war. Now a certain nobility seems to infuse his blank
verse line, which had formerly marched forward with an excess of
pomp and circumstance. Once more also, as at the beginning, his
sympathies extend beyond Germany's frontiers. In deploring the
war he could find virtue in foe as well as friend, could write in
sorrow without anger against the occupying forces who 'ravaged'
his land and place his hopes for Germany's true greatness in the
coming generation—which was to disappoint him also in his
last years:

> O Land
> Zu schön als dass dich fremder tritt verheere:
> Wo flöte aus dem weidicht tönt aus hainen
> Windharfen rauschen, wo der Traum noch webt
> Untilgbar durch die jeweils trünnigen erben . .
> Wo die allblühende Mutter der verwildert
> Zerfallnen weissen Art zuerst enthüllte
> Ihr echtes antlitz . . Land dem viel verheissung
> Noch innewohnt—das drum nicht untergeht![1]

In 'Das Neue Reich' George regains some of his old lyrical
charm. Didacticism, while not absent, is softened by grief, and
grief has made George a poet again. The ghost of Maximin still
walks, but now it is in the familiar autumnal gardens, and
George's poems repeat the autumnal dying fall;

> Du bist mein wunsch and mein gedanke
> Ich atme dich mit jeder luft
> Ich schlürfe dich mit jedem tranke
> Ich küsse dich mit jedem duft
>
> Du blühend reis vom edlen stamme
> Du wie ein quell geheim und schlicht
> Du schlank und rein wie eine flamme
> Du wie der morgen zart und licht.[2]

[1] Oh land too beautiful to be ravaged by a foreign foot, where flutes sound from the willow-thicket, and aeolian harps sound on the heath, where dream still weaves inextinguishable, among its now scattered inheritors, where the all-flowering mother of the white art that is now overthrown and runs wild, first revealed her true countenance, land that is still full of great promise—and therefore will not perish.

[2] You are my wish and my thought, I breathe you with every breath, I gulp you down with every drink, I kiss you with every scent. You flowering shoot from a noble branch, you, secret and simple as a spring, you slim and pure as a flame, you tender and light as the morning.

George's rhythms are now close to those of German nineteenth-century poetry; his words are no longer abrupt or
declamatory but sing themselves. In his defeat and disappoint-
ment he has regained contact with nature. No longer does it
seem possible to him that everything shall be controlled and
cultivated. In 'Der Mensch und der Drud' (The Man and the
Satyr) he at last acknowledges the existence of an untamed force
—the Satyr which speaks to man with a consciousness of
superiority:

> Du bist nur mensch . . . wo deine weisheit endet
> Beginnt die unsre. Du merkst erst den rand
> Wo du gebüsst hast für den übertritt.
> Wenn dein getreide reift dein vieh gedeiht
> Die heiligen baüme öl und trauben geben
> Wähnst du dies käme nur durch deine list.[1]

Once man has broken the bond which unites him with
animals and with the soil, warns the Satyr, then his mind, which is
all-powerful in the clouds, trips itself up. Man, however, defies
this 'monster with a crooked mouth' and tells him his time is past.
But the Satyr is left with the last word:

> Nur durch den zauber bleibt das leben wach[2]

George's final acknowledgement of this force of magic, might
even at the last have made him a great poet. But his movements
were hampered by the prophetic mantle. He failed still to distinguish between his personal fate and the crisis through which
the world was passing. In 'Der Gehenkte' (The Hanged Man) one
of the most impressive of these final poems, he sees himself once
more as the martyr who has suffered for art and for truth, the
scorn and obloquy of an uncomprehending world.

To the last, George did not regret that his manner of writing,
his esoteric vocabulary, his difficult symbolisms, and also his
deliberately eccentric spelling and punctuation, had of necessity

---

[1] You are only man; where your wisdom ends ours begins; you only notice the
boundary when you have atoned for overstepping it. When your corn ripens and your
cattle prosper and your sacred trees yield oil and grapes, you boast that this is due only
to your cunning.

[2] It is only through magic that life remains awake.

kept his public smaller than it might have been. He prided himself on his hermeticism, and at the same time he poured scorn on the uncomprehending readers whom he deliberately kept at bay.

When the Nazis came to power they courted George, seeing in his New Empire a possible harbinger of their own. In his nationalism, his rejection of democracy, his theoretical scorn for human life and his cult of heroism, George was not far from their ideals. He was, however, an aristocrat in spirit, conscious even at his most Germanic of his country's debt to the Latin world, from which its civilization sprang. Moreover there was too great a contrast between his memory of the dead Maximin and the coarse presence of the Nazi leaders who wished to do him honour. George rejected their overtures, retired to Switzerland, and in the year after Hitler's seizure of power, died in exile.

Rainer Maria Rilke (1875-1926) did not live to be confronted by any such tragic choice. Had he lived into his sixties one can have no doubt that he would have remained in Switzerland, where he had made his home after the Kaiser's war, and that no telegrams of invitation would have come to him from Berlin. Rilke stood further apart from the German tradition than any poet who has written in German since Heine. Both Goethe and Hölderlin at times influenced his writing, but so to a greater extent did the French Symbolist poets. His overriding desire was to give his muscle-bound native tongue some of the flexibility of French. Nevertheless he took advantage also of the German superiority in the expression of abstract thought. His *Elegies* indeed draw on the strength of both languages. Though born in Bohemia, a citizen of the Austrian Empire, he did not share Hofmannsthal's regret for the passing of the Habsburgs. He was before everything a European, with affinities to the art of France, Italy and Spain, though with a singular ignorance of Britain, against which he felt some prejudice.

Rilke's first experiences to take the form of poetry were vaguely mystical. On a visit to Russia, his imagination was captured by the lives of the wandering pilgrims, to whom he devoted a section of his first important book, *Das Stundenbuch* (The Book of Hours) (1903). Repelled, like George, by urban materialism, Rilke found his first ideal in the life of the primitive Russian village, which he had in fact seen only as a stranger. But at the same time he rejected the simple Christianity in which

that life was rooted; his ideal landscape at this point contained
no churches:

> Alles wird wieder grosz sein und gewaltig.
> Die Lande einfach und die Wasser faltig,
> die Bäume riesig und sehr klein die Mauern;
> und in den Tälern, stark und vielgestaltig,
> ein Volk von Hirten und von Ackerbauern.
> Und keine Kirchen, welche Gott umklammern
> wie eine Flüchtling, und ihn dann bejammern
> wie ein gefangenes und wundes Tier.[1]

There must be no preoccupation with the beyond, he concludes,
no gazing up to heaven, only a resolution not to come to death
unprepared,

> und dienend sich am Irdischen zu üben,
> um seinen Händen nicht mehr neu zu sein.[2]

Although preoccupied with death, Rilke laid much more
importance than would a Christian mystic on the importance of
the experience to be gained from living. As living beings, he
believed men to be as essential to God as He to them. Not only
must they mature by 'accustoming themselves to the things of
earth', they must at the same time act as His senses, giving Him a
contact with things, of which at His level he could not otherwise
be aware. It was in this spirit that he asked,

> Was wirst du tun, Gott, wenn ich sterbe?
> Ich bin dein Krug (wenn ich zerscherbe?)
> Ich bin dein Trank (wenn ich verderbe?)
> Bin dein Gewand und dein Gewerbe,
> mit mir verlierst du deinen Sinn.[3]

Death was for Rilke the supreme experience for which the
whole of life was a preparation; it was the moment in which the

[1] Everything will be great and strong again. The lands will be simple and the waters
will ripple, the trees will be huge and the walls very low; and in the valleys, strong and
various, a people of shepherds and ploughman. And no churches to cling to God as to
a fugitive, and weep round him like a captured and wounded beast.

[2] And humbly to accustom oneself to the things of the earth, so as no longer to be
new to death's hands.

[3] What will you do, God, if I die. I am your jug (What if I am smashed) I am your
drink (What if I go bad?) I am your cloak and your trade, if you lose me you lose your
purpose.

seed that is within a man comes to ripeness. 'Everyone carries
inside him his own death,' he wrote in a passage of the *Notebooks
of Malte Laurids Brigge* that describes the last illness of the poet's
grandfather. The idea was to be greatly developed in his later
writings. He was also, from the first, concerned rather with the
moment of experience than with vistas into the past or future.
When the past comes into Rilke's poetry it is in the form of a
work of art that has survived to tell us of another way of life.
Everything that he describes is immediate: a situation, a statue,
a legend, a simple object are for him all immediate doorways
leading into the field of eternal values. In *Das Stundenbuch* a
degree of self-dramatization seems still to be present; the poet
assumes the cloak of a monk, a pilgrim, a beggar and a dying
man by turns. Like George, he is composing pictures, but they are
less contrived; and Autumn is not for him only a season of decay,
but contains its own promise:

> Jetzt reifen schon die roten Berberitzen,
> alternde Astern atmen schwach im Bett.
> Wer jetzt nicht reich ist, da der Sommer geht,
> wird immer warten und sich nie besitzen.
>
> Wer jetzt nicht seine Augen schlieszen kann,
> gewisz, dasz eine Fülle von Gesichtern
> in ihm nur wartet bis die Nacht begann,
> um sich in seinem Dunkel aufzurichten:—
> der ist vergangen wie ein alter Mann.[1]

The hidden purpose of life being to ripen the seed that will
spring up at the moment of death, the method of nourishing it
becomes evident in this Autumn poem. It is to gather impressions
from the visible world that can be transformed, and arise in the
darkness within a man once the night has set in. The process is
akin to that of poetic creation, which was for Rilke a transformation of the visible object into an invisible essence. Where
George had wished to reject life and retire behind the palings of
art, Rilke believed the whole process of living to be one of
creation. This idea, which was fundamental to him, was far more
fully expressed in his *Elegies*. It is already implicit, however, in

---

[1] Already the red berberis berries are ripe, aging asters breathe weakly in the bed.
Whoever is not rich now that summer is going will wait for ever and never possess
himself.
  Anyone who cannot now shut his eyes, in the certainty that a plethora of faces is
only waiting within him till night sets in, to arise in his darkness, has decayed like an
old man. . . .

Das Stundenbuch. Confirming his belief in his poetic mission, it also heightened his anxiety in those years when the gift of creation seemed to have been withdrawn from him. He feared that he might have to wait for ever and never possess himself.

In the *Buch der Bilder* (Picture Book) (1902) the writing of which had proceeded alongside that of *Das Stundenbuch*, the poet seems to have attempted to remove himself from the foreground of his poems. The collection was intended to be one of objective pictures, but these are in fact often no more than a pretext for personal statements. The few fine poems in the book are those in which Rilke makes no attempt to disguise his subject; and among them 'Der Lesende' (The Reader) stands out for the statement of his fundamental problem of expression in its last lines:

> Und wenn ich jetzt vom Buch die Augen hebe,
> wird nichts befremdlich sein und alles grosz.
> Dort drauszen ist, was ich hier drinnen lebe,
> und hier und dort ist alles grenzenlos;
> nur dasz ich mich noch mehr damit verwebe,
> wenn meine Blicke an die Dinge passen
> und an die ernste Einfachheit der Massen,—
> da wächst die Erde über sich hinaus.
> Den ganzen Himmel scheint sie zu umfassen:
> der erste Stern ist wie das letzte Haus.[1]

Rilke's problem was to express in poetry this new-found unity between his inner and his outer life, to find symbols which, while expressing both, would at the same time make more profound statements than would be possible either by means of personal confession, after the manner of the *Stundenbuch*, or of objective picture-drawing, such as he was attempting in the *Buch der Bilder*.

In three poems of 1904, which were later incorporated in the *Neue Gedichte* (New Poems) of 1908, Rilke for the first time succeeded in finding symbols capable of bearing the full weight of his discoveries. It is remarkable that two of these pieces, 'Orpheus, Eurydike, Hermes', and 'Alkestis' are fresh treatments of old legends, and only one, 'Die Rosenschale' (The Rose-cup), an invention of his own. In contrast to George, whose Maximin

---

[1] And now when I lift my eyes from the book, nothing will be strange, and everything will be great. There outside is everything that I am experiencing within, and nothing has limits either within or without; only that I weave myself more closely into things when my glance harmonizes with them, and with the serious simplicity of their shapes—then the earth outgrows itself. It seems to enclose the whole sky; the first star is like the last house.

legend, being founded in the poet's private experience, was
incapable of carrying any impersonal statement, Rilke here
succeeds in completely harmonizing his outer and inner vision.

Rilke's greatest need, at this moment when he had left Paris,
quarrelling with the sculptor Rodin, whose secretary he had been,
was for withdrawal. Pulled by the worldly claims of a wife and
child, and with no method of earning a living, everything seemed
to demand that he should abandon poetry. But something even
more urgent within him compelled him to reject these objective
demands and 'weave himself more closely into things', so that
the world that had seemed divided could be brought together,
with all boundaries abolished, and the last house and the first
star could be one. He had, therefore, to make real his acceptance
of death, which had perhaps hitherto remained for him in the
realm of ideas, and go into isolation.

The theme of Rilke's three great poems is one of reconciliation through withdrawal. 'Die Rosenschale' opens with an image
of two boys fighting, his symbol of the divided world, from which
he turns to contemplate the opening of a rose, which when most
open still encloses some secret that is withheld. The flower stands
for the union of all opposites, as does also Alcestis' smile, when
she departs to Hades as a substitute for her husband Admetus:

> Aber einmal sah
> er noch des Mädchens Antlitz, das sich wandte
> mit einem Lächeln, hell wie eine Hoffnung,
> die beinah ein Versprechen war: erwachsen
> zurückzukommen aus dem tiefen Tode
> zu ihm, dem Lebenden—[1]

Alcestis knows herself to be predestined for death. She is merely
acting out a part that has been long ago assigned to her. Nothing
remains to her now of what she once was; and she goes with the
messenger from the Underworld, not in order to save her
husband from death but to release him from his clamouring for
life:

> Ich ging ja,
> damit das alles, unter dem begraben
> der jetzt mein Gatte ist, zergeht, sich auflöst—[2]

[1] But yet he took one glance at the girl's face, that turned with a smile, bright as a
hope, which was almost a promise that she would come back when she was grown, out
of deep death, to him who was living.

[2] I have gone so that all that is buried in him who is now my bridegroom may melt
and be dissolved.

And as Alcestis goes, she gives Admetus that smile that is almost a promise to return. Yet she will not return in her own shape, one supposes, but as one of those faces that he will call up in the darkness of his mind when the night has set in.

Neither 'Alkestis' nor 'Die Rosenschale' is a perfect poem. The first is marred by an unfortunate image in its opening lines whereby the messenger is compared to a superfluous ingredient thrown into the brew of Alcestis' marriage-feast. And 'Die Rosenschale' is somewhat uneven in its language, which is by turns metaphysical and sensual. So anxious was Rilke to extend the range of German poetry, and to naturalize the vast resources accumulated by the French poets since Baudelaire, that he lapsed into more than an occasional tastelessness. Every detail of 'Orpheus, Eurydike, Hermes', however, is successful. It is a poem of greater depth than any that Rilke had yet written, and he was not to equal it until he completed the *Elegies* twenty years later.

A Russian Symbolist, Valery Bryussov, writing in the same year on the same subject, describes Eurydice as a shadow, with only shadowy memories of earth and of her husband's love. In Rilke's poem, on the other hand, though wedded to death she is more real than the living Orpheus, who has come to rescue her. He, like Admetus, is distracted by his clamouring senses. All impatient to possess his wife again, he lets his gaze rush forward to the next bend in the path while his hearing stays behind, following after him like a scent. He was a musician no longer, for his hand was unconscious of the lyre which had become one with it, like a rose-shoot that clings to the trunk of an olive. But she, as she came after him, clinging to Hermes' hand, was 'like a sweet and dark fruit, so full was she of her great death that was so new she understood nothing.'

There was no profit for Orpheus now in regaining his dead wife; only her loss could aid the ripening in him. Only in isolation could he sing again; only in mourning her could he effect that transformation of reality into idea, which was for Rilke the essence of the poet's task. Eurydice in death had returned within herself; but as Orpheus's lost bride, she could inspire him, and through his song create a new world:

Die So-geliebte, dasz aus einer Leier
mehr Klage kam als je aus Klagefrauen;

dasz eine Welt aus Klage ward in der
alles noch einmal da war: Wald und Tal
und Weg und Ortschaft, Feld und Flusz und Tier;
und dasz um diese Klage-Welt ganz so
wie um die andre Erde eine Sonne
und ein gestirnter stiller Himmel ging,
ein Klage-Himmel mit entstallten Sternen—:
diese So-geliebte.[1]

With that half of himself which he had embodied in Orpheus,
Rilke rejected the death of the clamouring senses which was
necessary if he was to pass beyond the stage of the *Buch der
Bilder*. But before the two volumes of *Neue Gedichte* were
completed, he had accepted the idea of isolation completely.
Henceforth all that mattered was that poetry should be written;
he would take sufficient money to procure himself the right conditions from anyone who offered it. Fortunately there was no
lack of patrons.

Rilke was in part prompted to this denial of common egoism
by the suicide of his friend Paula Becker-Modersohn, whose
husband, like his own figure of Orpheus, had pressed her to
return from the Elysian fields, in which she claimed, as a painter,
to be walking. Rather than comply with her duties as a wife, she
had taken her life; and Rilke in his *Requiem* for her, blamed the
husband as he had not blamed the Orpheus of his poem.

In a later poem, 'Todeserfahrung' (Experience of Death)
Rilke carried the idea of acceptance even further, and claimed
that death and life were in fact one, since it is only at the moment
of death that intimations of true reality reach the world, surging
upwards through the cleft that is opening to receive the departing
spirit:

Doch als du gingst, da brach in diese Bühne
ein Streifen Wirklichkeit durch jeden Spalt,
durch den du hingingst: Grün wirklicher Grüne,
wirklicher Sonnenschein, wirklicher Wald.[2]

[1] The so-beloved that more mourning came from one lyre than ever from mourning
women; that a world grew out of mourning, in which everything was reproduced:
wood and valley and road and village, field and river and beast; and that around this
mourning world as around the other world, a sun and a still starry heaven revolved,
a mourning heaven with stars in reversed places—this so beloved.

[2] Then as you departed there broke on to this stage a streak of reality through that
cleft whereby you went: green, real green, real sunshine, and real woodland.

This recreation of reality is the principal subject of the *Duineser Elegien* (Elegies of Duino), which were begun by Rilke in 1912, and finished in his most creative few days in February 1922. In the interval, the poet, thinking of himself as barren, frequently despaired and, longing only for the completion of his *Elegies*, rejected the majority of the poems that came to him independently of them. But in the end the renunciation of his own will, his willingness to subordinate his life to the unpredictable urge of creation, enabled Rilke to free his inspiration. Orpheus no longer desired the return of Eurydice, for she was alive within him, and he was dead to the 'world' and open only to the invisible 'open' region of idea:

> Engel (sagt man) wüszten oft nicht, ob sie unter
> Lebenden gehn oder Toten. Die ewige Strömung
> reiszt durch beide Bereiche alle Alter
> immer mit sich und übertönt sie in beiden.[1]

When the war came to interrupt Rilke's endeavours to finish the *Elegies*, he greeted it in the first moment as a cleanser and restorer. But already by September 1914 he was viewing it only with resignation, knowing that now, with poetic composition almost impossible—he wrote very little between 1915 and 1919— and with the likelihood of being called into the army, he was driven into an isolation very different from that of his desire. The magical fragment of that month, 'Ausgesetzt auf den Bergen des Herzens', ends with the same words with which it began: 'exposed on the mountains of the heart'; he had now reached a place above words, above feelings. It was his attainment of this place that made him free to receive that supreme burst of inspiration which gave to the world within a mere three weeks, in February 1922, the completed *Elegies* and the two sequences of *Sonette an Orpheus*.

The outstanding symbol of the *Elegies* is those Angels, in whom, as Rilke wrote in a letter, 'that transformation of the visible into the invisible which we are performing already appears complete.' Many of the themes have been suggested in the earlier poems: the interpenetration of life and death; the re-creation

---

[1] Angels, they say, often cannot tell whether they are moving among the living or the dead. The eternal torrent whirls all ages with it through both realms for ever, and sounds louder in both.

of beauty by the mourning of its loss, already described in
'Orpheus, Eurydike, Hermes'; the storing of impressions as the
purpose of life:

> Sind wir vielleicht hier, um zu sagen: Haus
> Brücke, Brunnen, Tor, Krug, Obstbaum, Fenster,—
> höchstens: Säule, Turm ... aber zu sagen, verstehs,
> oh zu sagen so, wie selber die Dinge niemals
> innig meinten zu sein.[1]

Here are stated the great themes of the Lover and the Hero,
whose supreme achievement is to transcend themselves before an
audience of the attendant dead: and in the Tenth Elegy—perhaps
Rilke's supreme achievement—there is the picture of the City of
Pain, his epitome of the common life, with the roaring fair on its
outskirts, with its rifle-ranges of happiness, and its curious booths
in which, for adults only, there is an anatomical display of the
breeding of money. In this last Elegy, Rilke appears to be
advancing from symbolism to allegory, and in it too, he makes
the final advance from pain and mourning to praise and joy.
Here out of a mourning landscape, overhung by mourning
constellations, named after life's hardest and most significant
experiences, joy breaks forth like a spring. And this miraculous
spring, further down, in the land of the living, will become a
navigable stream. The final motif is of praise and jubilation:

> Dasz ich dereinst, an dem Ausgang der grimmigen Einsicht,
> Jubel und Ruhm aufsinge zustimmenden Engeln.[2]

From this opening of the last Elegy to the *Sonette an Orpheus*,
which were rapidly written in those same February days that saw
the completion of the long unfinished Elegies, is but one step
forward. Though their ostensible purpose is to mourn a death,
their prevailing note is of praise. Orpheus emerges from Hades,
having eaten of poppy with the dead, and is now capable of
understanding the music of praise to which the world moves:

---

[1] Are we not here, perhaps, just to say: House, Bridge, Fountain, Gate, Jug, Olive-tree, Window—at the most, Pillar, Tower ... but to say it, understand, to say it in such a way as even the things themselves never inwardly imagined themselves to be.

[2] That one day, emerging from this terrible vision, I may burst into jubilant praise before assenting angels.

Nur wer die Leier schon hob
auch unter Schatten,
darf das unendliche Lob
ahnend erstatten.

Nur wer mit Toten vom Mohn
asz, von dem ihren,
wird nicht den leisesten Ton
wieder verlieren.

Mag auch die Spieglung im Teich
oft uns verschwimmen:
Wisse das Bild.

Erst in dem Doppelbereich
werden die Stimmen
ewig und mild.[1]

The best of these sonnets develop paradoxes like those of the mystical poets. But Rilke's vision remains on a psychological rather than a spiritual plane. The *double-sphere* is that in which object and reflection, reality and dream, life and death are one: and it is here that the poet comes to see objects in their true shape. True, he still feels himself threatened by the world of machines, and the ugliness of the City of Pain, but he has won through to an allegorical view of life, and to the certainty that all will in the end be well:

Heil dem Geist, der uns verbinden mag;
denn wir leben wahrhaft in Figuren.
Und mit kleinen Schritten gehn die Uhren
neben unserm eigentlichen Tag.

Ohne unsern wahren Platz zu kennen,
handeln wir aus wirklichen Bezug.[2]

A single stage further, and Rilke might have found a religious attitude. But with this supreme achievement of February 1922, his progress stopped. Some fragments of unfinished poems written in the last four years of his life show him to have been

---

[1] Only one who has raised his lyre even among the shades can divine and deliver unending praise.
  Only one who has eaten of their own poppy with the dead, will never again lose its slightest note.
  Even if the reflection in the pond often blurs for us, know the picture.
  Not till the double-sphere will the voices be eternal and mild.

[2] Hail to the spirit that can unite us, for in truth we live figuratively, and in comparison with our proper day the clocks move by little steps.
  Without knowing our real place, we act by true relationship.

developing the allegorical manner of the Tenth Elegy, and there are more exercises in the paradoxical manner of the Sonnets.

In his two great works Rilke not only created a world-picture more complete and profound than that of any contemporary poet with the possible exception of Yeats, but also enriched and extended the resources of German poetry to as great an extent as Goethe. In the *Elegies*, he made the long German line flexible, varying its pace and breaking up the fixed patterns in which the German poetic sentence is liable to fall. His variation of pace, his compact imagery, his abrupt changes from figurative to objective language, are for German absolutely original. They have given the first generation of German poets to learn from him—those of the post-Nazi epoch—a technical capital that is still far from exhausted. The *Sonnets* on the other hand are in a purely German tradition; they are indeed only sonnets in the number of their lines and their rhyme-schemes. Metrically and in length of line they are not sonnets in the conventional sense. The work is far more various also than an orthodox sonnet sequence, since the poems do not follow a single pattern.

If the *Sonnets* have any affinities with the past, it is with the sometimes irregular sonnet forms of the German Baroque poets. Their compressed statements also remind one occasionally of the final lyrics of the second *Faust*. They are thus in complete contrast to the *Elegies*, whose closest formal model, like that of Eliot's early poetry, is to be found in Laforgue's cadenced free-verse. Both Eliot's and Rilke's verses are, however, far more regular than Laforgue's. What Laforgue taught both poets was the art of counterpoint. Within their lines, and sometimes competing with their formal pattern, is a secondary organization of assonances, alliterations and echoes.

Over all Rilke's last poetry as over the *Sonnets* presides the figure of Orpheus who, failing to bring back his lost Eurydice, remained on earth as the symbol of transformation and of song:

> Errichtet keinen Denkstein. Laszt die Rose
> nur jedes Jahr zu seinen Gunsten blühn.
> Denn Orpheus ists. Seine Metamorphose
> in dem und dem. Wir sollen uns nicht mühn

Um andre Namen. Ein für alle Male
ists Orpheus, wenn es singt. Er kommt und geht.
Ists nicht schon viel, wenn er die Rosenschale
um ein paar Tage manchmal übersteht?

O wie er schwinden musz, dasz ihrs begrifft![1]

In his later life Rilke made some successful translations of
poems by Paul Valéry (1871-1945), with whom he felt a close
affinity. Yet these, sensitive though they are, show that even in
Rilke's hands, German lacks the subtlety to express the fine play
of the imagination which has been one of the chief qualities of
French poetry since Mallarmé. For the German poet an object is
present or absent, a symbol is firmly visual or tactile. For the
French poet, and to a lesser degree for the Spanish and Italian,
absence of a remembered object, if sufficiently dwelt on, almost
evokes its presence, and reality borders closely on dream.
Valéry is consequently a more difficult poet than Rilke, since even
after establishing his often elusive meanings, one cannot be
certain that the shimmer of his verse does not conceal other
meanings more evanescent still. His is a poetry of disappearances,
in which the natural objects observed and chosen as symbols
dissolve into an interplay of thought and feeling, that lies wholly
within the poet's mind. Valéry's principal concern is with the
tension between action and the philosophical contemplation of
which it is both the outcome and the destroyer. His Narcissus
gazing into the pool in the quiet of dusk, finds his absorbed
brooding disturbed by the thought of other men who have gazed
in the same water before him;

Ils respirent ce vent, marchent sans le savoir,
Foulent auz pieds le temps d'un jour de désespoir . . .
O marche lente, prompte, et pareille aux pensées
Qui parlent tour à tour aux têtes insensées!
La caresse et le meurtre hésitent dans leurs mains,
Leur cœur, qui croit se rompre au détours des chemins,
Lutte, et retient à soi son espérance étreinte.
Mais leurs esprits perdus courent ce labyrinthe
Où s'égare celui qui maudit le soleil!

[1] Set up no memorial stone. Only let the rose flower every year at his desire. For it is
Orpheus. His metamorphosis into this and that. We need not trouble ourselves for
other names. For he is once and for all Orpheus when he sings. It is not already much
that he often outlasts the rosecup by a few days? Oh but he must vanish for you to
understand it.

Leur folle solitude, à l'égal du sommeil,
Peuple et trompe l'absence. . . .[1]

Contemplation is impossible, since its purity is contaminated
by the ghosts of other men, whose passions and despairs, reflected
even in the stillest pool, break the Narcissus-image; the alternative is action. Life must be accepted, and the subtlest music of the
turning spheres be adapted to the coarse ears of men. From
contemplating the dead in their Mediterranean graveyard the
poet turns at the conclusion of his 'Le Cimetière Marin' (Cemetery
by the Sea), to a rejoicing in life and beauty, even though there
may be nothing beyond it:

Le vent se lève! . . . il faut tenter de vivre!
L'air immense ouvre et referme mon livre,
La vague en poudre ose jaillir des rocs!
Envolez-vous, pages tout éblouies!
Rompez, vagues! Rompez d'eaux réjouies
Ce toit tranquille où picoraient des focs![2]

Valéry's is a visual poetry of extreme compression—as witness
the double picture of the last line quoted—and is held together
by a pattern of ever varying mood. He does not reason, but turns
his mind, which moves always with overtones of feeling, from one
climate of thought to another. For him the sole positive achievement in life is poetic creation. But here lies a paradox, which is
set out in his poem 'La Pythie' (The Prophetess): the act of
creating a poem violates the calm of contemplation, which
represents a higher value still. Narcissus for ever gazes into the
pool, but the waters never grow quite still.

Valéry was in his youth a disciple of Mallarmé, under whose
influence he wrote a number of short poems afterwards published
as the *Album des Vers Anciens* (Album of Old Verses). For many
years he occupied an important position in the world of finance,
and wrote nothing more until 1917, when he published 'La Jeune
Parque' (The Young Fate). This fragmentary presentation of his

[1] They breathe this wind, walk without knowing it, tread underfoot the hours of a
despairing day. . . . Oh slow, sharp tread, that is like the thoughts that speak one after
another to the foolish brain! Kissing and murder hesitate in their hands, their heart
which believes it will break at each bend in the road, struggles and holds on to its hope
with clutching fingers. But their lost spirits walk this labyrinth, where strays the man
who curses the sun! Their crazy solitude, like sleep, peoples solitude and receives it.

[2] The wind rises . . . one must attempt to live. The vast air opens and closes my book,
the wave dares to spout from the rocks in spray! Fly away, my dazzled pages! Break
waves, break up with your rejoicing waters this quiet roof where foresails used to peck.

conflicting moods is already partially free from the aesthetic influence of his master, which prevailed in his early verses. It is, however, constructed after the manner of 'L'Après-midi d'un Faune', though with the important difference that the flux is one of thought rather than of sensual mood. 'La Jeune Parque' is, however, hermetic in Mallarmé's way; the poems of his next and final volume *Charmes* (Charms), while no less subtle, are almost entirely clear. Although still using a symbolist technique, Valéry reduces and simplifies, introducing into an atmosphere of dream a certain order and intelligence. The march of his verse has, in fact, classical affiliations and the use of a clinching phrase or rhyme often suggests that his aim is to produce a classical equivalent to Mallarmé's Romantic and associative verse. One can even detect Racinean echoes in the opening address to the spring in the second fragment of his unfinished 'Narcisse', and particularly in its fourth line:

> Fontaine, ma fontaine, eau froidement présente,
> Douce aux purs animaux, aux humains complaisante
> Qui d'eux-mêmes tentés suivent au fond la mort,
> Tout est songe pour toi, Soeur tranquille du Sort![1]

The shorter poems in *Charmes* start with the contemplation of some familiar creature or object. The image is then developed from plane to plane of diminishing reality. Compared with Rilke's Orpheus sonnets, Valéry's poems seem insubstantial; thought seems to be feeding on itself. Yet in 'Les Pas' (The Steps) one finds a symbol compactly developed to tell two stories at once: that of a delighted lover waiting for the steps of a woman who is coming to his bed, and that of an equally delighted poet awaiting the moment of inspiration:

> Si, de tes lèvres avancées
> Tu prépares pour l'apaiser,
> A l'habitant de mes pensées
> La nourriture d'un baiser,
>
> Ne hâte pas cet acte tendre,
> Douceur d'être et de n'être pas,
> Car j'ai vécu de vous attendre,
> Et mon cœur n'était que vos pas.[2]

[1] Spring, my spring, water coldly present, sweet to animals, who are pure, and condescending to humans who, self-tempted, follow death to the bottom, all is dream for you, quiet Sister of Fate.

[2] If with lips advanced you are preparing to appease the inhabitant of my thoughts with the nourishment of a kiss, do not hurry the tender act, sweet in its being and not-being, for I have lived by waiting for you, and my heart has been nothing but your steps.

Though Valéry may begin from a simple observation, his tendency is to refine his subject till it is raised to the plane of metaphysics. Rilke, when speaking of something like Valéry's kiss that both is and is not, attempts to present it more concretely, as in his poem of the unicorn, which advances from non-being to being by virtue of being loved:

> O dieses ist das Tier, das es nicht gibt.
> Sie wusztens nicht und habens jeden Falls
> —seinen Wandeln, seine Haltung, seinen Hals,
> bis in des stillen Blickes Licht—geliebt.[1]

The unicorn acquires so much life that it comes, in fulfilment of the legend, to be reflected in a maiden's mirror. Valéry's 'Habitant de mes pensées', on the other hand, remains completely mysterious to the end. It may stand for his love, which will be nourished by his mistress's kiss, or for himself as poet, or—by an even finer metaphysical interpretation—for the essence of himself, dwelling except at rare moments among his thoughts, but acquiring its own existence in the act of love or creation. Rilke moves from the abstract to the concrete, and Valéry in the opposite direction.

In 'Cantique des Colonnes' (Song of the Columns) unequalled among Valéry's poems except by 'Le Cimetière Marin', the movement towards abstraction is even more pronounced. The columns of some classical temple, described in the early verses in all the reality of their stone

> Par le ciseau tirées,
> Pour devenir ces lys![2]

become a principle of rhythm, a mathematical proportion, and finally a set of dancers, performing their figure not in space but in time, moving through the centuries with the inevitability of a stone falling into the sea.

> Nous marchons dans le temps
> Et nos corps éclatants
> Ont des pas ineffables
> Qui marquent dans les fables. . .[3]

---

[1] This is the creature that does not exist. They did not know it, and so loved it—its walk, its gait, its neck and the light in its quiet gaze.

[2] Drawn by the chisel to become these lilies.

[3] We move in time, and our radiant bodies take ineffable steps that leave their mark in fables.

Valéry's poetry advances beyond that of Mallarmé, from which it sprang, by reason of these powers of abstraction. The master refines on the sensual vision, becoming obscure at the moment when his private associations differ from those of any possible reader. Valéry, on the other hand, though his thought is dense in 'La Jeune Parque', quickly refines it. He is difficult only in so far as he is always arguing from observation to idea. He does not, however, entirely reject living for thinking. 'Le Cimetière Marin' and other poems are rich with the heat and sunshine of the Mediterranean scene. Nor is he on the side of the dead against the living. In 'Le Cimetière Marin' it is clear that neither the dead nor Zeno's timeless moment of contemplation embodies his ultimate values. Yet, although the poem ends on a note of mental affirmation, the progress towards it has not been unchecked. Valéry's poetry is the product of a conflict between thought and the powers of distraction, represented by the Serpent in 'Ebauche d'un Serpent' (Sketch of a Serpent), and it is the raw sensuality of the disturbing elements that gives it its warmth and brilliance. Were his the poetry of pure, abstract contemplation, Valéry would not be capable of the grandeur of his address to the sun, in his Serpent poem. Here he characterizes the nourisher of life as at the same time the raiser of an illusory world:

> Grand Soleil, qui sonnes l'éveil
> A l'être, et de feux l'accompagnes,
> Toi qui l'enfermes d'un sommeil
> Trompeusement peint de campagnes,
> Fauteur des fantômes joyeux
> Qui rendent sujette des yeux
> La présence obscure de l'âme,
> Toujours le mensonge m'a plu
> Que tu repands sur l'absolu
> O roi des ombres fait de flammes![1]

George, Rilke and Valéry revived Symbolist poetry, increased the range of its subject matter, and spread its influence beyond the boundaries of the French speaking world. Rilke, indeed, the

[1] Great sun, that sounds the waking blast to being, and accompanies it with fires, you who enclose it in a sleep deceptively painted with landscapes, protector of joyous phantoms that bring the obscure presence of the soul within the orbit of the vision, I have always been pleased by the lie that you spread over the Absolute, O king of shades made of flame!

greatest figure of the three, was translated in his lifetime, and sometimes with his own assistance, into a number of languages, and his influence extended throughout the whole field of European poetry. His *Elegies* are the supreme large-scale poem of the last fifty years, challenged only by Eliot's *Four Quartets*, These, indeed, and Ezra Pound's *Cantos*, are the only achievements of symphonic scale to be dealt with in this book; others such as Robert Bridges' *Testament of Beauty*, and various large-scale poems in German attempt rather to imitate the great works of the past than to speak in a new way of the spiritual discoveries of a new age.

4

To the remote Hesperides

THE new poetry, with its symbolism, its metaphysical interests, its kinship with the seventeenth century, and its capitalization of the technical experiments made by the successors of Baudelaire, spread in the second decade of the present century to the western edges of Europe, which had hitherto been slow to respond to new poetical movements and influences. Now for the first time Andalusia and Ireland, countries that still cherished memories of an older, pre-European culture, had each a major poet, and somewhat later the last and most consequent of the symbolist poets, Edwin Muir, brought even the remote Orkneys into the orbit of modern poetry.

Juan Ramón Jiménez (1881-1958), the poet of Moguer, near the Atlantic coast of southern Spain, transplanted himself midway through his poetic career to the further side of that ocean, as a consequence of the Civil War. Consequently, he is at present more highly valued in Spanish America than in Spain itself. So long as he remained at home, indeed, his work could not be compared to that of his major European contemporaries. The volume of his early production was large, but it was not till his old-age that he became capable of treating a major theme at any length. His countrymen, knowing his older poetry better than his more recent, which was published abroad, tend to praise him, therefore, for his impressionistic charm rather than for his metaphysical power.

Jiménez's development, through a variety of decadent, aesthetic and precious styles, in each of which he wrote remarkable poems of short flight, did not bring him to the stage reached by the mature Rilke and George around 1908 for almost another thirty years. The first of his poems, indeed, to fall clearly into the modern category date from 1935.

Jiménez's beginnings as a poet were under the influence of Verlaine and lesser French writers. Summoned from his remote corner of Andalusia by the fashionable poets of Madrid, he made his early reputation with an ease that would have been fatal to a less scrupulous and retiring craftsman. Rubén Darío, the prodigious Nicaraguan who had, almost single-handed, rescued Spanish poetry from provincial dullness, had been very far from Spanish in his tradition. His success lay in transplanting fashions that were already fading in Paris to a poetry which had discovered no new forms since the Romantic era. Though Jiménez's initial inspiration was French also, he had as a young man not only steeped himself in the atmosphere and tradition of his own province, whose history was deeply affected by the Arabic civilization of which it had been the centre. He read also with selective enthusiasm two almost forgotten poets of the nineteenth century, Gustavo Adolfo Bécquer and Rosalía Castro, who had emptied Spanish poetry of its prevailing rhetoric, and written with a sometimes harsh directness reminiscent of Thomas Hardy. He also read the half-forgotten folk-songs which were being collected, in his youth, from the various provinces of Spain. Familiarity with these folk-songs, which in their compression and their strange tricks of assonance, echoed their seventeenth-century origins, gave Jiménez an advantage that had been denied to the cosmopolitan Darío, as it had to others of the generation that came to maturity about 1908: he was from the first in touch with a submerged popular tradition, which had much to offer to Spanish poetry even up to the years of the Civil War.

Coming to Madrid as the poet of deserted parks and ghostly assignations, he brought with him a memory on which the scenes of his home had made a far stronger impression than had the vineyards of his youth on Stefan George's or the impressions of anything in the landscapes of his childhood upon Rilke's. Colour, light, perfume, the vastness of evening cloudscapes, the freshness of the wind from the Sierra, and the harsh midday sun on the treeless plain: all are conveyed with an immediacy that dispels the hazy impressionism of his adopted medium. Into the evening twilight of his deserted park with its dull golds, its indistinct voices and its hints of gnomes or satyrs with tragic gaze, breaks the sudden glory of sunset, piercing the clouds:

> Pero el cielo . . . El cielo no
> puede ser para este encanto;
> el jardín está partido
> a la altura de los brazos;
> y el cenit se va rompiendo
> de hoja en hoja . . . Sólo un algo
> de amatista, ¿ de qué mundo ?,
> de oro ignoto, de azul májico;
> una luz de pesadilla
> sobre los helechos blandos;
> una nieve de sol; no, un
> sol de luna . . . ¿ estrellas, nardos ? . . .[1]

The whole mood of the poem has changed: the park is rightly described in its title as 'Parque doble'. (Twofold Park).

This duality expressed in the double vision of a park runs through all Jiménez's early poetry. A man of poor health, readily subject to vague bodily disorders, he had in part the temperament of a true Decadent. On the other hand, the making of poetry was to him a positive activity from which he derived great energy; and the countryside, in which he was so deeply rooted, represented for him a landscape of ever-changing moods, liable to be struck at any moment, as was his park, by a shaft of sunlight, by the white beam of creation. Andalusia was, in fact, a concept of double meaning: a country of rock and harsh sunshine that was at the same time a metaphysical reflection of the poet's own barrenness at those moments when poetry did not come.

For many years Jiménez's inspiration was fugitive. He wrote many poems, and tried several mediums—the folk-song, the sonnet, the strict quatrain, and unrhymed vers-libre—in an endeavour to make his poetry more substantial. Music and visual imagery were always present, but the poet had needed to find a metaphysical certainty, like Rilke's; and for this a deepened understanding of the actual moments of creation seemed necessary. With his marriage in 1916, and his participation in the liberal cultural movement then developing in Spain, his poetry took a more consistently optimistic turn; autumn park yielded to sunsoaked fields, night to morning, autumn to spring. A new brightness of imagery, relying not on fashionable French theories concerning the confusion of the sense impressions, but

---

[1] But the sky . . . the sky can have no part in this enchantment; the garden is divided at arm's height, and the zenith breaks on one leaf after another. . . . Only a little amethyst,—from which world? a little unknown gold, and magic blue; a nightmare light on the soft ferns; a snowfall of sunlight. No, the sun like moonlight. . . . Are they stars or tuberoses?

on the folk-tradition of Andalusia, gave his poetry a sharp impact,
that it was later to transmit to an Andalusian of the next generation, Federico García Lorca. The following lines, indeed, might
well be Lorca's:

> Levantará el gallo
> su clarín de llama
> y la aurora plena
> cantando entre granas,
> prenderá sus fuegos
> en las ramas blandas[1]

But Jiménez was not satisfied with these powers of invention;
what he wanted was a limpidity that he had never yet attained,
like that of a pool, as he wrote, into which the spray of a fountain
has disappeared leaving no trace on the surface that has received
it. Always his endeavour was for *depuración:* a purification that
would eliminate all decorative detail. Already adjectives of colour
and substance had yielded to those of light and absence: a rose is
described in terms not of its present beauty, but of its scent that
lingers on the memory. Jiménez's aim is like that of Rilke, to
transmit the essence of things, divorced from their temporal
appearance. But where Rilke in 'Die Rosenschale' sets out to
distil the idea of a rose from its physical development in time
from bud to overblown flower, Jiménez starts from the imprint of
an already vanished rose on the poet's memory. The method
might seem to be derived from Mallarmé's, but Jiménez's purpose
is his own. Not satisfied with mastery of rhythm and sensual
imagery, he is striving to call out from himself the missing
intellectual quality, without which he cannot bring substantiality
to his writing. It was this that he demanded at the point, in about
1919, when his self-imposed task of *depuración* was almost
complete:

> Intelijencia, dame
> el nombre exacto de las cosas!
> . . . Que mi palabra sea
> la cosa misma,
> creada por mi alma nuevamente.
> Que por mí vayan todos
> los que no las conocen, a las cosas. . . . [2]

[1] The cock will raise his trumpet of fire, and full dawn, singing among crimsons, will
set fire to the tender branches.

[2] Intelligence, give me the precise name of things. . . . Let my word be the thing itself,
newly created by my soul. Through me let all those who do not know things approach
them.

C

Now the search for metaphysical truth, and a growing delight in the poetic gift itself, which had formerly appeared painful, began slowly to bring more colour into Jiménez's poetry. Adjectives signifying brightness and transparence give place to nouns, unqualified and sometimes repeated, that suggest the existence of isolated and significant objects in an otherwise empty world. As Rilke in his *Elegies* suggested that man must transform nature by means of art to a condition in which it can be perceived by angels, so Jiménez now suggests that by total devotion to the task of writing his own nature will one day arise remade like the phoenix, a pure immortal ember.

> Día tras día, mi ala
> —¡ cavadora, minadora!
> ¡ qué dura azadón de luz!—
> me entierra en el papel blanco. ..
> —¡ Ascensión mía parada
> en futuros del ocaso!—
> ... De él, ascua pura inmortal,
> quemando el sol de carbón,
> volaré refigurado![1]

At the moment of writing this poem, 'La obra' (Work) the poet's ascension still seemed to him far in the future; perhaps the mention of sunsets is meant to suggest that he will have to wait till his old-age. For in the same year of 1923 he wrote to the German critic Ernst Robert Curtius: 'At the age of 42, and after twenty-five years of ceaseless labour with Beauty—I feel, think, and clearly see that this is where I begin; and if I live fifteen or twenty years more, I believe that I shall see my work—which all exists in an inchoate state today—realized.'

The first step forward was marked by *La Estación total* (All Seasons in one), which contained poems written between 1923 and 1936, and was published in Buenos Aires. Jiménez makes no attempt to build a mythology; his symbols are few. What he does is to recall to life the birds and creatures that perished in his *depuración*. Now they appear not as reflections of his moods, but objectively seen, with wonder and reverence, as part of a divine order with which the poet is in tune only in his moments of

---

[1] Day after day, my wing—an excavator, a miner, with how hard a pickaxe of light—buries me in the white paper—My slow ascension into a future of sunsets. From it a pure immortal ember, burning the coal of the sun, I shall fly transformed!

creation. The central experience of this book and its unfinished successor, *Dios deseado y deseante*, is that timeless moment that is central also to T. S. Eliot's *Four Quartets*. The life of a flower is shown in 'Flor que vuelve' (Flower that returns) to be just such a moment:

> ¡ Florecer y vivir, instante
> de central chispa detenida,
> abierta en una forma tentadora;
> instante sin pasado,
> en que los cuatro puntos cardinales
> son de igual atracción dulce y profunda;
> instante del amor abierto
> como la flor!
> Amor y flor en perfección de forma. . . . [1]

Jiménez had always been the enemy of history, had only valued his perceptions in so far as they gave him admittance to immediate truth, without past or future. It was to this that he attained in his moments of creation, and it is in these timeless and selfless moments that he had in his last poems his desired and desirous God, who is not the God of the Catholics. Rather is He akin to that spirit which Blake characterized as Eternity, and which he said was in love with the productions of Time. Evidence of this God he finds in the processes of creation, in the sea and in that glory of nature that Jiménez had praised in his early poetry, and then neglected as he pursued his search for abstractions. Once more He appears to the poet in the colours of the night sky:

> Todas las nubes arden
> porque yo te he encontrado,
> dios deseante y deseado;
> antorchas altas cárdenas
> (granas, azules, rojas, amarillas)
> en alto grito de rumor de luz.
> Del redondo horizonte vienen todas
> en congregación fúljida,
> a abrazarse con vueltas de esperanza
> a mi fe respondida.[2]

[1] Flowering and living, the moment of a central spark, prolonged and open in a tempting form; a moment with no past, in which the four points of the compass exert equal attraction, both sweet and deep, a moment of love open like a flower. Love and flower in perfection of form. . . .

[2] All the clouds burn because I have found you, God desirous and desired, tall, livid torches (crimson, blue, red and yellow) in a high shout like the sound of light. From the round horizon they all come in a bright assembly to embrace one another with return of hope that answers my faith.

Jiménez's God is present in the bird at dawn, in all nature and in the love of man and woman. He is the desirer when the poet desires, and He is at the same time the object of that desire. On this note of mystical paradox Jiménez's poetry concluded. It had not become a religious poetry, though it was now firmly grounded in metaphysical understanding. Having begun in the half-light with hints and impressions, it had become a poetry of major statement. Though now austere and undecorated, it yet retained some echoes of its early music, and recaptured some of the colour of its Andalusian beginnings. God had found his way back into nature:

> Mar verde y cielo gris y cielo azul
> y albatros amorosos en la ola,
> y en todo, el sol, y tú en el sol, mirante
> dios deseado y deseante. . . .[1]

In this poetry of the last decade of his life, Jiménez stood far apart from the poets of Spain and if not also of Spanish America. Twenty years before, at the moment when Gerardo Diego's first anthology aroused the world's interest in contemporary Spanish poetry, all the younger men owed something to Jiménez. Only one, however, Jorge Guillén (b. 1893), consistently followed him in his concern for essences; others imitated his music, but favoured bolder imagery and practised repeated changes of style. Guillén alone slowly put together a single collection, *Cántico* (Song-book), which was published in its final form in Buenos Aires in 1950. For he had followed Jiménez into exile, and has been for more than twenty years teaching in the United States.

The poems of *Cántico* have a deceptive transparency; white seems to be laid on white, mirror to reflect mirror. For Guillén the essence of a loved person or thing, or of an event, can be held only in the depths of the stilled mind, which like the water of a limpid pool catches the image of the heavens. The poem 'Presagio' (Presage), from the section *Aquí mismo* (Here and nowhere else) of this book conveys the metaphysical intensity of a poetry which, like that of Jiménez, is non-religious:

---

[1] Green sea and grey sky and blue sky and loving albatrosses on the waves, and the sun over everything, and you in the sun, gazing down, desired and desirous God.

Eres ya la fragancia de tu sino.
Tu vida no vivida, pura, late
Dentro de mí, tictac de ningun tiempo.

¡Qué importa que el ajeno sol no alumbre
Jamás estas figuras, sí, creadas,
Sonadas no, por nuestros dos orgullos!
    No importa. Son así más verdaderas
    Que el semblante de luces verosímiles
    En escorzos de azar y compromiso.

Todo tú convertida en tu presagio,
¡Oh, pero sin misterio! Te sostiene
La unidad invasora y absoluta.

¿Qué fue de aquella enorme, tan informe,
Pululación en negro de lo hondo,
Bajo las soledades estrelladas?
    Las estrellas insignes, las estrellas
    No miran nuestra noche sin arcanos.
    Muy tranquilo se está lo tan oscuro.

La oscura eternidad ¡oh! no es un monstruo
Celeste. Nuestras almas invisibles
Conquistan su presencia entre las cosas.[1]

The poetry of Guillén moves in an opposite direction from
that of Valéry, which has, no doubt, to a slight extent influenced
it. Guillén knew the French poet, and made a fine translation of
'Le Cimetière marin'. But where Valéry proceeds from object to
abstraction, Guillén, like Rilke, beginning with metaphysical
statement, ends in the world of objects. Though the beloved of
this poem has become for him a mere scent, though their souls
are so detached from even the starry night as to be quite transparent, holding no secrets, yet eternity itself, he insists, can only
be experienced among things.

Guillén's poetry is full of reflections of rooms, of scenes, of
landscapes and even of political events, which are caught in this
mirror of eternity, and presented in the absolute present. It is a

[1] Now you have become the scent of your fate, your pure and unlived life pulses
within me, a ticking of no time.
What does it matter that the alien sun never lights these shapes, which are created,
not dreamed, by our twin prides? It does not matter. In this way they are truer than the
semblances of lights one can believe in, foreshortened by disaster and difficulty.
All of you transformed into your presage—oh, but with no mystery! The invading
and absolute unity supports you.
What has become of that enormous, that shapeless pulsing in the deep blackness,
beneath the starred solitudes? The famous stars, the stars do not gaze on our night,
which has no secrets. The great darkness has become quite unperturbed.
Dark eternity is not, no is not a monster of the heavens. Our invisible souls capture its
presence among things.

poetry of the moment of greater clarity that comes on waking from sleep, of sudden ecstasies, in which the cause is forgotten and only the greater intensity of sensations is remembered, of light seeping in through closed eyelids, of breeze and iridescence, of hard outlines dividing hardly perceptible colours, which nevertheless denote real objects seen in their essential being.

What separates Guillén from Jiménez is his closer kinship to the Baroque poetry of essences. The older poet experimented with Gongorism in his *Sonetos espirituales* (Spiritual Sonnets), and then, in the course of his self-imposed *depuración*, put aside his seventeenth-century models. Guillén, on the other hand, whose poetry shows no perceptible development, poems of 1919 being indistinguishable in style from those of 1950, has long ago perfected his own *depuración* of the Baroque technique, without sacrificing the essential strength of metre, metaphor and wordplay that he owes to Góngora and his contemporaries.

The conclusion of Guillén's 'Tarde mayor' (The Greater Evening), which tells of the triumph of nature over history, of ultimate freedom over the cruelties of the Civil War, is compact in an altogether seventeenth-century manner though with little trace of actual Baroque mannerism:

> Y pasará el camión de los feroces.
> Castaños sin Historia arrojarán
> Su florecilla al suelo—blanquecino.
>
> Un ámbito de tarde en perfección
> Tan desarmada humildemente opone,
> Por fin venciendo, su fragilidad
>
> A ese desbarajuste sólo humano
> Que a golpes lucha contra el mismo azul
> Impasible, feroz también, profundo.
>
> Fugaz la Historia, vano el destructor.
> Resplandece la tarde. Yo contigo.
> Eterna al sol la brisa juvenil.[1]

Guillén's poetry often shimmers with hints and half-meanings, only to shine out suddenly with positive statements. In these it

[1] And the cruel men's lorry will pass. Chestnuts with no history will shed their small flowers on the ground—which will be almost white. A circle of evening in its perfection, thus disarmed, opposes its fragility to—and finally conquers—this merely human disorder that beats against the invulnerable sky itself, which is cruel also and deep. History is transitory, the destroyer works to no avail. The evening shines. I am with you. The young breeze is eternal in the sunshine.

goes far beyond that of Jiménez. But in his search for essences, Guillén is certainly nearer to Jiménez or Valéry than to his slightly younger contemporary Lorca. He is more sparing also in the development of his anecdote. One finds in his poetry little trace of his reading, his opinions, his beliefs, his history. Beside Lorca, or even beside Jiménez, he is almost anonymous. All one can postulate about him with certainty is that, like Rilke, Jiménez, and Valéry he unhesitatingly believes in the hegemony of the creative act.

The progress of W. B. Yeats (1865-1939) in many ways subsumes that of the other great Symbolists. Like George, but rather less convulsively, he dispelled his early dreams and woke to an agonized concern for the events of his day; like Rilke, he abandoned a picturesque and sentimental myth for an individual one; like Valéry, he composed a personal music, setting abstruse ideas to the lightest and surest of lyrical measures; and like Jiménez, he found his greatest strength in old age. Unlike all these, however, except Stefan George, he was never a 'pure' poet. Indeed, he introduced extraneous images into even the finest of his poems; and there are few that do not become clearer by the exploration of his philosophical beliefs.

So long as poets shared the general ideological background of their readers, such cosmological metaphors as they might introduce presented no difficulties. But Yeats's theosophical hypotheses were, even as Theosophy, unorthodox; and it is difficult to know what degree of faith he put in them himself. His imagery can seldom be treated, however, like that of Rilke, as a purely poetic system, revolving around the fixed star of the creative act. Yeats's system depended on the almost equal pull of two poles, that of poetry and that of semi-religious belief. Only in very few poems, of which 'Byzantium' is one, does strength of vision draw these opposite poles into a complete relation with one another. It is not by chance that Yeats thought of life and creation as a dance of opposites.

Before *The Green Helmet* of 1910, Yeats was a minor poet, a survivor from the days of *The Yellow Book* who used Irish myth and theosophical theory as a picturesque decoration for essentially Decadent poetry. Through Arthur Symons, the first propagandist for Symbolism in Britain, he had heard of Mallarmé; and he knew some French poems of the period in

Symons' translations. Later in life too, he became curious about the aristocratic attitudes of Stefan George, which seemed to chime with his own. But Yeats had small knowledge of foreign languages; he had little French and no German. Whereas Rilke, George and Jiménez were well read in French, and Valéry had knowledge of the Greek and Latin classics, Yeats began only with the capital he derived from those English poets who appealed to him; Spenser, Shelley and his own contemporaries of the 'nineties. He was at first, in fact, so little attuned to the new fashions which were to come that his interest was rather in the texture of a poem than in the impact of its individual images. His treatment of the Rose, a symbol of central importance to Rilke and Jiménez, is strangely distant. The flower itself is not even visualized. Nor can Yeats go so far as Jiménez, and treat it in absence, as a scent that has vanished from the air. Yeats's rose is no more than a counter marked with the outline of a flower, intended to represent certain qualities or moods in an abstract philosophical scheme.

Yeats was from the outset fascinated by such schemes; that set out in his prose work, *The Vision*, is only one of several successive and compendious world-pictures, by which he set out to explain to himself the varied phenomena of life. First he was attracted to Irish mythology, which he blended with some ideas taken at second hand from Hinduism. Later he made some connection with Madame Blavatsky and the Theosophical movement, to which he attached himself somewhat loosely; its method of thought influenced his way of reasoning, however, throughout his life. For central to Theosophical theory was a belief in esotericism; the truth about the Universe was, according to the all-too-often conflicting teachings of the Society, known only to the few, who could pass it on only to the initiated. Its philosophy like Yeats's own was essentially magical.

In his earliest poetry Irish myth, theosophical speculation, and some unorthodox Christian imagery were combined with a certain 'ninetyish languor'. In 'The Secret Rose', the flower is perhaps intended to be a symbol of Esotericism itself:

> Far-off, most secret and inviolate Rose,
> Enfold me in my hour of hours; where those
> Who sought thee in the Holy Sepulchre,
> Or in the wine-vat, dwell beyond the stir

And tumult of defeated dreams; and deep
Among pale eyelids, heavy with the sleep
Men have named beauty. Thy great leaves enfold
The ancient beards, the helms of ruby and gold
Of the crowned Magi; and the king whose eyes
Saw the Pierced Hands and Rood of elder rise
In Druid vapour and make the torches dim;
Till vain frenzy awoke and he died; and him
Who met Fand walking among flaming dew
By a grey shore where the wind never blew,
And lost the world and Emer for a kiss. . . .

So loose is the poem's argument, and so insubstantial its associations, that the symbol never becomes clear. One is reminded of the easy manner of William Morris, whose *Earthly Paradise* contains many such shadowy invocations, composed of echoes from earlier poets, than of the later Yeats, the master of the compressed line. One of his prevailing defects, however, is already in evidence: his habit of assuming in his reader an acquaintance with ideas and symbols which were private to himself. Here one may ask who is the king 'whose eyes saw the Pierced Hands and Rood', and wonder what connection the poet has found between the Druids and the Holy Sepulchre. Again, his selection of adjectives is conventional and only vaguely emotive: 'the helms of ruby and gold of the crowned Magi' confuses helmets and crowns; 'flaming dew' raises a paradox that can only be resolved by reference to the story from which Yeats took his detail. This dream world, indeed, is more literary even than Rilke's imaginary Russia. There are, however, in these early poems occasional lines on which sensual observation has made a mark:

I have heard the pigeons of the Seven Woods
Make their faint thunder. . . .

is a statement that is only slowly weakened by the allusiveness of the poem that it introduces.

By 1910, however, the year of *The Green Helmet*, Yeats had grown dissatisfied with the vague poetic language in which he had hitherto been writing; he accused himself of having for too long pursued a mere sentimental beauty, which he considered unmanly. Now he advocated 'homely phrases' and 'the idiom of common speech'; and he shocked the management of the Abbey Theatre,

c *

Dublin, for which he was writing plays, by his harsh attempts to dispel his habitual Celtic Twilight by the introduction into '*The Shadowy Waters*' of bold sexual statement. Moreover a sentimentally poetic interest in Ireland's past was now beginning to yield to strong partisanship in some of his country's present controversies.

Yeats's early love poetry, though addressed to a living and very characterful woman, had borne very little imprint of her personality. She might have been as ethereal as the Queen of the Fairies, whom Yeats is seen introducing to the sceptical George Moore in Max Beerbohm's cartoon. But now controversy, the difficulty of suiting his lines to the mouths of living actors, and the very real loves and hatreds of his Dublin friends, reinforced his theoretical desire to make a *depuración* of his language, even to some extent of his imagery. 'No Second Troy' shows this revolution taking place. In speaking of his old love, Maud Gonne, now like himself approaching middle age, he removes her from the realm of abstractions, to relate her to a legend with universal associations:

> Why should I blame her that she filled my days
> With misery, or that she would of late
> Have taught to ignorant men most violent ways,
> Or hurled the little streets upon the great,
> Had they but courage equal to desire?

Along with a tautening of language, there is here the beginning of a new myth, in which, following Dante, the poet uses his friends and enemies, together with such figures from the Anglo-Irish past as Swift and Parnell, as characters in a cosmological scheme. Here he made little distinction, however, between living people or historical characters, and the half-legendary neighbours and ancestors who had peopled his childhood imagination in County Sligo. He had little of Dante's power of relating the drama in which he was himself involved to eternal principles.

Yeats's new mythology, though far more striking than the old, was to prove in many ways as abstruse and wayward. But henceforth ironic and often sharply rendered pictures of reality balanced the theoretical abstraction that had robbed his Rose poetry of any firm impact. Henceforth there was always a hard edge to at least some of any poem's images. Henceforth, too,

Yeats would express his moods, even those of exasperation,
clearly, as in 'The Fascination of What's Difficult', in which he
records his disgust with the practical job of suiting his reflective
line to the simpler needs of the theatre:

> My curse on plays
> That have to be set up in fifty ways,
> On the day's war with every knave and dolt,
> Theatre business, management of men.
> I swear before the dawn comes round again
> I'll find the stable and pull out the bolt.

Fortunately Yeats could not release the colt of his inspiration
from 'the lash, strain, sweat and jolt' of everyday controversy.
The next six years, up to the time of the tragically unsuccessful
rebellion of Easter Week 1916, saw him more, not less deeply
involved. Though he remained for the most part in England,
Yeats's feeling became increasingly bound up with Irish affairs,
the more so since the actors in them were not only performing
their own roles but at the same time playing parts in a mythological study of his own composition. They were for him at the same
time men and symbols.

'In dreams begins responsibility', a line that Yeats claimed to
have found in an old play, appears as epigraph to his collection of
1914, *Responsibilities*. The new Ireland was both his dream and
his responsibility. But in its early unheroic days, he only cursed it
for failing to revive the glories of its legendary past. He can find
little of the spirit of his childhood's heroes in the chaffering
Dublin of 'September 1913'. Yeats the spiritual aristocrat has
little sympathy with the petit-bourgeois revolutionaries who were
to win Ireland her independence:

> Yet they were of a different kind,
> The names that stilled your childish play,
> They have gone about the world like wind,
> But little time had they to pray
> For whom the hangman's rope was spun,
> And what, God help us could they save?
> Romantic Ireland's dead and gone,
> It's with O'Leary in the grave.

Romantic Ireland, however, was reborn in the events of
Easter 1916, and the responsibility for the pathos and the folly of

those days rested with the poets. The Irish movement had still to learn political realism, Yeats's first reaction was of disgust. Little though he subscribed to the English point of view in the First World War, which was then raging, he was almost as indifferent to the Irish rebellion in the form that it took. He dwelt in imagination in a past century, in which the responsibility for Ireland's fate had rested with his own class, the Protestant Anglo-Irish. The Ireland of his dream, if it were to take shape, would be as far from any of the present political alternatives as George's Third Empire from the realities of Hitlerian politics. Yeats was no democrat, and despised the people. The one quality he respected was heroism, and this he now discovered in the fighters around the Four Courts and the Post Office in that hopeless week, when men whom he had once scorned and

> passed with a nod of the head
> Or polite meaningless words. . . .
> Being certain that they and I
> But lived where motley is born

were suddenly transformed into heroes:

> All changed, changed utterly:
> A terrible beauty is born.

The transformation, however, was short-lived, and existed principally in Yeats's thoughts. The history of Ireland reverted to its unheroic way, and Yeats, though honoured by the Republic with a seat in the Senate, remained generally aloof. The real transformation was in himself, and synchronized with his marriage in 1917. This, like Jiménez's marriage in the previous year, brought a new directness. Both poets had hitherto been too prone to seek for essences not as the fruit of experience but as a substitute for it. The immediate effect was to bring Yeats closer to reality, but to enmesh him at the same time in his final and most elaborate system of symbolical speculations. His wife proved to be a medium, capable of producing automatic scripts. In these certain 'communicators' set out for Yeats that most compendious world-system which he explained in his prose work, *The Vision*, and which he used, in varying degrees of complexity, in several poems. The purpose of these communications was made clear at the outset by the mysterious dictating agency: 'We have come to give you metaphors for your poetry.'

The material written down by Mrs. Yeats under these trance conditions was of a piece with her husband's previous metaphysical speculations. One cannot but think that the active mind behind the manifestations was his own. Furthermore, the ideas were clearly elaborated at later stages either by husband and wife together, or by the poet alone. He speaks indeed in *The Vision* of having thought out part of it in All Souls' Chapel at Oxford. What degree of credence he himself placed in it is not clear. The pattern of 'phases of the moon', which explained the psychological differences of humanity, by reference to a succession of incarnations through which each passed, is in fact a variant of theosophical theory, probably influenced by the symbology of the Tarot cards. Other constituents were drawn from occultist writing with which Yeats was already familiar. It was at least therefore generally consonant with the poet's previous ideas; the originality lay in its application to his poetry.

Here the nodal point lay not in the theory of types and incarnations, which merely permitted Yeats to cast his friends once more for parts in a drama of his own composition. It lay in the field of opposites. The great Wheel of Incarnations was a prison in which man would continue to revolve, unless at certain 'phases of the moon' when personality was weakest, an escape could be made. Yeats had hitherto thought of himself as a heroic figure; now he brought into play his opposite or anti-self, symbolized as the Hunchback, the Saint or the Fool, representives of those phases in which escape from a recurrence of lives was possible.

> Hunchback and Saint and Fool are the last crescents.
> The burning bow that once could shoot an arrow
> Out of the up and down, the wagon wheel
> Of beauty's cruelty and wisdom's chatter—
> Out of that raving tide—is drawn betwixt
> Deformity of body and of mind.

Yeats himself was proud of his physical beauty; he remained on the side of the Hero, but the dualism appears in the poetry; something in Yeats cried for self-abnegation, and the throwing down of the poetic mask. Perhaps it expressed itself best in the folk-like simplicity of some of his latest songs, which he put into the mouths of creatures like Crazy Jane, whose position on the wheel lay somewhere between deformity of body and of mind.

This same dualism appeared again in the contradiction which Yeats found between philosophy and the life of the senses. Generally he speaks for the flesh, rating beauty, as he had done in his earliest poems, as a spiritual blessedness in itself. But the dilemma is never resolved. It is in fact accepted into the system of *The Vision*, in the loosely Platonic theory of contradictory gyres or spirals; subjectivity and objectivity, space and time, Will and Creative Mind, appear as opposing forces, or 'intersecting states struggling against one another'. Life is, in Yeats's view, the product of these tensions.

At moments, even in his finest poems, ideas from this system are introduced somewhat crudely; the symbolism never became as natural to the poet as Rilke's purely poetic symbolism in the *Elegies:* In 'The Second Coming'—already mentioned—a poem inspired by the Irish troubles of the 'twenties, in which Yeats prophesied the end of civilization, a bald quotation from his theoretical authority abruptly breaks the initial enchantment half way through.

> The Second Coming! Hardly are those words out
> When a vast image out of *Spiritus Mundi*
> Troubles my sight. . . .

The term *Spiritus Mundi* requires the same extra-poetic explanation as the various references assembled around the idea of the Rose in his earliest writing.

Compared with Hofmannsthal's vision twenty years before of the breakdown of civilization 'The Second Coming' is imperfect; there is some intellectual interference with the poetic vision; and it must be admitted that intellectually Yeats was often a bungler. What the ideas of *The Vision* taught him however was that, even though opposites could not be reconciled in life, and the Hero in him would always wrestle with some weaker longings to play the part of the Saint or Fool, at the moment of poetic inspiration a synthesis could and did take place. The supreme moment, in Yeats's belief, was that of creation: the moment in which he came nearest to some great power outside himself. Herein was the true escape from the orbit of the moon.

Yeats however was not concerned only with poetry. As a poem could be created to enjoy its own kind of immortality, so he had read that something could be made out of a man himself which would survive death. The way to this lay through self-abnegation. The first requirement was that the poet should lay down his mask, and renounce the outward personality that he had for so long valued as in itself a work of art.

At first Yeats rebelled against this newly discovered truth. It only increased his awareness that, as a poet, he was on the side of his ageing heart against all the philosophers. Indeed, as age advanced on him, he became ever more reluctant to accept it; he would not

> bid the Muse go pack,
> Choose Plato and Plotinus for a friend
> Until imagination, ear and eye
> Can be content with argument and deal
> In abstract things.

It was some time indeed before he concluded that the Muse was not exclusively on the side of the heart. Though his 'passionate, fantastical imagination' might still be young, it was subject to mortality. What he must now create, therefore, is a body in which to exist out of time, an image that will survive both his passion and his philosophizing. He sees it in the poem 'Sailing to Byzantium', in

> such a form as Grecian goldsmiths make
> Of hammered gold and gold enamelling
> To keep a drowsy Emperor awake;
> Or set upon a golden bough to sing
> To lords and ladies of Byzantium
> Of what is past, or passing, or to come.

The heart has suffered, the mind has taken the philosopher for friend, and a poem is created that is made both of feeling and thought, a work of art that is both permanent and prophetic. But even here some shadow of duality still remains, for the bird is both a toy 'to keep a drowsy Emperor awake' and a supernatural image endowed with knowledge of past, present and future. Truth and beauty, spirit and intellect, though not entirely reconciled, are here brought together in one symbol, in which the poet 'once out of nature' will survive or be reborn. The idea of magic remains; the world of artistic creation is finally identified with the world beyond the grave. This identification of poetic vision with the state after death is carried much further in the companion poem 'Byzantium', which was composed after the poet's recovery from a severe illness, in his own words 'to warm myself back to life'. Here the artificial bird hanging in the emperor's tree, which in terms of 'Sailing to Byzantium' would seem to signify the finished work of art, may be thought of also as the purified soul singing on the topmost bough of the tree of life, and capable of choosing whether or not to be reincarnated into material existence. With this interpretation the verse assumes great depth:

> Miracle, bird or golden handiwork,
> More miracle than bird or handiwork,
> Planted on the star-lit golden bough,
> Can like the cocks of Hades crow,
> Or, by the moon embittered, scorn aloud
> In glory of changeless metal
> Common bird or petal
> And all complexities of mire or blood.

This may seem to express Yeats's detachment from the world at the height of his illness. The poem may then be seen, on one level of meaning, to chart the stages of ascent from life, through a purgatory of

> Flames that no faggot feeds, nor steel has lit,
> Nor storm disturbs, flames begotten of flame

to that higher fire, 'God's holy fire' of 'Sailing to Byzantium', and so back, with the poet's physical recovery, to the world of 'mire and blood' and to

> Those images that yet
> Fresh images beget,
> That dolphin-torn, that gong-tormented sea.

In 'Sailing to Byzantium' it is the work of art that must be separated from the world of dream in which image succeeds image with mechanical repetitiveness, and yet must be made out of those images. In 'Byzantium' there is superimposed the statement that the spirit which is to survive death must similarly be separated from, yet forged out of the events of common life. All Yeats's later poetry was devoted to a search for the 'reality' which was to be born out of the 'mire and blood'—the phrase is Platonic—and which was to be not only a perfect work of art but a living principle. What he now aimed to create was a lyricism as profound and as free from reasoned argument as Blake's *Songs of Innocence*. He did not abandon his theosophical theories, but viewed them with greater detachment. As his public importance grew and his hold on life weakened, he came to think even more of the heart, and to aim at writing a poetry which would speak directly for it, with all the rant and rage of youth harnessed to the wisdom of his reluctant old age.

Yeats could not, to the last, consent to grow old; the more trivial he saw the preoccupations of mind and body to be, the more passionately he clung to them. Such a poem as 'Meru' may seem to accept the claims of pure spirit. But in 'The Circus Animals Desertion' he reviews the themes that he has once turned into poetry, and while accepting their supernatural inspiration, insists that their origin for him was in the heart.

> Those masterful images because complete
> Grew in pure mind, but out of what began?
> A mound of refuse or the sweepings of a street,
> Old kettles, old bottles, and a broken can,
> Old iron, old bones, old rags, that raving slut
> Who keeps the till. Now that my ladder's gone,
> I must lie down where all the ladders start,
> In the foul rag-and-bone shop of the heart.

It was not true that the ladder whereby he climbed had gone. Although the poems written in his sixties, which include the two Byzantium pieces, represent the peak of Yeats's production, there is no failure of originality to the end. The development of his poetry never stopped, because his receptivity to events and ideas was continuous. The youth that he was so reluctant to part with lay principally in just this capacity for reacting freshly to new impressions. He was never at the entire mercy of his theories, and they did not harden into dogma, as those of Stefan George did when he began to preach the religion of Maximin.

Yeats's poetry is on the whole less simple than that of his great European contemporaries, and this because he was seldom capable of unifying his vision. Contradictions run through his work from beginning to end. The Romantic ego appears, disappears and returns in a new shape; myths are adopted, broken, recombined and again melted down in the fire of feeling. Yeats wore many masks, but was never satisfied with any of them. Like Baudelaire, he was by turns clairvoyant, prophet, fool and dreamer, and it was perhaps his constant unrest that made out of the minor poet of 1908, the greatest figure in English poetry since the death of Tennyson.

Edwin Muir (1887-1959) occupies a similar position in British poetry to Jorge Guillén's in Spanish. After Jiménez and Yeats, poetry had to make fresh connexions with the past. Guillén reforged the broken links with the Baroque style without imitating that style. In the same way Muir, while owing the deepest debt to Rilke, comes much closer to the great Victorians than any other poet of the century. His preoccupations, in fact, are theirs. Browning, to whom Muir is most closely akin, while ostensibly telling stories and reading morals, was sometimes—especially in 'Childe Roland'—writing a kind of parable that foreshadowed those of Rilke's *Neue Gedichte*. The characters and the action, though presented as objective creations, really act out a struggle between conflicting personalities in the poet himself. Browning denied that 'Childe Roland' had any subjective meaning, and he may even have supposed that he was speaking the truth. Muir, on the other hand, uses the technique of 'Childe Roland' or Rilke's 'Orpheus, Eurydike, Hermes' to express situations that are both personal to him and, so he believes, common to Western man. He is both a symbolist and a writer of parables in the Biblical spirit. Into these he attempts to weave meaning behind meaning, and is encouraged to do so by his familiarity with the Bible itself. His love of the Biblical parable, clearly the product of his Scottish upbringing, was, however, reinforced in middle life by an acquaintance with psychoanalytical theory, first acquired as a patient after a bout of mental strain.

Muir, the son of Orkney crofters who met with misfortune, lived a hard life in Scotland before coming south to earn his living as critic and translator. None of his poems written before 1921 is included in this collected volume. Before that date, indeed, he had little leisure to produce anything so unsaleable as poetry.

In his reading and translating, however, he was attracted to such authors as Nietzsche, Rilke and Kafka. While for half a century the chief foreign influence on English literature had been from France, Muir was attracted to the fundamental questionings of Central Europe. His early poetry had solidity, though little originality of expression. His principal themes were of childhood remembered, and turned into a fable. The early Muir is haunted by fear; and his greatest fear is that as things are so they will ever be. 'The Recurrence' argues against the theory advocated by Nietzsche that all things recur eternally, and that life is consequently a trap from which there is no escape. Yeats had been perturbed by such thoughts and had found his solution in his theory of the phases of the moon. The Fool, the Hunchback and the Beggar could escape by throwing off personality. Muir, though at that time not a Christian poet, put his faith in the fact of the Crucifixion:

> the heart and the mind know,
> What has been can never return,
> What is not will surely be
> In the changed unchanging reign,
> Else the Actor on the Tree
> Would loll at ease, miming pain,
> And counterfeit mortality.

To Muir life is no dream, but a reality, in which, however, the true and the ostensible drama are not the same. Actions are, as he was encouraged to feel by the theory of psychoanalysis, figurative. But the meanings he eventually found were far more Christian than Freudian.

One of Muir's primary preoccupations is with the Fall, and with the intimations of primal innocence that we receive in childhood, and may continue to receive as adults. In 'The Labyrinth' a voice within him repeats the argument of eternal recurrence that

> there's no exit, none,
> No place to come to, and you'll end where you are,
> Deep in the centre of the endless maze.

But an answer comes from his heart that this is illusion:

> It is a world, perhaps; but there's another.
> For once in a dream of trance I saw the gods

> Each sitting on the top of his mountain-isle,
> While down below the little ships sailed by,
> Toy multitudes swarmed in the harbours, shepherds drove
> Their tiny flocks to the pastures, marriage feasts
> Went on below, small birthdays and holidays,
> Ploughing and harvesting and life and death,
> And all permissible, all acceptable,
> Clear and secure as in a limpid dream.

Muir's poetry is a poetry of search for this other world. Like Baudelaire, he sets out on a voyage, but in pursuit of a truth more clearly envisaged than the Frenchman's shadowy *repos*. Nor is Muir as ignorant of the nature of his *wound* as Baudelaire. The *wound* or *evil destiny* from which he suffers was received at the expulsion from Eden. This can be healed only by an individual return to a state in which 'all is acceptable'. It is paradoxical that in the theory of eternal recurrence, properly understood, just this way of escape is provided.

Muir sees man's evil destiny not only in his personal but in his political situation. Like Guillén, he is at times a social poet. He comments with a similar universality on the cruelties and devastations of war, and on the growing cloud of horror and fear that has enveloped the world. He himself saw not only the war in Britain but the Communist coup in Czechoslovakia. In 'The Usurpers', he characterizes the men who plot and carry through such deeds, men capable of almost forgetting eternity so deeply are they immersed in time, yet haunted sometimes by 'fluttering dreams' that they cannot entirely push aside. They defiantly proclaim their liberty, yet at the poem's conclusion recognize that their 'wild flight through nothing' will 'tumble down at last on nothing', that they are nihilists in a world where nihilism is not the ultimate value:

> These fancies trouble us.
> The day itself sometimes works spells upon us
> And then the trees look unfamiliar. Yet
> It is a lie that they are witnesses,
> That the mountains judge us, brooks tell tales about us.
> We have thought sometimes the rocks looked strangely on us,
> Have fancied that the waves were angry with us,
> Heard dark runes murmuring in the autumn wind,
> Muttering and murmuring like old toothless women
> That prophesied against us in ancient tongues.
> These are imaginations. We are free.

The poem is not merely a portrait of the fascist or communist mentality. It speaks of all men who are immersed in time and oblivious of eternity; and Muir, in the tradition of Wordsworth, sees in nature perpetual reminders of a different reality.

Up to the last of the *Collected Poems*, fear and assurance are equally balanced in Muir's poetry. But in his last book, *One Foot in Eden*, faith predominates, and something in the nature of a second coming is seen on the further side of disaster. Many of the poems in this volume are very carefully worked out parables. A Biblical or classical legend is re-enacted against the background of Muir's childhood landscape in Orkney. Like Rilke, Muir derives fresh truths from these ancient stories, which he tells with the freshness that they must have held for him as a boy. Orkney and Eden, childhood and the new clarity of old age, are drawn together, and the conclusion is now as then:

There is no trust but in the miracle.

Muir's method is deliberate; and this he sees both as an advantage and a danger. It is an advantage because he subordinates every detail of his poem to his overall purpose. Like Browning and unlike almost all modern poets, he secures his effects by the paragraph rather than by the single line or image. Like Rilke or the Metaphysicals, he is content to develop one idea throughout a whole poem. That of 'The Horses', one of the finest poems in the collection, treats a theme that has already been the subject of an early poem. In the first version, these animals on his father's farm were 'both bright and fearful presences'. But now they are harbingers of a new simplicity. The poem tells of some breakdown in civilization. Deserted tractors, lying about the fields, 'look like dank sea-monsters couched and waiting' when

that evening
Late in summer the strange horses came,

bringing with them that lost communion with nature, and that release of natural emotion, the absence of which has been one of the principal themes of Muir's poetry. The willing incorporation of these animals that had never known the Fall into the life of guilt- and remorse-ridden man, who has now met and survived his last earthly disaster, is the theme of this poem's magnificent conclusion:

> In the first moment we had never a thought
> That they were creatures to be owned and used.
> Among them were some half-a-dozen colts
> Dropped in some wilderness of the broken world,
> Yet new as if they had come from their own Eden.
> Since then they have pulled our ploughs and borne our loads,
> But that free servitude still can pierce our hearts.
> Our life is changed; their coming our beginning.

This poem and Guillén's 'Tarde mayor' mark the conclusion of a movement which began with Hofmannsthal's vision of the disorderly ship and Hardy's dismissal of the whole human experiment. On the plane of society great disasters may continue to occur, but individually men may find their way back to Eden by way of a new simplicity and a new subordination to nature. 'History' says Guillén, 'is transitory, and the destroyer works to no avail'; and Muir repeats his intimations of another way of living:

> And yet sometimes
> We still, as through a dream that comes and goes,
> Know what we are, remembering what we were.

An answer has been found to some of the questions that have been asked by the poets since Baudelaire. But our age of fear and disaster has led other poets to ask other questions, for which they have found answers of a very different kind.

5

The vision of the Apocalypse

In the year 1908 the world of politics, as well as that of poetry, was approaching crisis point. The first great European war was still six years away, but a series of incidents, each centred around the rival claims of the Imperialist powers to control the few corners of the world which were still free from their domination, threatened at intervals of only a few months to precipitate hostilities. The effect of this growing tension was first felt among the writers of those countries that were to suffer worst: in Russia, whose social system had already been shaken by the loss of the Japanese war, the abortive revolution of 1905, and the stubborn refusal of the ruling caste to meet any reasonable demands for reform; in Austria, whose destruction had already been foreseen by von Hofmannsthal; and in Germany, where growing militarism had already destroyed all respect for individual values. In all these countries the artist was driven into opposition, and remained there, an anarchic rebel against the blindness of rulers, and the philistinism of officialdom. Even those who when the revolution came rallied to the conservative side opposed, scorned and attacked their rulers up to the last moment before the crash.

The poets Alexander Blok, Georg Trakl and Georg Heym, who, in different ways, prophesied the disaster that was to overtake their countries, cannot be matched by contemporaries in the comparatively healthier societies of England, France and the United States; only in Italy, where demoralization by war was to lead to corrupt dictatorship, is there some approximate parallel in the restless and unhappy poems of Dino Campana. For the rest the poetry of apocalypse corresponds to a poetry of national defeat.

Alexander Blok (1880-1921), the only great poet among the

apocalyptics, was a contemporary of Rilke and Yeats, whose work might be considered with theirs were it not for the effect on it of his more violent political background. Starting where they did, he was nevertheless unable to subject his poetry to a systematic *depuración* on account of the more violent events around him, to which he was compelled to respond. Furthermore, the Russian poetic tradition stood very much further apart from the growing internationalism of style than those of Spain and England, the two countries which still preserved a fair measure of independence. Blok's poetry, indeed, is Russian in style and tradition to a far greater degree than that of Stefan George is German; any affinities he might claim with the French symbolists were in fact slight. He began in the tradition of the Russian romantics, Tyutchev and Fët.

In the very last years of the nineteenth century, when the adolescent Blok was beginning to write, very little good poetry was being produced in Russia. Even the novel, after giving birth to a supreme masterpiece in each of the opposing Russian styles, 'War and Peace' in the classical, and 'The Brothers Karamazov' in the romantic, was in decay. There was still life in the theatre, where Chekhov's work was not yet complete, but the most insistent voices among Russian intellectuals were those of the pseudo-mystics and theosophists, and of all the self-styled Symbolists who were attempting to naturalize the style of the French decadents to a language which was still somewhat too robust to accept it. Blok, in passing, interested himself in the theories of his French contemporaries. His acquaintance with foreign literature however, was principally with the Germans, though he had some Latin and enough English at one point to make some short translations from Byron. He had however a far closer kinship with the more ambivalent genius of Heine, whom he translated more successfully at two epochs in his life, than with any French writer.

Among his Russian contemporaries he was chiefly impressed by the visionary philosopher Vladimir Soloviev, whom he valued, however, entirely as a poet. His philosophical writings, with their schemes for a union of all the churches and the mystical reconciliation of religion and science, Blok found quite unreadable. His attitude to other men's books, indeed, was like that of many poets; they served him only as quarries for imagery or ideas that he could use in his own writing. He was impatient of sustained influences, and his discipleships to other writers can be measured in months, not years. For he was from the first what he only later acknowledged himself to be, a solitary in a gregarious world.

Blok's first important volume of poetry, his *Verses about the Beautiful Lady* (1904), is full of those half-hidden significances that he found in the semi-philosophical poetry of Soloviev. It is, by Blok's definition, a symbolist book. For although it owes nothing to the French Decadence, its central figure, the Beautiful Lady, not only embodies a living woman, the daughter of the chemist Mendeleev, whom the poet was to marry, but stands also for the principle of beauty, and for Soloviev's idea of Sophia, the Divine Wisdom. It is very difficult, in this period of his writing as in all others, to separate the several strands of his symbolism, and say with any certainty that one poem is addressed to a woman, another to an idea, and a third to his native country; in his multiple meanings he is a typically modern poet.

The texture of the *Beautiful Lady* is akin to that of nineteenth-century poetry in its uncomplicated language, which is, however, sometimes conventionally poetical, and in its lyrical simplicity. It is nearer to Rossetti than to Rilke or Yeats. If such a poem as 'Sudden Light'—

> I have been here before,
> But when or how I cannot tell:
> I know the grass beyond the door,
> The sweet keen smell,
> The sighing sound, the lights around the shore. . . .

were translated into Russian, it could easily take its place in Blok's book. Like Rossetti, Blok saw in his work resemblances to the *Vita Nuova*; he even contemplated writing a prose commentary to the *Beautiful Lady* to strengthen the parallel. But, unlike Rossetti, he saw also, almost from the beginning, beside the ideal figure of his wife, his inspiration and his goddess, her shadow, a figure of evil. Already in 1901 he speaks of a 'white-faced ghost', that wanders through the fields of his native place, but is driven away by the blessed lady. But there came a moment, immediately after the conclusion of this book, when fortunes were reversed. The vision broke, and the ghosts were left in possession of the field. Blok felt that he was under a spell. The

heavenly figure to whom he had been joined in mystical marriage,
had become a fleshly enchantress:

> In you lie hidden, on the watch,
> The great light, and a baleful darkness,

he wrote: and here the philosopher Soloviev's influence abruptly
ended. With it went too his exemplary domestic life, and the cult
for his wife, to which many of his friends had also subscribed.

Henceforth Blok knew himself to be solitary, drank heavily,
mixed with low company, and found his female companions in
the theatre or among the gipsies. The girls he now addresses are
at least half-depraved. In their still innocent eyes they reflect
their kinship with the *Beautiful Lady*. But they are learning bad
ways. Blok tells of one whose ribbons are too bright and who
will meet him in the churchyard if he calls. She cracks sunflower
seeds and gives bunches of flowers to the telegraph clerk in the
yellow-piped uniform. Blok was rapidly becoming master of the
telling realistic detail. Deriving this facility, perhaps, from a
short-lived apprenticeship to Strindberg, he came to find hidden
significances in the sordid life of the town just as he had formerly
seen them in his idyllic converse with the Divine Wisdom.

In 1905 came the abortive revolution, with whose ideals Blok
proclaimed himself in sympathy. But the chief importance of this
event for him lay in its correspondence to an upheaval that was
taking place in his own soul. The first signs of this had appeared
in the doubling of the Beautiful Lady's figure. Subsequently it
became more visible as a total contrast between dream and
reality. Blok was, like Yeats, a poet of tensions. He was not
capable, however, of inventing any myth that would bring his
opposites together. Swinging from one to the other, his poetry
took as violent a turn as his life; and his principal endeavour
from this point onwards was to find some alternative embodiment
for the forces of good that his Lady had once represented. She
continued for a while to appear, though in such disguises as that
of the mysterious stranger who passes through the café where the
poet is drinking with his friends in one of his best known poems,
'The Stranger':

> Slowly she passes through the drunken rabble,
> Companionless and fair,
> And by the window sits, a mist of perfume
> Spread round her in the air.

Her silken waist, her hat of sable feathers,
Her narrow hand with rings,
Seem to exhale a breath of long-forgotten
And legendary things.

Tranced by the wonder of her nearness, striving
To pierce her shadowy veil,
I look on an enchanted shore, a distance
Beyond some magic pale.

Unspoken mysteries to me are given,
Another's sun is mine:
Transfused through every corner of my being,
Steals the astringent wine.

                    (transl. Frances Cornford)

The secret that she carries is not communicated to the poet, or remains with him only during his intoxication. Yet persistently there recurs in the poems an intimation that there is some hidden truth to be discovered. Blok lacked Yeats's persistence; he could not search in books or pursue cults for long. True to the tradition of Orthodox mysticism, to which, though a dissident, he was psychologically attuned, he expected truth to come to him as a striking revelation. A gleam of it might occur on a spicy March morning during the thaw, while he was walking in the marshes outside St. Petersburg—now his habitual landscape. Beneath the dark sky he hears the far away sound of a gipsy dance, the music of his 'evil' side, and receives a mysterious intimation from the opposite forces, embodied in the figure of some successor to his Lady:

And suddenly you are here, distant and strange,
And tell me—in your gaze the lightning gleams
—'Once the soul enters on her final path
She foolishly weeps for her former dreams'.

For Blok, suffering something like the dark night of the senses, the chief hope for a positive force to replace that of his early dreams lay, as he saw it, in *music*: an all-embracing term, which stood in his symbolism for a release of emotion, either in poetic inspiration or, on the social scale, in revolution. Blok stood opposed to intellectualism, humanism and middle-class values. He developed however a strong and mystical patriotism.

Indeed, after the uprising of 1905 had failed, by a curious switch in his poetic thought, Blok came to regard Russia as another incarnation of his Beautiful Lady and as the leader of those forces of *music* which were to triumph after a further revolution. For then they would bring, first at home and then to the whole world, a release from the oppressive forces of civilization, which he believed to have taken a wrong path at the end of the Middle Ages.

Henceforth Blok was a revolutionary poet, though no Communist critic of his own time or today supposes him to have understood the forces that he applauded, and though the revolution, when it came, disappointed his hopes almost from the start. The new Russia was, as Blok saw it, to lead the anti-humanist crusade. But at the same time, he saw her, in a rare gleam of genuine prophecy, building factories in the Siberian waste, and challenging the West on its own materialistic field. Russia was to be both the land of a new faith and 'The New America'.

The common life of man was, in Blok's eyes, sordid and exasperating. In the poem 'Humiliation' he describes it in terms of an over-furnished brothel, full of merchants, students and cardsharpers into which a young man comes—a projection of the poet himself—in search of a girl. When he has slept with her, he is overwhelmed with disgust. He feels himself to be stifling in her embraces, while her breath whistles in her throat with a sound that reminds him only of the grave. A winter sunset enters the room and floods her bed with a gaudy glow. It is as vulgar as the brothel furniture. Like a gorged snake, the train of her dress slides, heavy and dusty, from the chair on to the carpet, as he steals away. But even here the opposing set of values is hinted at. Her white face reminds him of some holy image that he has profaned.

The symbolism of the sunset outside, which stands for the decaying world, and of the girl's falling dress, is clear in itself. There is no comment from the poet.

By 1911, the date of 'Humiliation', Blok was increasingly concerned with death. If the Beautiful Lady had, in one aspect, taken on the features of his native land, on the other she had begun to assume the character of death. A year or two before, he had come to look back on his whole life as past, and to speculate only on the manner of its ending. Will he fall beside the Kremlin, the symbol of his country's greatness?

> Some Easter-night beside the Neva,
> In wind and ice and snowstorm, shall
> Some beggar-woman with her crutches
> Move my still body where I fall?
>
> Or in the countryside I love so,
> When the grey autumn rustles round,
> In rain and mist shall the young vultures
> Devour my body on the ground?
>
> Or in an hour of starless anguish,
> Inside some room's four walls, shall I
> Give in to iron fate's compulsion
> And lie down on white sheets to die?
>
> (transl. C. M. Bowra)

Blok returns to this subject several times. His search for the lost ecstasy of childhood, a theme common to himself, to Baudelaire and to Muir, is the subject of an untitled poem that calls up a vivid memory from his early youth. Mysteriously one morning, there entered into a silent bay a squadron of cruisers, only to depart just as suddenly. But when they had gone, the semaphore-station continued to wink out its signals, though everything else had fallen still. *Music* had appeared and suddenly disappeared, leaving no trace of its mysterious presence, except these code signals. Such memories, now increasingly rare, were rich in what Blok treasured most: the promise that *music* would break into his life once more. The poem ends with a hint of this possibility; he remembers how it used to happen:

> Perhaps upon a pocket-knife
> You'll find a speck of foreign dust;
> And then the world seems strange again,
> Swathed in a brightly coloured mist.

But perhaps the appearance of these battleships portended also the coming of *music* in another form, that of war and revolution. The poem 'On the Field of Kulikovo' mentioned in my second chapter, states a theme which unites many of those he has touched on in the past. The sense of approaching disaster, the national destiny, the linking of mood and landscape, produce a far more closely knit sequence than those he has hitherto attempted:

> Once more, swept by an ancient grief,
> The cotton-grass is bent to earth,
> Once more beyond the misty stream,
> You call upon me from afar.
>
> Droves of wild horses on the steppe
> Flash by and vanish, leave no mark,
> And savage passions are unloosed
> Beneath the high moon's crescent yoke.
>
> I too am swept by an ancient grief,
> A wolf beneath the crescent moon,
> All power over myself is lost,
> How can I fly to follow you!
>
> I hear the clash of bloody strife,
> Afar the Tartar trumpet brays,
> I see the distant spreading fires
> And Russia's fields softly ablaze.

The conflagration spreading through Russia became an increasingly constant theme of Blok's poetry, and the collection *My Country*, in which 'On the Field of Kulikovo' takes its place, contains some of his finest poems. These are at times tender, as when he remembers a visit to an old gentleman who seemed to exemplify the peaceable Russia of long ago, at times invocatory, at times impressionistic, at times, as in 'New America', factually prophetic. But the burden of his feeling for the Beautiful Lady, who had now reappeared as the figure of his native land, was of hopeless love.

It was with objective hopelessness that Blok saw the opening of the First World War, and watched the troops entraining at St. Petersburg to be slaughtered on the plains of Galicia. This was not the true battle; the defeated revolution of 1905 was more real to the poet, the battering of the wind on the shutters of his house more elemental and closer to the *music* that he was listening for. When the revolution of 1917 broke out, though never accepted by the Bolsheviks, he applauded them; and his final great poem 'The Twelve' can be read as a political manifesto in their favour.

'The Twelve' is a loosely strung sequence, written in the measures of popular tunes, which describes a ragged column of revolutionaries parading the streets of Petersburg in the first revolutionary winter. Priests, gentry, reactionaries are jeered at; an officer's kept woman is casually killed, while the wind blows through the whole poem, sweeping away a great placard inscribed with a Liberal or Constitutional slogan, whipping up the snow, and driving it into the eyes of the ragged marching column. This column has become an impersonal force like the elements, and at its rear the old world tags along like a hungry dog. 'The Twelve' differs from almost all Blok's previous work in its colloquial catchiness. His mysterious symbolisms seem to be forgotten until at the very last they reassert themselves in a passage that has puzzled Blok's critics ever since its first publication.

For as he marches his hungry and destructive group out through the blinding storm, which represents the *music* of the revolution even more faithfully than the soldiers themselves, he suddenly introduces the figure of Christ walking at their head:

> On they march with sovereign tread,
> With a starving dog behind,
> With a blood-red flag ahead—
> In the storm where none can see,
> From the rifle bullets free,
> Gently walking on the snow,
> Where like pearls the snowflakes glow,
> Marches rose-crowned in the van
> Jesus Christ, the Son of Man.
>
> (transl. C. M. Bowra)

Throughout the poem there have been snatches of vituperation against the Church. Blok had ceased to be a Christian at the same time as he had thrown off the influence of Soloviev. But the figure of Christ seems to have remained in his thoughts as another embodiment of that emotional release that he found in music, in the storm, and in slaughter and revolution. The paradox of introducing Christ to resolve an atheistic poem succeeds by its very violence. It shows perhaps the extent of Blok's continued debt to Heine, the only poet of the nineteenth century capable of attaining a poetic effect by such shock tactics. Blok himself, questioned shortly afterwards as to his reasons for introducing this image, said that it had come to him as a surprise. 'But the more I gazed the more clearly I saw Christ.'

After 'The Twelve' Blok wrote hardly any more poetry. One piece alone, 'The Scythians', which dates from the same month,

January 1918, in which 'The Twelve' was finished, makes an appeal to Europe to join hands with the revolution and be saved by Russia, the Sphinx who gazes at western man with hatred and with love. As for the Revolution itself, Blok compares it to such natural convulsions as the earthquakes at Lisbon and Messina. The poem is rather a warning and a threat than an invitation. If Blok offers the West love, it is a burning and consuming love:

> For the last time, reflect, O ancient world!
> To a feast of work and peace in brotherhood,
> For the last time, to a gay feast of brothers
> The lyre of the barbarian summons you.

Blok was no longer able to hymn the revolution, for the events had failed to coincide with his hopes. He sank into a dispirited silence. 'All sounds have stopped', he told Gorki. 'Can't you hear that all sounds have stopped?' It was chiefly thanks to Gorki's intervention that he was supported by the Party for the last three years of his life. During this time he wrote some pamphlets and essays, and made various public appearances. But the Bolsheviks, Gorki included, continued to think of him as a Decadent. He died in 1921 at the age of 40.

Despite his claim to be a Symbolist, Blok up to the last developed themes and techniques that sprang from the Romantic poetry of the nineteenth century. His modernism lay principally in his awareness of the crisis into which civilization was falling. In the same way Georg Trakl, an Austrian poet of lesser range, but his closest European counterpart, depended almost entirely on his nineteenth-century models, at first on Lenau and other lyricists, and afterwards on the earlier and more Classical Hölderlin. He, even less than Blok, learnt to master a new style.

Georg Trakl (1887-1914), though a native of Salzburg, was of entirely Slavonic descent. In this he resembled Lenau, the outstanding poet of the Austrian Empire in the nineteenth century. His failure, like Lenau's, arose from his close imprisonment in his own imaginary world. Blok is at moments obscure, with an obscurity which is organic, not deliberate. One is in doubt as to the significance of his symbols, at a loss to understand the shifting meanings of his central feminine figure. But he is never wilfully difficult, out of a Mallarméan desire to refine his experience, and present only those aspects that are beyond the range of philistine humanity. Trakl in the same way, is obscure only because one is uncertain what value to attach to a particular symbol.

Trakl's range is much more restricted than Blok's. It is true that like his Russian contemporary he read idealistic philosophy; he was familiar with Nietzsche and Kierkegaard. But he was never interested in the world and its problems. War, revolution, the survival or death of humanity, existed for him principally as events in his inner world. The cataclysm that he expected and prophesied was merely the onset of his own threatened madness. Even as late as 1912 Blok could write poems of acceptance, could say that he was grateful for life as it was, that he had never looked for a better fate, and that in the end he realised there was no need of happiness, an unrealizable dream which half-way through his life he had never captured. But Trakl rejoiced in nothing. It is possible that he too thought of happiness as unseizable. But he could never say that he wished for no better life than he was living. Trakl received no such half-illuminations as Blok received walking in the marshes, beside his bay, or on the battlefield of Kulikovo. The best state he knew was a kind of autumn stillness in which he was faintly reminded of a childhood that had not been innocent. Then certain signs—the flight of birds across the sky, for instance, that seemed to him like files of pilgrims— suggested to him the existence of some paradisaical realm which might be entered, if only in dreams.

Trakl had little in common with his literary contemporaries, the German expressionists who, whatever their emotional limitations, concerned themselves with the fate of man as a race. Where their verse is violent his is drugged and languid. A closer parallel exists however between his autumn landscape, with its strong primary colours, and that of the Blaue Reiter school of painters, their equivalent in the field of art. The resemblance is, indeed, extremely strong, Both make their effects by the use of a few symbols rawly presented. Both insist rather than insinuate. The Van Gogh sunflowers are, furthermore, an inheritance common to both:

> Im roten Laubwerk voll Gitarren
> Der Mädchen gelbe Haare wehen
> Am Zaun, wo Sonnenblumen stehen.
> Durch Wolken fährt ein goldner Karren.[1]

[1] In the red foliage full of guitars the girls' yellow hair blows against the fence, where sunflowers stand. A golden wheelbarrow travels through the cloud.

D

In contrast to this brightness some old people are shown in brown shadow. The poem is, in fact, composed as a painting with strong visual contrasts. Each object is briefly recorded without comparisons, and it is only when one has read several poems that one realizes how limited the number of these objects is. One then sees also how closely they fit into Trakl's single pattern of symbols, which is held together by a single mood. The poet's prevailing mood is made up of one quarter bemused wonder, and three quarters agonized and haunted regret.

Trakl's poems do not develop; they lack argument. To Rilke it did not seem inevitable that he should have expressed his feelings through the medium of words. 'A Trakl who could have exercised his genius in painting or music,' he wrote, 'would not have perished under the over-great weight of his creation, and the darkness which it brought upon him.' But the darkness did not arise from Trakl's efforts to write; it had enveloped him in his childhood, before he was a poet at all. No deflection into another medium could have saved him.

Trakl's unrelieved gloom and his narrow range of intellectual interests limit his choice of subject, but heighten the intensity of his vision. By the very economy of his means he creates a landscape all his own. 'One quickly sees,' wrote Rilke of the poem 'Sebastian im Traum' (Sebastian in Dream), 'that the circumstances governing this rising and falling music were individual and unrepeatable, like the conditions giving rise to a dream. Even a close spectator sees the poet's vision and insights as through a window-pane, and as if shut outside. For Trakl's experience is like the reflections in a glass; it fills the whole of his room, which is inaccessible, like the room in a mirror.'

Rilke received Trakl's poems in Paris. Later, in 1915, knowing nothing about him, he asked for information. For though he saw that the subjectivity of the symbols was a condition of the poetry itself, he would still have liked 'a pointer for many of the lines, in order to be confirmed here and there in my instinctive reading'. These pointers are now provided by the known facts of Trakl's biography. But for a reader who lacks an instinctive understanding of his poetry such facts will do little to reinforce its appeal.

The details of Trakl's short life were sordid and unhappy; in the finest of his poems, however, he distilled from the disorder of his earthly existence a liquor of limpid clarity. He was capable of expressing the totality of his vision in very few lines. Indeed an early sonnet, 'Traum des Bösen' (Dream of Evil), contains it all, though not in its final intensity.

Verhallend eines Sterbeglöckchens Klänge—
Ein Liebender erwacht in schwarzen Zimmern
Die Wang' an Sternen, die im Fenster flimmern.
Am Strome blitzen Segel, Masten, Stränge.

Ein Mönch, ein schwangres Weib dort in Gedränge.
Gitarren Klimpern, rote Kittel schimmern.
Kastanien schwül in goldnem Glanz verkümmern;
Schwarz ragt der Kirchen trauriges Gepränge.

Aus bleichen Masken schaut der Geist des Bösen.
Ein Platz verdämmert grauenvoll und düster;
Am Abend regt auf Inseln sich Geflüster.

Des Vogelfluges wirre Zeichen lesen
Aussätzige, die zur Nacht vielleicht verwesen.
Im Park erblicken zitternd sich Geschwister.[1]

The waking lover is clearly the poet himself; and his waking is in fact no waking at all, but a sinking into dream. In his dream, there passes before him a procession of symbols of evil, which can only be related one to another in the light of Trakl's own childhood and background. His native city of Salzburg in the late afternoon heat, suggestive whisperings at dusk, ugly and menacing figures, and finally the hint of a guilty relationship between brother and sister: the sordid secret of Trakl's adult life.

Not only is Trakl the brother of the last line; he is also on account of his love for his sister Margarete, the leper who is trying to read the auguries of the birds. For Trakl was always hoping to read some signs of hope in a generally gloomy prognostic. But he was from the start, in his own eyes a 'poète maudit'.

Georg Trakl was born at Salzburg of a prosperous trading family who were able to give him a French governess, from whom he learnt enough to read the French poets. He learned little else, alarmed his friends by taking almost fatal doses of

[1] As the sound of a passing-bell dies away, a lover wakes in black rooms, his cheek turned to the stars that sparkle in the window. On the river flash sails, masts and ropes.
A monk, a pregnant woman there in the crowd. Guitars twang, red dresses shimmer, chestnut trees languish stiflingly in the golden brilliance; the melancholy splendour of the churches stands out black.
The spirit of evil looks out from pale masks. A square grows horribly and gloomily dark; at evening whispering arises on islands.
Lepers, who are perhaps rotting in the night, read the confused signs of the birds' flight. Brothers and sisters gaze tremblingly at one another in the park.

chloroform, failed his school examinations, and consequently found no profession open to him but pharmacy. He wrote poetry, however, from his earliest schooldays, at first submitting himself to the influence of Lenau, as Blok had to that of the Russian romantics. But Lenau was a less satisfactory master; his few successful lyrics are monotonously autumnal, his range of symbols even smaller than Trakl's own. In the poems written between 1909 and 1912, therefore, Trakl turned for examples to Baudelaire, Verlaine and Rimbaud's 'Bâteau Ivre'.

Such a poem as 'Menschliches Elend' (Human Misery)—which was later renamed 'Menschliche Trauer' (Human Grief), while it presents a scene of suburban squalor that might derive from Baudelaire, is free from that quality of self-dramatization that pervades *Les Fleurs du Mal*. Either because his own personality was weak, as the result of drug-taking, or because he welcomed rather than fought against the horror he saw, Trakl succeeds in removing himself from the foreground of his poems. He remains oppressively present in his symbols, yet is apparently writing of the fate of his fellow-men rather than of his own:

> Im Hasel spielen Mädchen blasz und blind,
> Wie Liebende die sich in Schlaf umschlingen.
> Vielleicht, dasz um ein Aas dort Fliegen singen,
> Vielleicht auch weint im Mutterschosz ein Kind.
>
> Aus Händen sinken Astern blau und rot,
> Des Jünglings Mund entgleitet fremd und weise;
> Und Lider flattern angstverwirrt und leise;
> Durch Fieberschwärze weht ein Duft von Brot.[1]

The pale, blind girls like Marie Laurencin figures, who play in the bushes, the strange and knowing youngster who dodges a guilty kiss, even the bright asters—the flowers of autumn—that fall from limp hands, all reinforce the picture of corruption, overtly presented in the third line. And to counterbalance this feverish sexuality, Trakl presents only the clean smell of bread—which occurs in others of his poems—as a symbol of good. But even the good is only perceived through the fever of an evil dream. Perhaps the child cries not so much in its mother's lap

---

[1] In the hazels pale, blind girls play, like lovers who embrace in sleep. Perhaps flies are humming round a carcass there, perhaps too a child is crying in its mother's lap.
Blue and red asters fall from hands, the boy's mouth slips away, strange and knowing, and lids beat gently, pained and bewildered: through the darkness of fever drifts a smell of bread.

as in her womb (for *Schosz* has both meanings). Perhaps all life is evil from the start. Yet though the symbols are all drawn from Trakl's nightmares, there is, overflowing them, a pity for mankind, and also—a motive that develops in the poetry of his last years—some hint that the poet's personal disaster was matched by some external catastrophe which threatened the world. Trakl's apocalypticism has never the strength of Blok's; there is nevertheless present even in his Salzburg poems, some intimation of a fallen state common to himself and to the world.

The most beautiful of these poems is 'Der Herbst des Einsamen' (Autumn of a Solitary), an autumn landscape of harvest ripeness closer to the spirit of Lenau than to Baudelaire; a piece which in the solemn beat of its lines comes near to suggesting that somewhere there is some relief for Trakl's despairs, somewhere a salvation for the guilty spirit of man:

> Der dunkle Herbst kehrt ein voll Frucht und Fülle,
> Vergilbte Glanz von schönen Sommertagen.
> Ein reines Blau tritt aus verfallner Hülle:
> Der Flut der Vögel tönt von alten Sagen.
> Gekeltert ist der Wein, die milde Stille
> Erfüllt von leiser Antwort dunkler Fragen.[1]

But Trakl heard no whispered answers to his questionings. Short spells of work in Viennese chemists' shops alternated with longer periods during which he stayed with or sponged upon friends. Finally he settled at Mühlau, near Innsbruck, with a well-to-do editor of a periodical which was printing his work. With him he remained until the outbreak of war. His move into the Tyrol had an important effect on his poetry. Whereas hitherto it had contained only occasional echoes from Hölderlin, henceforth he wrote in the free metres and with many of the mannerisms of that master. Perhaps the change from the gentler landscape of Lower Austria to the starker mountains seemed to him to call for a more rugged style; perhaps his own suspicions that he was on the verge of madness caused him to identify himself with a poet who ended his life mad. But, whatever the reason, Trakl began to write Hölderlinian pastichë:

[1] Dark autumn comes in full of fruit and plenty, the yellowed brilliance of fine summer days. A pure blue emerges from its decayed husk; the flight of birds rings with old legends. The wine is pressed, the mild stillness fills dark questions with whispered answers.

Und es leuchtet ein Lämpchen, das Gute, in seinem Herzen
Und der Frieden des Mahls; denn geheiligt ist Brot und Wein
Von Gottes Händen, und es schaut aus nächtigen Augen
Stille dich der Bruder an. . . . [1]

This is too close to its model, Hölderlin's 'Brot und Wein',
to possess much virtue. But soon, although still not completely
independent, Trakl succeeded in filling Hölderlin's forms with a
myth of his own. This was more elusive than the simple legend of
the guilty boy lost in the autumn park which informs his earlier
poems; and it was at the same time more intense in its premonitions of doom. There are aspects of Trakl's last poems that have
been lately described as Existentialist. Certainly he had read
Kierkegaard; certainly there are images from Christian myth in
that enigmatic sequence, 'Helian', for which Rilke demanded a
key. But the Christian symbols were mere arbitrary constituents
of his own dreams. The crisis which he foresaw was not a crisis of
faith, nor the threat to civilization of the approaching war. It
was rather the fear of his own approaching madness, a terror of
the consequences of his own guilt. And in his fear he glimpsed a
way back, not as Nikolaus Lenau had done under similar circumstances, to the innocence of childhood, but into his private
dream-world, the vision of which is concentrated in the twelve
lines of 'Ruh und Schweigen' (Rest and Silence):

Hirten begruben die Sonne im kahlen Wald.
Ein Fischer zog
In härenem Netz den Mond aus frierendem Weiher.

In blauem Kristall
Wohnt der bleiche Mensch, die Wang an seine Sterne gelehnt;
Oder er neigt das Haupt in purpurnem Schlaf.

Doch immer rührt der schwarze Flug der Vögel
Den Schauenden, das Heilige blauer Blumen,
Denkt die nahe Stille Vergessenes, erloschene Engel.
Wieder nachtet die Stirne in mondenem Gestein;
Ein strahlender Jüngling
Erscheint die Schwester in Herbst und schwarzer Verwesung. [2]

[1] And there shines a lantern of goodness in his heart, and the peace of the meal; for
bread and wine are hallowed by God's hands, and a brother gazes quietly upon you
with the night's eyes.

[2] Shepherds buried the sun in a bare wood. A fisherman dragged the moon out of the
freezing pond with a hair net. In the blue crystal dwells the pale man with his cheek
leaning against his star; or he bows his head in purple sleep.

But the black flight of birds still moves the watcher, the holy (relic) of blue flowers,
the near-by stillness thinks of what is forgotten, an extinguished angel.

The brow darkens again in moonlit rock. The sister appears, a shining girl, in
autumn and dark decay.

It is a dream in which the familiar flight of the birds, the forgotten thing remembered, and the angel whose brightness has been dimmed, are outweighed by the black corruption of the last line, in which Margarete appears with attributes of autumn less peaceful than those in 'Herbst des Einsamen'. The sequences 'Helian' and 'Sebastian in Traum' are composed of this same elusive material, interspersed with hints, echoing from poem to poem, of secrets that are never revealed, with symbols imprecise in meaning, and threats, positive and brutal, that break the fine music of the dream.

When war broke out Trakl rejoiced. He had just been on the point of attaining some financial security. A fund for writers had been tapped for his benefit. But at the last moment he had refused to take the money. A recall to the army, in which he had already spent a tedious compulsory year, restored him to independence and commissioned rank. Almost immediately he was drafted up to the Galician front, to which Blok had, from St. Petersburg, seen the troops departing. It was on the eve of a bloody but inconclusive battle, the slaughter of which he accepted in his last poem 'Grodek' as the fulfilment of his dream. The crisis had come; the murderous outbursts that he feared in himself had infected the world; perhaps he would be vicariously saved:

> Umfängt die Nacht
> Sterbende Krieger, die wilde Klage
> Ihrer zerbrochen Münder.
> Doch stille sammelt im Weidengrund
> Rotes Gewölk, darin ein zürnender Gott wohnt,
> Das vergossene Blut sich, mondne Kühle;
> Alle Strassen münden in schwarze Verwesung.
> Unter goldnem Gezweig der Nacht und Sternen
> Es schwankt der Schwester Schatten durch den schweigenden Hain,
> Zu grüssen die Geister der Helden, die blutenden Häupter.[1]

Though the poem seems to envisage salvation, and in its last line looks forward to the unborn grandchildren of the dead, the solution is unreal; Trakl's transformation of Margarete into a

---

[1] The night encircles dying warriors, the wild laments of their torn mouths. But quietly there gather in the willow-wood red cloud-masses in which a raging god dwells, the spilt blood gathers, cool of the moon. All roads lead to black corruption. Under the gold boughs of the night and stars, the sister's shadow sways through the silent wood to greet the spirits of the heroes, and their bloody heads.

blessed figure who receives the spirits of the slain into Valhalla did not give him the strength to endure war at first hand. A few days before writing this poem, the poet had found himself in charge of a forward hospital to which the wounded were being brought. There was a lack of medical equipment and anaesthetics. At the sight of so much blood and suffering, he broke down, and was removed to Cracow for observation. The doctors suspected schizophrenia. On the edge of that madness which he had always feared and foreseen, and from which the war had not saved him, Georg Trakl poisoned himself. He lay for many hours in a coma before he died.

Trakl's power lies in the hallucinatory nature of his disordered dreams. The choice of his pictures is small, and his view of the outer world restricted by the narrow slit of his own temperament, through which he peers. With crazy simplicity, he presents this vision as if it shows rather more of known reality than it actually does. The Expressionist movement, on the verge of which he existed, was similarly simple and limited in its range of interests. It aimed also at powerful writing, though in the service of an external rather than an internal vision. Essentially a German movement, it had few followers elsewhere, the causes of its brief success and subsequent failure lying in the Central European situation itself. It was, in effect, a repetition of the Sturm und Drang movement of the early nineteenth century. This too had been the product of a moment of national crisis: that of the Napoleonic wars. But whereas from Sturm und Drang, there emerged two great writers, Goethe and Schiller, each the richer for an experience that had been outlived, German Expressionism produced nothing that outlasted it. The crisis from which it was born did not end.

The grip of German literary conformity had by the first decade of the twentieth century haidened to an unprecedented degree. Rebellion against weak academicism, against provincial ivory towers and stuffy intellectual standards went side by side with an anarchic reaction against Prussian militarism, as violent and immoderate as the force that it opposed. Rilke moved unnoticed to Paris, and remained a stranger to Germany; George, except to the initiated, appeared to inhabit the tallest and most unapproachable of all ivory towers.

Expressionism began at the moment when a World War

appeared inevitable. It ended at the point when it became abundantly clear that defeat had brought no change of spirit to Germany. Yet even as it attempted in the months of blockade and hardship to break the stranglehold of German academicism, Expressionism was already a spent force. Of the two dozen poets whose work appeared in its principal anthology *Menschheits-dämmerung* of 1920, the best, among them Georg Trakl, were dead. It is possible that if George Heym (1887-1912) or Ernst Stadler (1883-1914) had survived, the movement would have produced some better poetry. Heym, technically the most promising of the group, had however perished in a skating accident before the war. In the first campaign in France, Stadler, the best balanced of the group, was killed. The rest wrote fervently, excitedly and without great powers of construction for as long as they had an audience, but eventually drifted into politics, Communist or Fascist, or into other fields of literature. One, Franz Werfel, became a novelist of distinction, and another Max Brod, did much to further the reputation of his friend Franz Kafka, whose novels share with Trakl's poetry the sense of damnation for an unspecified crime. Both accept their guilt, but torture themselves with apprehension; neither can see a prospect of setting a foot back in Eden. It is their preoccupation with this situation that makes Trakl and Kafka, the only two writers at all close to the Expressionist movement who are widely read. The rest were concerned with less fundamental problems.

The prime aim of Expressionism was to write powerfully of matters within the experience of the majority. It was, in fact, an attempt to reverse the esoteric drift of Symbolism. For this it had to break more violently with the German poetic tradition than Rilke or George, who had merely assimilated French influences. The Expressionists found it necessary to sacrifice the whole stiff syntax of their language. August Stramm (1874-1915), the most extreme of them, evolved a concentrated style that recalls that of the Imagists who were working on more peaceful themes at the same time in Britain and America.

Stramm's simple intention is to communicate the sights, sounds and horror of war more directly than would be possible in a reasoned and punctuated statement. He chooses his words to act as missiles that will explode in the reader's mind, with the impact of a shell. In describing a trench-attack he attempts with raw immediacy to convey not a picture or a recollection but the actual sensations of the moment itself:

> Aus allen Winkeln gellen Fürchte Wollen
> Kreisch
> Peitscht
> Das Leben
> Vor
> Sich
> Her
> Den keuschen Tod
> Die Himmel fetzen
> Blinde schlächtert wildum das Entsetzen.[1]

Each word is used in isolation and, lacking punctuation, most lines can be read in more than one way. Stramm uses nouns as verbs, and sometimes verbs as nouns. The alliteration is crude, the line-breaks arbitrary. The attempt to convey excitement succeeds, but there is no statement. A number of Expressionist poets adopted this technique, and some dramatists wrote plays in which their characters shouted in this way from various corners of the stage. Ernst Stadler, a poet of far greater capacity, uses it at the climax of his ' Fährt über die Kölner Rheinbrücke bei Nacht' (Journey over the Rhine bridge at Cologne by Night).

Stadler begins by describing with visionary intensity the passage of an express train through the bowels of the night. He catches the fragmentary sights outside the carriage window, and reproduces in his long rhythms the rumble of the train, which suddenly changes to a roar as it leaves the bank and rushes high above the river. But in its conclusion the poem dissolves into breathless stuttering:

> Nackte Ufer, Stille. Nacht. Besinnung. Einkehr. Communion.
> Und Glut und Drang.
> Zum Letzten, Segnenden. Zum Zeugungsfest. Zur Wollust. Zum
> Gebet. Zum Meer. Zum Untergang.[2]

Stadler's aim is, like Stramm's, to convey immediacy, to show a succession of sights, sounds, events and nervous processes

---

[1] From all corners fears yell will shriek whips life before it pure death the heavens shred blindly terror slaughters wildly on all sides.

[2] Naked banks, Quiet. Night. Recollection. Withdrawal into oneself. Communion. And fire and stress as a final blessing. As a feast of reproduction. As delight. As prayer. To the sea. To destruction.

succeeding one another, each caught as with a flash-lamp at the moment of its impact. The poet, sitting in the train, withdraws into himself, and then, in a moment of communion, accepts the whole of life, even to his final merging, at the moment of highest fulfilment, with the sea, the element from which all life rose.

Stadler, though an experimental poet who had read Whitman and Verhaeren, was essentially a conservative. Georg Heym (1887-1912) on the other hand, a Silesian living in Berlin, was a would-be radical who failed to make the break with traditional measures and rhythms that his new content required. Heym was, like Baudelaire, the poet of the great city; he was indeed the first to look on slums and docks like those of East Berlin as subjects for poetry. But he had not the objective eye of Baudelaire; his vision came closer to that of the excitable and haunted Verhaeren. When he wrote of a mortuary, he took the part of the dead body, awaiting like Beckett's tramps the coming of an absent God. He could not look down the streets without imagining some presiding evil spirit who will extinguish the lamps; the sky for him is a leaden pall that will soon fall to crush the houses, Urban life to him is horrible, and evil spirits brood over everything:

Einer steht auf. Dem weiszen Monde hängt
Er eine schwarze Larve vor. Die Nacht,
Die sich wie Blei vom finstern Himmel senkt,
Drückt tief die Häuser in des Dunkels Schacht.

Der Städte Schultern knacken. Und es birst
Ein Dach, daraus ein rotes Feuer schwemmt.
Breitbeinig sitzen sie auf seinem Furst
Und schrein wie Katzen auf zum Firmament.

In einer Stube voll von Finsternissen
Schreit eine Wöchnerin in ihren Wehn.
Ihr starker Leib ragt riesig aus den Kissen,
Um den herum die groszen Teufel stehn.[1]

Heym's vision is of pure life-denying horror. Already in 1911, he had conjured up another spirit of the same family as his town demons, the herald of approaching war. The poem 'Der Krieg'

[1] One stands up. He hangs a black mask before the white moon. Night, which falls like lead from the dark sky, presses the houses deep into the shaft of the dark.
The city's shoulders crack. And a roof bursts, gushing forth red fire. They sit astride on the ridge, and howl like cats to the firmament.
In a room full of dark shapes, a woman in childbed howls in her pains. Her strong body towers like a giant over the pillows, and the great devils stand around it.

(War) is probably his most powerful. It is not, however, technically in advance of 'Die Dämonen der Städte'. The images are crude as those of a poster; the language Baudelairean, and the form that of George, lopped of its antiquarian decorations. Heym's imagined refuge from the horrors of the city was, like Baudelaire's, some land overseas, to be reached only perhaps after a long voyage of discovery. When he writes of dream it is in a lighter measure; his regret for a lost love in 'Mit den Fahrenden Schiffen' (With the voyaging ships) is charming, almost wistful. Whereas in his haunted poems the repeating quatrains with their rhymes become monotonous, in one or two of his love poems he seems to be feeling out towards a new unrhymed measure.

It is possible to imagine that if the war had not killed Stadler, and if Heym had not sunk under the ice, either might have matured into a poet of greater quality. Stadler might have found subjects to suit his forms, and Heym's vision might have grown less conventionally excitable. The example of Gottfried Benn (1886-1956), however, a survivor from the Expressionist group, despite his later adherence to a new school of realism (Die neue Sachlichkeit), does not suggest that there was any way out of Expressionism that did not lead either to political propaganda or to nihilism. There was in none of these German poets the blind urge to seek a solution for their own problems and the world's, which took Blok past the stage of disgust marked by 'Humiliation' to renew his search for the Lady; none of them could recall an experience as pure as that which Blok records in his poem about the warships. The Expressionists dispel their emotion in excitability, or descend into a trough of self-pity. Benn, however, attempts to be objective; his nihilistic pity is for the world, which seems capable of yielding no pleasures more intense or lasting than a warm day by the Mediterranean or a casual amorous conquest.

Benn's line, nevertheless, even from the beginning is less monotonous than Heym's or Trakl's. He drew his imagery from life, and first from the hospital wards that he was walking when his fellow Expressionists were preoccupied only with literature. His description of a cancer-ward is one of the most hideous poems in modern literature. Reality oppresses the young doctor. Yet throughout his life he seems to have been even more bitterly tortured by the fear that ultimately nothing may be real at all.

To protect himself against this fear, he tried to put his trust in the creative spirit. But here too he was overtaken by doubts. 'Works of art are phenomena, historically ineffective, without practical consequences. That is their greatness.' Yet one cannot be sure that he really believes in art, or is sufficiently hard-driven by his own dread to commit himself utterly to his writing. Much of it appears cynical and is more remarkable for its form than for its content. Benn absorbed all the innovations of the Expressionist group, even the staccato utterance of Stramm. He introduced foreign words, strange technical expressions and sometimes a knowing tourist's patter. Often, in his endeavour to reach the absolute of poetry, he drained away the original content to leave only allusions and self-questionings. The object that has aroused his pity disappears to leave him despairing only over a 'Verlorenes ich' his lost ego:

> Die Welt zerdacht. Und Raum und Zeiten
> Und was die Menschheit wob und wog,
> Funktion nur von Unendlichkeiten—,
> Die Mythe log.[1]

There are moments, however, in Benn's poetic development when the pool is less muddy. Even though the myth is a lie, it has moments of elegiac beauty, even though his farewell is neither to the world nor to a loved object, but merely to a departing mood, it has its own nobility:

> Ein letzter Tag—: spätglühend, weite Räume,
> Ein Wasser führt dich zu entrücktem Ziel,
> Ein hohes Licht umströmt die alten Bäume
> Und schafft im Schatten sich ein Widerspiel,
> Von Früchten nichts, aus Ähren keine Krone
> Und auch nach Ernten hat er nicht gefragt—,
> Er spielt sein Spiel, und fühlt sein Licht und ohne
> Erinnern nieder—alles is gesagt.[2]

A poet seems to be taking leave of powers in which he has never fully believed, and from which he has expected neither

[1] The world thought to pieces. And space and time, and what wove and weighed mankind, only a function of eternities—the myth lied.

[2] One final day—: broad spaces in an evening glow, a stream leads you to a goal out of reach, a high light bathes the old trees, and makes itself an opposite in the shadows, not a fruit and no crown of wheat-ears, but indeed it asked for no harvest. It plays its game, is conscious of its light, and sinks without memories—everything is said.

honour nor harvest. He is conscious of the light of the evening
sun, and perhaps of another light, one half-glimpsed, that seemed
to betoken some abiding reality. But now he accepts his loss.
Experience has been painful, and he refuses to preserve memories.
What surprises is Benn's complete isolation in the last decade of
his life. This poem was written shortly after the loss of Hitler's
war, yet there is little reflection in it, or in any of his poems, of
the long Nazi nightmare and the chaos in which it ended. Benn
was attacked by the dictatorship which he had at first supported,
and took refuge in the army where he served as a doctor; this
he called an escape into the 'inner Emigration'. As a poet, however, he had made this escape thirty years earlier.

The elegiac nihilism of the Italian poet Dino Campana
(1885-1932) is less obsessive then Benn's. Even though for large
stretches of his life Campana was confined in lunatic asylums,
his poems are open to the world, through which he wandered
from Russia to Argentina. Campana can, in fact, in a verse or
two call up a scene, as he does that of a passenger ship bearing
him through the night to Buenos Aires. While he sometimes
confuses mood and vision, unlike Trakl he does not live in a
subjective prison.

At the end of a poem of farewell, 'Giardino autunnale'
(Autumn garden), Campana summons a memory, which he does
not reject:

> E in aroma d'alloro,
> In aroma d'alloro acre languente,
> Tra le statue immortali nel tramonto
> Ella m'appar, presente.[1]

His autumn garden is, perhaps, but another version of the
Decadents' park. Yet in the short lines of Campana's poem,
there is a suggestion of life outside the gates. His poems are full
of suggestion; a wind passes with the sound of broken words
spoken from some deep anxiety. Wandering through the babel of
a fair, the poet is reminded by a song of some girl who 'is not born
and yet is dead', and who has 'brought grief to his heart'. 'We
know life as it is,' he wrote, 'now let us make a dream of life as a
whole.' Campana's poems have a visionary lucidity. As one reads,

---

[1] And in the odour of laurel, in the bitter, failing odour of laurel from between the
statues immortal in the sunset, she appears to me, present.

one seems to know their meaning, but they are as difficult to translate into prose statement as Valéry's or Mallarmé's. For always the outlines are blurred; one thing is transformed into another, or stands for another, and behind every statement there is a suggestion of deeper possibilities. More various and more involved in the world than Trakl, he yet shared with him a fatal insanity, whose central symbol was the girl he loved, pitied, feared, desired and despised. She is the figure brought to life in the best of his longer poems, 'Una strana zingarella' (A Strange Gipsy):

E tu piangi in ginocchio per terra colle mani sugli occhi
E i tuoi piedi lunghi e brutti
Allargati per terra come zampe
D'une bestia ribelle e mostruosa.
Che sapore avranno le tue lacrimucce?
Un puoco di fuoco? Io vorrei farne
Un diadema fantastico e portarlo
Sul mio capo nell'ora della morte
Per udirmi parlare in confidenza
I demonietti dai piedi forcuti.[1]

The girl is real in a way that a similar temptress in a poem by Swinburne would be purely fictional. And there is pity here as there would not be in a poem by Benn. The true comparison might be with Blok's 'Humiliation' were it not that Campana does not give the girl an existence in her own right. Campana, moreover, remains absent from most of his poems; the chief reason for their difficulty, indeed, is that there is no constant recording agency. Campana's senses mark an impression but, like those of a madman, fail to relate it to the rest. The poetry if full of hints, therefore, yet makes no more positive statement than in the concluding lines of the poem to the Gipsy. They immediately follow those I have just quoted:

Povera bimba come ti calunnio
Perchè hai i capelli tragici
E ti vesti di rosso e non odori.[2]

[1] And you weep kneeling on the earth, your hands over your eyes, and your long, ugly feet splayed on the earth like the paws of some monstrous, defiant beast. What taste will your little tears have? A touch of fire? I would like to make a fantastic diadem of them, and wear it on my head at the hour of my death, to hear the little demons with cloven hooves speak to me in confidence.

[2] Poor child, how I wrong you with words, because you have tragic hair, and you dress in red, and have no scent.

While it is only possible to relate Campana to the poets of apocalypse on account of the intimations of disaster that he shared with Blok and Trakl, the link which connects the one great English poet of the Kaiser's war with them is even more tenuous. Yet Wilfred Owen (1893-1918) comes near to the German expressionists in his interpretation of war's landscape, a picture which he drew more truly than any of them, since he survived till the very last days of the fighting. Owen was in his beginnings, a Romantic poet of limited power, prone to echo the cadences of Keats. As Georg Heym remained fixed to the last in an outworn convention, so did Owen until the moment when a new vision was suddenly matched for him by new technical discoveries. Owen's assonances and half-rhymes reproduce the broken sounds of the battlefield. His vision of the trench landscape was necessarily new, since the lunar waste of the Somme was a thing hitherto unknown. Heym's devouring city had been described by Baudelaire and Verhaeren before him; Owen saw a new horror:

> My soul looked down from a vague height with Death,
> As unremembering how I rose or why,
> And saw a sad land, weak with sweats of dearth,
> Gray, cratered like the moon with hollow woe,
> And pitted with great pocks and scabs of plagues.
>
> Across its beard, that horror of harsh wire,
> There moved thin caterpillars, slowly uncoiled.
> It seemed they pushed themselves to be as plugs
> Of ditches, where they writhed and shrivelled, killed.

In this poem, 'The Show', the poet is master of his vision, but not of his attitude to it. He is still in the position of Heym, who, foreseeing a war, was horrified. He resembles Heym also in that he is not yet master of his own language. His personified Death is no more real, for all Owen's greater experience of war, than Heym's demon sitting astride the roof of a burning house. The final stage in his development, when he surpassed all those poets whose central experience was of world disaster, excepting only Blok, is revealed in hardly more than two poems, one compassionate and indignant, and the second compassionate in a mood of resigned acceptance. The first is the sonnet 'Anthem for Doomed Youth';

What passing bells for these who die as cattle?
  Only the monstrous anger of the guns.
  Only the stuttering rifles' rapid rattle
Can patter out their hasty orisons.
No mockeries for them from prayers or bells,
  Nor any voice of mourning save the choirs,—
The shrill demented choirs of wailing shells;
  And bugles calling for them from sad shires.

Here everything is achieved that was attempted by the Expressionists. The sharp juxtaposition of the harsh and the poetic word—
cattle following on *passing bells*—is in the Baudelairean tradition.
But the disturbingly imperfect rhyme *guns, orisons;* the Stramm-
like onomatopœia of the third line, which reproduces the
sounds of rifle-fire, and of the seventh which suggests the whine
of shells passing overhead; these outstrip the achievements of the
whole apocalyptic generation, though still within the traditional
framework of the sonnet. Owen's greatest poem, the unfinished
'Strange Meeting' with its picture of the underground warrens
of trench fortifications, goes even further. Here is a myth of
uncertain equivalences, and to match it a complete pattern of
half-rhymes which breaks more conclusively with the conventions
that had obtained since the Renaissance than anything except the
as yet unpublished work of Gerard Manley Hopkins. Moreover
in this poem Owen accepts with resignation a vision of complete
disaster. He sees himself as the last poet. Henceforth no man will
be capable of reconciling killer and killed:

Now men will go content with what we spoiled.
Or, discontent, boil bloody, and be spilled.
They will be swift with swiftness of the tigress,
None will break ranks, though nations trek from progress.
Courage was mine, and I had mystery,
Wisdom was mine, and I had mastery;
To miss the march of the retreating world
Into vain citadels that are not walled.
I would go up and wash them from sweet wells,
Even with truths that lie too deep for taint. . . .

The loss was absolute. Owen watched the sufferings of the
men he had returned to the front to lead. He interpreted them
finally, without the indignation with which he had written only a
few months before.

Owen was killed exactly a week before the armistice was

signed. 'He was one of those destined beings,' wrote Edmund Blunden, a friend, 'who, without pride of self (the words of Shelley will never be excelled), see, as from a tower, the end of all.' This is true not only of him, however, but of Blok, on the field of Kulikovo. It is in their failure to exclude 'pride of self'— or at least to transcend the personal—that Trakl, Heym, Stadler, and even Campana, fail to equal him. Yet the comparison is in one important aspect unfair; Blok and Owen met and confronted events, which for the others existed for the most part as mental fictions. Trakl collapsed utterly on his first sight of a reality that matched the auguries which he had read in the passage of the birds across the sky. It was consequently as men capable of accepting experience that the Russian and the Englishman triumphed over the rest; and it is by reason of this acceptance that their poetry is both more positive and greater.

The poetry of Robert Graves (b. 1895) seems like a pendant to that of the Apocalyptics in general, since it owes its quality largely to his refusal to draw conclusions from an emotional experience of war that threatened to pull him in their direction. Graves's poetry is full of doubt and self-distrust; it is ironic, though chiefly at the expense of the poet himself, and of his mission. Seeing the disaster about to befall western culture, Graves feels that it is no part of a poet's duty to make a public prophecy.

> It behoved us, indeed, as poets
> To be silent in Siloam, to foretell
> No visible calamity,

he states in 'The Fallen Tower of Siloam'; and at moments, as in 'Act V, Scene 5' he seems to welcome the catastrophe. He even delights in imagining the slaughter of those few minor characters who survive to moralize at the end of the bloodiest Jacobean play. Graves's own attitude is that of a survivor from a slaughter in which he saw so many of his generation perish. The theme of ghosts still appears in poems written thirty years after the first war, in the years that followed the second:

> Is this joy? to be doubtless alive again,
> And the others dead? Will your nostrils gladly savour
> The fragrance, always new, of a first hedge-rose?
> Will your ears be charmed by the thrush's melody
> Sung as though he had himself devised it?

Graves is forever surprised at finding himself alive, and forever doubtful whether his experiences are anything but those of a ghost. In 'The Terraced Valley', a poem of his middle years, he argues away a moment of experience that appears similar to Eliot's vision of the rose-garden, in 'Burnt Norton'. For him it was merely a moment of strangeness:

> The unnecessary sun was not there,
> The necessary earth lay without care—
> For more than sunshine warmed the skin
> Of the round world that was turned outside-in.

The poet missed the familar things and by crying to his companion, who had disappeared with the coming of this 'more than sunshine',

> broke
> This trick of time, changing the world about
> To once more inside-in and outside-out.

Faced with possibilities of transcending common experience, the poet resorts to truculent nihilism:

> No escape,
> No such thing; to dream of new dimensions,
> Cheating checkmate by painting the king's cheek
> So that he slides like a queen.
> Or to cry, 'Not true, not true!'
> Like a corpse in the cholera-pit
> Under a load of corpses . . .

Only love seems to excite Graves to any more positive attitude than that of a dogged struggle to survive. But usually he presents it too as a thwarted and painful experience. In a late piece 'Through Nightmare', however, there is a rare quality, the recognition in a loved woman of something more precious than the mere persistence needed for survival:

> The untameable, the live, the gentle,
> Have you not known them? Whom? They carry
> Time looped so river-wise about their house
> There's no way in by history's road
> To name or number them.

In your sleepy eyes, I read the journey
Of which disjointedly you tell; which stirs
My loving admiration, that you should travel
Through nightmare to a lost and moated land,
Who are timorous by nature.

Graves's poetry is witty in the Metaphysical sense; it is tighter in argument and subtler, though less adventurous in technique than Owen's. In its restraint indeed, it stands in the tradition of Thomas Hardy, and to some extent outside modernism altogether. Graves also is less reluctant than most modern poets to speak in the first person. His *I* is not, like that of Yeats, a mask, yet in his distrust of his own personality, his refusal to dramatize, or even to believe in, his own experience, he has, perhaps involuntarily, taken his stand among the moderns. He has seen and accepted the same vision of the end of an epoch that came to Blok, but, taking an opposite attitude, has decided that it is the poet's business to remain uncommitted, the last cuirassier on the frontier of an Empire that has already fallen by internal decay.

In Peter's Church there is no faith or truth,
Nor justice anywhere in palace or court.
That we continue watchful on the rampart
Concerns no priest. A gaping silken dragon,
Puffed by the wind, suffices us for God.
We, not the City, are the Empire's soul:
A rotten tree lives only in its rind.

The rest of the English war-poets saw events more narrowly. Siegfried Sassoon (b. 1886) wrote bitterly and Edmund Blunden (b. 1896) sadly of the purposeless destruction of life and country-side in the years of trench warfare. The best poems of both either record or look back on the Flanders campaigns. In fact, like Robert Graves, they too at times regard themselves as ghosts surviving from that time. The peaceful world appears in their poetry to exist rather as a refuge from fear than in its own right. Probably war poetry in this age can only achieve greatness if the slaughter is seen in relation to man as a whole and his place in history. It is because no poet arose with this breadth of vision that the Second World War, even more than the First, lacked poets of stature in all countries.

6

In the waste land

THROUGHOUT a great part of Europe the First World War and its attendant revolutions passed from men's minds with surprising rapidity, and with them faded the extremes of the apocalyptic style. Symbolism re-established itself as the dominant convention of the 'twenties, whose greatest poets, Yeats, Rilke and Valéry had already gone far towards perfecting their styles before 1914. New experiments and theories, which had received some impetus in the war years, were for a while confined to a very small circle centred on Paris. Being the product of social tensions, they could not make much headway in the decade of false prosperity, but waited for the onset of the next crisis, the slump of 1929. The years that followed the armistice were a period of aestheticism, in which it was even claimed in many quarters that the mission of art had in the present age received an unexampled extension, and that it was now in the artist's power to provide a substitute for religious experience. The divorce between the poet and the public was, nevertheless, almost universally accepted on the plea that since he was compelled to explore territory in advance of any that was ready for general occupation, he must for the present, like any pioneer, remain out of touch with the mass of his future followers.

There was, however, from the outset, an opposition to this point of view on the part of writers who, although unable to accept the claims of religion, put no trust in any aesthetic solution. For them uncertainty and doubt were a lot that must be accepted, though with varying degrees of hope that out of the pain of disbelief some flash of faith might be born. In the case of T. S. Eliot a resolute facing of doubt led to religious faith; in that of the Russian poet Mayakovsky the move was from an exaggerated and flamboyant egotism to a partly ironic, partly naïve belief in his country's new destiny. The group who passed through the *waste land* in the years up to 1930 were in no sense a unified body; it is indeed doubtful whether they would have acknowledged any common aims or attitudes beyond a growing willingness to experiment and a general dissatisfaction with Symbolism. All, however, though unlike in their aims and sympathies, resolutely refused to build any myth. Rejecting prophecy and making no claims or statements, they rely solely on their moments of experience, basing on them alone any conclusions they may reach.

This new movement gained its first strength in Spain, a country whose destiny had remained on the whole divorced from that of the rest of Europe, and which had hardly been penetrated by any new thought since the Counter-Reformation. While it was possible for Juan Ramón Jiménez to adapt the Symbolist style to the Spanish language, it is doubtful whether he made any real links for it with the Spanish tradition. It is noteworthy that while he spent the last twenty years of his life in exile, as have most distinguished Spaniards who accepted the Europeanizing tendencies of the Republic, his two greatest contemporaries were both victims of the Civil War. The Spanish tradition is violent and uncompromising, and it is not out of keeping with it that Miguel de Unamuno should have died after upbraiding the rebel generals, with whom he had at first felt some sympathy, or that Antonio Machado should have perished in the first village beyond the frontier, after struggling into France, a sick man, with the retreating Republican armies.

Both these poets are poets of doubt, painfully and honestly accepted. Miguel de Unamuno (1864-1936) stands midway between modernism and tradition. His techniques are no more revolutionary than those of Thomas Hardy, with whom he shares a tough distaste for the *poetic* phrase, and a habit of expressing recalcitrant thought in broken language. The rigours of his unsuccessful struggle for faith are reflected in the frequent imperfections of his line. This has earned him the reputation of being no true poet, but a prose-writer who chose at times to write in verse. The judgement is unfair since it is in his roughness that his very real originality lies. Unamuno is one of the few poets of doubt to refuse Heine's consolation of irony. Modern in this, and in his rejection likewise of Romantic self-dramatization,

Unamuno became, despite his wide reading in fourteen languages, ancient and modern, the poet of his adopted landscape of Castile—he was by birth a Biscayan—and of his own recurrent situation: a state of agonized uncertainty in face of the problem of death and survival. Despite his almost Protestant familiarity with the Bible, it was not the Christ of the Gospels that Unamuno addressed in his most sustained poem, the sequence 'El Cristo de Velazquez' (The Christ of Velazquez), but Velazquez's painting of the crucified Saviour which hangs in the Prado. The burden of his question was one already old in Spanish literature: Is life a dream?

> Es sueño
> Cristo, la vida, y es la muerte vela.
> Mientras la tierra sueña solitaria,
> vela la blanca luna; vela el Hombre
> desde su cruz, mientras los hombres sueñan;
> vela el Hombre sin sangre, el Hombre blanco
> como la luna de la noche negra.[1]

The poem is a long metaphysical struggle with Unamuno's abiding problem, and it suffers somewhat from a lack of concrete imagery. In his desperate longing for immortality, Unamuno seized on every possible argument and analogy. In writing of the death of his dog, he translated the situation into one in which it is the man who dies, to live perhaps in the memory of his God, as the dog in that of his master. Poetry itself thus derives its chief importance from its power of perpetuating a voice that is now silent. Yet even here, there is in Unamuno no egoism of the Romantic sort, since he is imprisoned in the modern dilemma: he cannot believe in his own existence as a concrete and unchanging personality.

Unamuno could find no way out since, unlike such a later poet as T. S. Eliot, he was entirely bound by a humanistic attitude to time. The survival he wished to prove was a survival in time, which be believed Christ to have achieved for Himself, and through His Passion for other men. Christ was therefore for Unamuno a hero rather an aspect of God, and could be compared to the moon that, in the darkest night, vouches for the sun's

[1] Life is a dream, O Christ, and death a watch. While the earth is in solitary sleep, the white moon watches; the Man watches from his cross, while men sleep; the bloodless Man watches, the Man white as the moon on a black night.

continued existence by reflecting its rays. Intellectually, however, Unamuno could not convince himself of truths that he perceived emotionally. His poetry, therefore, like much that has followed it, is one in which emotion and intellect are at odds. He is indeed the type of the religious poet of today whose religion lies in a few rare moments of experience, and in his wish to believe in them. But his writing is at its finest when he confronts death not in the imagination but in the bare Castilian countryside, where the cross above a deserted cemetery seems to give him assurance that there is a Providence watching over the dead as over the living:

> Después que lento el sol tomó ya tierra,
> y sube al cielo el páramo
> a la hora del recuerdo,
> a toque de oraciones y descanso,
> la tosca cruz de piedra
> de tus tapias de barro
> queda, como un guardián que nunca duerme,
> de la campiña el sueño vigilando.[1]

Here the cemetery serves as a symbol for the state of death, which Unamuno had considered in the abstract in 'El Cristo de Velazquez'. It is in this recording of the Castilian landscape in which death is ever present that the deepest emotion finds its way into Unamuno's poetry.

Antonio Machado (1875-1939), once the pupil of Unamuno, was also, despite his Sevillan birth, primarily a poet of Castile. Indeed the rugged restraint of his lines compares with the colour and flow of his friend Jiménez's as the landscape of the *meseta* with the greater dramatic richness of Andalusia. Moreover, where Unamuno resorted to metaphysical argument only because of the nature of his problem, Machado was by nature a metaphysician, prone to compare and relate aspects and appearances in any situation. But a situation for him was, more constantly than for Unamuno, embodied in a landscape. Machado was a poet of far greater visual power than his Biscayan contemporary, and far more various in the music of his verse. His landscape was one of sky and cloud, of rocks and water; and it coloured not

---

[1] After the sun has slowly sunk to the earth, and the high tableland is mounting to the sky at the hour of remembrance, at the bell for prayer and rest, the rough stone cross on your clay walls remains as an unsleeping guardian, watching over the countryside's sleep.

only his waking vision but his dreams. It was a landscape of nature
and the spirit together, of vision and of memory:

> Allá, en las tierras altas,
> por donde traza el Duero
> su curva de ballesta
> en torno a Soria, entre plomizos cerros
> y manchas de raídos encinares,
> mi corazón esta vagando, en sueños. . . . [1]

Machado's delineation of the landscape is as exact as a
painter's, and in his anatomy of Spain and her people he has a
similar exactness, that of a psychologist with a sense of history.
Machado was a radical and an agnostic, who believed in his
country's future even as he despaired of her present. Her spirit
was, as he saw it in the years of the First European War, hollow
and degraded, yet ultimately heroic. The typical Spaniard whom
he drew in 'Del pasado efímero' (Of the Transient Past) is in a
waste land from which he can never emerge. He sits in a provincial café thinking only of yesterday's gambling or the bull-
fight, and watching the sky only for the rain that may fall to
nourish his olive-trees.

> Lo demás, taciturno, hipocondríaco,
> prisionera en la Arcadia del presente,
> le aburre; sólo el humo del tabaco
> simula algunas sombras en su frente.
> Este hombre no es de ayer ni de mañana,
> sino de nunca; de la cepa hispana
> no es el fruto maduro ni podrido,
> es una fruta vana
> de aquella España que pasó y no ha sido,
> esa que hoy tiene la cabeza cana. [2]

Here is the portrait of a man as hollow as T. S. Eliot's
Sweeney, capable only of repeating the worn phrases of café-
conversation, and rotten without ever having ripened. Imprisoned in a shabby moment of time, he has neither present nor

---

[1] There in the high country, where the (river) Duero makes a curve like a crossbow
around Soria, between leaden hills, and patches of threadbare holm-oak woods, my
heart is wandering, in dreams.

[2] For the rest, taciturn hypochondriac, imprisoned in the Arcadia of the moment,
everything bores him; only the smoke of his cigar gives the illusion that there are some
shadows on his forehead. This man is neither of yesterday nor of tomorrow, but of no
time at all. On the Hispanic stock he is neither a ripe nor a rotten fruit, he is an empty
fruit of that Spain which is past and has never been, a Spain that is today grey-haired.

future. Machado too was limited by his vision of time. A better future seemed to him very far away; happiness could be won, he believed, only by the pursuit of the unattainable. Though God could never be found, faith could be born in the search for Him. This he states in the conclusion of a poem in praise of Spain and her tradition, 'Desde mi rincón' (From my Corner):

> Desde un pueblo que ayuna y se divierte,
> ora y eructa, desde un pueblo impío
> que juega al mus, de espaldas a la muerte,
> creo en la libertad y en la esperanza,
> y en una fe que nace
> cuando se busca a Dios y no se alcanza,
> y en el Dios que se lleva y que se hace.[1]

Despite the magnitude of his own crisis, the loss of his young wife after only a few years of marriage, Machado is less insistent than Unamuno on receiving an answer to his questions. He is content to remain in uncertainty. Though many of his finest poems are, in effect, explorations of the *galleries* of his own mind, he does not in his solitude look only inward. Much that he has seen remains with him to be recollected:

> ¡Oh!, os conmigo vais, campos de Soria,
> tardes tranquilas, montes de violeta,
> alamedas del río, verde sueño
> del suelo gris y de la parda tierra,
> agria melancolía
> de la cuidad decrépita,
> me habeis llegado al alma,
> ¿o acaso estabais en el fondo de ella?
> ¡Gentes del alto llano numantino
> que a Dios guardáis como cristianas viejas,
> que el sol de España os llene
> de alegría, de luz y de riqueza![2]

Many times in his life, even before he had written his best poems, Machado had feared that his talent would desert him, and

[1] From a town that starves and amuses itself, prays and belches, from an impious town that plays cards, turning its back on death, I believe in liberty and in hope, and in a faith that is born when one seeks a God and does not come to one, and in a God who bears himself and creates himself.

[2] Oh, you go with me, fields of Soria, quiet evenings, violet mountains, lines of poplars along the river, the green dream of a grey soil and brown earth, sour melancholy of the decrepit city, you have touched my soul, or perhaps you have lain in its depths? People of the high Numantine plain who preserve your God like women of old Christian stock, may the sun of Spain fill you with joy, love and riches!

that he would be left with 'only coppers for the gold he had changed the day before'. He was a poet of hope. He believed, as a radical and a republican, that 'happiness, light and riches' would in the end come to his cruel and backward country. But he was out of sympathy with the next generation which looked not to him but to Jiménez as their leader. His poetry was becoming increasingly intellectual: it had become a dialogue between characters of his own invention, of whom the chief were the erotic metaphysician Abel Martín and the rhetorician Juan de Mairena, the inventor of a poetry-making machine. Machado attempted to transform himself into such a machine, writing mechanical *coplas*, or Andalusian folk-songs. But with another side of his nature he wrote a few metaphysical poems, whose central symbol was *the great Zero*. For it was only in the absence of the loved object—be it God, his dead wife, his yet unborn country, or a landscape he had once known—that he found that object again. Nothing, he believed can be remembered unless it has first been forgotten.

> Al Dios de la distancia y de la ausencia,
> del áncora en la mar, la plena mar . . .
> El nos libra del mundo—omnipresencia—,
> nos abre senda para caminar.[1]

The path can only be found when the poet is freed from the world; truth can only be found when the ego has ceased to demand it. Towards the end of his life, indeed, Machado stated that the lyric of personal feeling had no more importance in the modern world. His idea of a poetry-making machine arose from a wish for anonymity. His attempts at folk-song, however, failed, since his mind was too philosophical to catch the popular note. He failed indeed even to make so much contact with the people whose cause he had adopted as the less politically conscious García Lorca. He shared with them, however, the ordeal of the Civil War, and found his new idiom, perhaps, in this participation rather than in the writing of his few final poems.

The discovery of a new idiom both up-to-date and traditional, both intellectually pliant and colloquial, was beyond the power of any Spanish poet, since the loyalties of all were to the country,

[1] To the God of distance and absence, of the anchor in the sea, the sea at high tide— He frees us from the world—from omnipresence—and opens us a path to travel.

where language is slow to develop, rather than to the town. In France, however, the work had already been done in the 'seventies and 'eighties of the previous century by two successors of Baudelaire, Jules Laforgue and Tristan Corbière. For a while, however, it was the Mallarméan side of the Symbolist movement that had most influence in France. The first poet, indeed, seriously to exploit the innovations in language and rhythm that these two had left, was a writer of mixed nationality who was French only by adoption, Guillaume Apollinaire (1880-1918).

In contrast to the Symbolists, Apollinaire drew his inspiration from the surface of life. The movement of his verse is rapid, his allusions often puzzling and his technique apparently off-hand. In fact he was a more careful craftsman than he wished to appear, and more intellectual in his approach than his rather modish subjects suggest. Being a close friend of the Cubist painters, he learnt from them to despise common appearances, and to see any given object as an assemblage of aspects, rather than as something bound by space and time. In 'L'Emigrant de Landor Road', for instance, the time sequence of the departing emigrant's life is seen in a series of snapshots drawn indifferently from past, present and future. This figure is Apollinaire's counterpart to Machado's bored clubman, a man of no nationality drifting from a trivial present to an equally trivial future. As he buys a suit off a dummy in a tailor's shop, he dreams of the money to be gained 'dans les prairies lyriques', but in fact he has nothing to look forward to, nothing to believe in. He is one of Eliot's 'hollow men', and the dummies on which the tailor displays his clothes stand for his wasted life:

> Au dehors les années
> Regardaient la vitrine
> Les mannequins victimes
> Et passaient enchaînées

> Intercalées dans l'an c'étaient les journées veuves
> Les vendredis sanglants et lents d'enterrements
> De blancs et de tous noirs vaincus de cieux qui pleuvent
> Quand la femme du diable a battu son amant[1]

---

[1] Outside the years looked through the shop window at the victim dummies and passed in chains.
Intercalated in the year were the widowed days, the bloody and slow Fridays of funerals some white some all in black vanquished by skies that weep when the devil's wife has beaten her lover.

The images are assembled as in a Cubist picture patches of newspaper, guitars and distant vistas of columns or streets that suggest Romantic possibilities, are pulled together by an overriding sense of pattern and a limited colour pallette. 'L'Emigrant' is written in the greys and browns of ironic melancholy, but lit all the time by flashes from another world unknown to the emigrant, that of the poet himself. Before the end of the poem, indeed, Apollinaire has abandoned his subject to indulge in a mockery of the Romantic style that is itself Romantic:

> Gonfle-toi vers la nuit O Mer Les yeux des squales
> Jusqu'a l'aube ont guetté de loin avidement
> Des cadavres de jours rongés par les étoiles
> Parmi le bruit des flots et les derniers serments[1]

The mixture of irony and Romanticism, which was present in Heine and in Jules Laforgue, leads the poet to attempt a great extension of subject and vocabulary. Whatever struck the painter's eye of Guillaume Apollinaire served him for an image; and in any curious and random piece of knowledge collected in his reading might be made to enrich a line. He was in fact imitating his friends Picasso and Braque in their use of *collage*.

There is a prevailing uncertainty, however, throughout Apollinaire's poetry, founded in a fundamental lack of standpoint. Anxious to break with the past, he resorts to what is often no more than modishness. In refusing to punctuate his poems, he responded to no organic need; it is always clear where the stops would be, if he would allow himself to put them in. In his war poems, also, many of which were written on post cards in lines that take the form of a fountain, a watch, or of falling rain, the device is unimportant. It has merely been invented to amuse a friend. Written out in regular form these verses prove, unlike similar exercises by George Herbert and others in the seventeenth century, to be quite conventional in the length of their lines. In his desire to break with symbolism, however, Apollinaire makes fresh links with the Middle Ages on which he draws both for metres and for imagery. The last valid contact between sophisticated poetry and folk-song lying so far back in French history,

---

[1] Swell towards the night, O Sea The eyes of sharks have watched avidly from afar till dawn the corpses of days gnawed by the stars amidst the noise of waves and last promises.

Apollinaire is forced to look to the old song-books for motifs whereas Machado has only to listen to singers in the streets of Seville.

Apollinaire's truest claim to originality lies not in his technique, which is eclectic, but in the vividness of his response to scenes as different as London and the Rhineland, the artists' quarter of Paris and the wartime desert of dug-out and shell hole in which he took a grim delight. There is zest and an astringent self-irony in his most sustained poem 'Le Chanson du Mal-aimé' (The Song of the Ill-beloved), in which he commemorates an unhappy love-affair with an English girl called Annie, which occurred when he was acting as tutor to a German family. He appears to have come to London to find her, and it is here that the poem begins. But Apollinaire attempts something more than to tell the story of an unhappy passion; he tries to put the event into some sort of historical context, even though he knows that in fact Annie herself will soon be out of his mind. He attempts, half-ironically, by the incantation of verse, and the introduction of echoes from past poets, to transcend the triviality of what he knows to be a trivial affair.

> Regrets sur quoi l'enfer se fonde
> Qu'un ciel d'oubli s'ouvre à mes vœux
> Pour son baiser les rois du monde
> Seraient morts les pauvres fameux
> Pour elle eussent vendu leur ombre
>
> J'ai hiverné dans mon passé
> Revienne le soleil de Pâques
> Pour chauffer un cœur plus glacé
> Que les quarante de Sébaste
> Moins que ma vie martyrisée
>
> Mon beau navire ô ma mémoire
> Avons nous assez navigué
> Dans une monde mauvaise à boire
> Avons nous assez divagué
> De la belle aube au triste soir[1]

[1] Regrets on which hell is founded May a sky of oblivion open to my prayers For her kiss, the kings of the world would have died the poor men of fame would have sold their shadows for her.

I have wintered in my past May the Easter sun return to warm a heart more frozen than Sebastes' forty less martyred than my life.

My lovely ship O my memory haven't we sailed enough in a world that is bad to drink Haven't we wandered enough from fair dawn to sad evening.

From this point, after one more verse, Apollinaire passes to what is in effect the refrain of the whole poem, which calls up echoes of Villon's ballades:

Voie lactée ô soeur lumineuse
Des blancs ruisseaux de Chanaan
Et des corps blancs des amoureuses
Nageurs morts suivrons-nous d'ahan
Ton cours vers d'autres nébuleuses[1]

The construction of 'Le Chanson du Mal-Aimé' stands half-way between that of Blok's 'Twelve' and of Eliot's *Quartets;* the poet's intention is to connect a number of moods and incidents by a musical structure. The image, which has predominated with the Symbolists, is to yield to the rhythmical passage; development is to give way to abrupt contrast within an overall context. Where Blok carries the sequence of his poem through time, tracing the march of his revolutionaries through the streets of Petrograd, and Apollinaire breaks off his story, reflects and resumes it again, still within the framework of time, Eliot, by contrast, though using the same method as Apollinaire of quoting and referring to the poetry of the past, abandons the time-sequence altogether: 'The Waste Land' contains no one character through whose mind it is reflected, but a number of voices, male and female, the sum of whose statements amounts to that of Antonio Machado describing his bored clubman.

There is deeper feeling in Apollinaire's laconic war-poems than in his 'Chanson du Mal-aimé', though the pity in them is much more muted than that of Wilfred Owen. It is in them that Apollinaire catches the folk-song directness for which Machado was even then, in neutral Spain, trying in vain:

Vers un village de l'arrière
S'en allaient quatre bombardiers
Ils étaient couverts de poussière
Depuis la tête jusqu'aux pieds

Ils regardaient la vaste plaine
En parlant entre eux du passé
Et ne se retournaient qu'à peine
Quand un obus avait toussé

[1] Milky Way O shining sister of the white streams of Canaan and of the white bodies of mistresses Dead swimmers shall we follow exhausted your course towards other nebulae.

Tous quatre de la classe seize
Parlaient d'antan non d'avenir
Ainsi se prolongeait l'ascèse
Qui les exercait à mourir[1]

Only in the last couplet is the spell of modern folk-song abruptly broken by the poet's own sophisticated voice. The purpose of this shock is to place the incident in the context of history by pointing a parallel between these dusty soldiers and the desert fathers of the Thebaid.

This shock treatment was first recommended as a poetic device in the Futurist Manifesto of 1909, in which a number of Italian poets, whose actual achievement amounts to very little, sought to define a poetry suitable for the machine age. 'No work can be a masterpiece', they stated, 'that has not an aggressive character'. The Futurists declared war on museums, libraries and academies of every sort; they glorified war itself as the only cure for the world. On the purely literary side they demanded 'Freedom for the Word', which involved a breaking down of all logic and sentence construction. The war-poems of August Stramm, quoted in the last chapter, are in this respect futuristic, though the movement itself had no following in Germany. In France, it encouraged Apollinaire and others in their break with Symbolism, and was no doubt responsible for the exaggerated cult of the Eiffel Tower, noticeable in the poetry and painting of the epoch. Apollinaire himself devoted a poem to that Futuristic monument.

The one Italian poet to take advantage of the new freedoms then in the air was Giuseppe Ungaretti (b. 1888) who was born in Egypt and was, during his pre-war residence in Paris, a member of the Apollinaire circle.

An early enthusiast for the war, Ungaretti saw service as an infantryman, and it was in the isolation of the trenches that he threw off the shreds of rhetoric which still hung about him owing to his contacts with the Symbolists and the even more declamatory enthusiasts for the 1909 Manifesto. Ungaretti's poetry has a most remarkable purity; all inessentials have been pruned away

---

[1] Towards a village behind the lines four artillerymen were going They were covered with dust from head to foot.
They looked at the vast plain as they discussed the past and scarely turned their heads after a shell had coughed.
All four of the 1916 class spoke of long ago not of the future Thus was prolonged the asceticism which was compelling them to die.

from such a poem as 'Monotonia' (Monotony), which is dated
from the battlefield of 1916:

> Fermato a due sassi
> languisco
> sotto questa
> volta appannata
> di cielo
>
> Il groviglio dei sentieri
> possiede la mia cecità
>
> Nulla è più squallido
> di questa monotonia
>
> Una volta
> non sapevo
>
> ch'è una cosa
> qualunque
> perfino
> la consunzione
> del cielo
>
> E sulla mia terra africana
> calmata
> a un arpeggio
> perso nell'aria
> mi rinnovavo[1]

This poem of Ungaretti's makes a single statement, but its
implications are manifold. From the last verse quoted, for
instance, we are to understand that in the poet's native Egypt the
sun would go down like a full chord at the end of a song, and thus
bring the poet relief, whereas the slow fading of the heavens at
evening in the north gave him only a feeling of monotony.
Ungaretti is in fact the first of a new group of poets who in their
desire for purity of line, reject every superfluous thread in the
strand of their reasoning. This new purism is related on the one
side to Valéry's poetry of bare ideas, on the other to the *Waste
Land* situation, which rendered all the D'Annunzian flourishes
then predominant in Italian poetry, suspect. Ungaretti's version
of the hollow man of Machado, Apollinaire and Eliot is 'the
wounded man' of the poem 'La Pietà' (Pity):

[1] Stopping at two rocks I languish beneath this dulled vault of sky. The knot in the
paths masters my blindness. Nothing is more dismal than this monotony. I did not
know that there is such a thing as the evening's consumption of the sky. And on my
own African soil soothed by an arpeggio at the close of an aria, I would take fresh life.

E

Sono un uomo ferito

E me ne vorrei andare
E finalmente giungere
Pietà, dove si ascolta
L'uomo che è solo con sè

Non ho che superbia e bontà

E mi sento esiliato in mezzo agli uomini[1]

Ungaretti's hero perhaps received his wounds in the war, but his plight is that of Unamuno, and of all those who cannot accept the Church's answer in a society where there is no alternative.

'Vorremmo una certezza', he says—we would have certainty, but perhaps God will prove nothing but a dream. The pathos of this poetry lies in the bareness of its language. In the poet's own words: 'Any soldier at grips with the blindness of things, with chaos and with death, became a being who in a flash recapitulates from the beginning.' One is reminded of the experience which is said to come to drowning men; the events of a whole life return to the memory in their essentials. Ungaretti entitled his complete poems, Vita di un uomo (the Life of a Man). Many of the war-poems are dated like diary notes: although their statements appear abstract, they in fact present the compressed account of actual situations.

Ten years after the war the vividness of these situations had faded. Involved in ceaseless literary disputes, Ungaretti remained certain that he, and he alone, had rejuvenated Italian poetry. However, his output in the post-war years amounts only to one book, Sentimento del Tempo (Perception of time), of which 'La Pietà' strikes the elegiac note. But the predominant feeling is of quiet, of an absence of pain rather than a conquest of certainty. In 1937 Ungaretti left Italy, going first to Egypt, then to Argentina, and finally settled in Brazil as Professor of Italian at the University of São Paulo. From here he returned in 1942, unwilling to remain an exiled spectator of his country's tragedy. On arriving in Italy he found himself acclaimed by Fascists and anti-Fascists alike, and was elected to a chair at the University of Rome.

[1] I am a wounded man. And I would go away and finally come, Pity, where the man who is alone with himself is heard. I have only pride and goodness. And I feel exiled among men.

From the tragedy of Italy's defeat and occupation, and from his own loss of his son in Brazil, Ungaretti's poetry regained depth, and with it a richness of language that had been absent till then. The volume *Il dolore* (Pain) is coloured by an acceptance of grief that seems to lift the poet out of the *waste land*. The poem 'Terra' (Earth) presents in great compression the picture of a civilization in decay, haunted by premonitions of a violent break-up:

> Potresti la chiglia sommersa
> Dislocarsi udire nel largo
> O un gabbiano irisi a beccare,
> Sfuggita la preda, lo specchio . . .
>
> Del grano di notte e di giorni
> Ricolmo mostrasti le mani,
> Degli avi tirreni delfini
> Dipinti vedesti a segreti
> Muri immateriali, poi, dietro
> Alle navi, vivi volare
> E terra sei ancora dei ceneri
> D'inventori senza riposo.[1]

Here the foreshortened history of Italy is presented in a series of seemingly disparate images. The dolphins of the Etruscans seem to stand for some primitive urges, painted on the immaterial walls of the unconscious mind, yet also still living; and the restless inventors, the men of the Renaissance are also the Fascists who have aped them, and are reducing their country to ashes. The associations are richer and more mysterious than in the earlier poems, where it is chiefly the sound of guns that booms in the background. But throughout the poems of this last volume the dead are present again, and their voices are louder even than those of the land into which they have been absorbed:

> Il vento continui a scrosciare,
> Da palme ad abeti lo strepito
> Per sempre desoli, silente
> Il grido dei morti è più forte.[2]

---

[1] You might hear the sunken keel break up out at sea, or a gull in its fury peck the mirror when its prey has escaped.
  You showed your hands full of the grain of days and nights, you saw the dolphins of Etruscan ancestors painted on the secret immaterial walls, then fly alive, straight to the ships, and you are again a land of the ashes of restless inventors.
[2] The wind continued to storm, from the palms to the poplars the sound ever grieved, but the silent cry of the dead is stronger.

From the palms of his native Egypt to the poplars of Northern Italy, Ungaretti hears the grieving of the wind; the dead and the ashes of cities are omnipresent in waking and in dream.

A second Italian poet, equal in stature to Ungaretti, is Eugenio Montale (b. 1896), like him a poet of small output. But Montale's experience of the first war, in which he served as an officer, counts for little in his poetry. The landscape in which he found his equivalent of a 'waste land' is a strip of desolate country near his native Genoa.

Montale's line is as closely compressed as Ungaretti's, and of all modern poetry his is, perhaps, the most difficult to reduce to a prose statement. His style, which has not varied from the beginning, is extremely complex. A Montale poem is a collection of motifs bound together by an overall mood, and by an anxiety, betrayed rather by the restlessness of the rhythms, to find a solution to a situation in which evil predominates. Sometimes, as in the poem 'Eastbourne', a description of that town on Bank Holiday, two forces can be seen in conflict; that of goodness, symbolized by the flashing glass of hotel-doors and by the sudden quiet after the band had 'put away its clamour', and evil by the continuous revolving of the roundabout. It is evil that conquers:

Vince il male . . . La ruota non s'arresta.

Anche tu lo sapevi, luce-in-tenebra.

Nella plaga che brucia, dove sei
scomparsa al primo tocco delle campane, solo
rimano l'acre tizzo che già fu
Bank Holiday.[1]

The 'light-in-darkness' refers perhaps to the flickering of the hotel-doors that has seemed to signal some mesage of peace and hope. A Montale poem, however, is always in flux, and so reproduces the poet's vision of the Universe. Montale is much freer than Ungaretti of the feeling of time. His assemblages of motifs are related psychologically, rather than by sequence of events. Even his Ligurian landscape, which predominated in his first book *Ossi di Seppia* (Cuttlefish bones) of 1925, yields to a more psychological field of connections in its successor, *L'Occasione*

[1] Evil conquers . . . The turning will not stop. You knew this too, light-in-darkness. In that burning streak, where you have vanished at the bells' first peal, only the bitter torch is left that once was *Bank Holiday*.

(Occasions) of 1939, in which 'Eastbourne' appears. Here, sometimes as in the poem 'Dora Markus', the drama almost comes into the open; the incident, or *occasion*, is almost clear. In 'Notizie dall' Amiata' (News from La Amiata), the poet speaks to a dead woman. In 'La Casa dei doganieri' (The Shore-Watchers' House) the subject is one of forgetting, in which the poet fails to hold up the thread of memory since his friend has dropped the other end; the shore-watchers' house in its decay is a symbol for the decay of their relationship; and again symbols of evil—the crazy turning of the compass—prevail over those of good—the lucky throw of the dice in the past:

> Libeccio sferza da anni le vecchie mura
> e il suono del tuo riso non è più lieto:
> La bussola va impazzita all' avventura
> e il calcolo dei dadi più non torna.[1]

Montale is frequently concerned with relationships, and with their decay. But in decay or destruction lies the supreme opportunity of survival or preservation:

> Svanire
> è dunque la ventura de venture.[2]

In one of 'Mottetti' it seems to follow that hell is incurred by the refusal to lose again what is already lost. Memory for Montale may stand marked with either a plus or a minus sign; the past must be forgotten in order to be reformed in the memory or as a poem. But the accent is not, as with the Symbolists, on the act of creation; there is for Montale no distinction between the recollection and the recording. A poem merely reproduces the flux of life as it is reflected in the equally inconstant mind. This movement of thought is perfectly rendered in the poem 'Barcche sulla Marna' (Boats on the Marne).

> Il sogno è questo: un vasto
> interminato giorno che rifonde
> tra gli argini, quasi immobile, il suo bagliore,
> e ad ogni svolta il buon lavoro dell'uomo,
> il domani velato che non fa orrore.
> E altro ancora era il sogno, ma il suo riflesso
> fermo sull'acqua in fuga, sotto il nido

---

[1] South-winds have thrashed the old walls for years, and the sound of your laugh is gay no longer: the compass turns crazily, at random, and the dice no longer turn up lucky.

[2] To vanish then is the chance of all chances.

del pendolino, aero e inaccessibile,
era silenzio altissimo nel grido
concorde del meriggio ed un mattino
più lungo era la sera, il gran fermento
era grand riposo.[1]

Into one dream of a perfect day in childhood in which there was
no fear, and in which man's work was good, enters another, the
repose of which is contrasted with the ferment of the first. Though
it appears to come from a deeper level of consciousness, though
its reflection is steady while the water flows past it, and though it
is a silence after the clamour of noon, yet it too lies beneath the
rule of time, and it is time (the inaccessible pendulum) that
prevails in the end. For evening falls, the poet and his shadowy
mistress descend from their boat, and in the last lines the incident
is fixed in time and peace. Dream yields to reality.

Montale's rhythms are modulated to these changing textures
of thought. They are rich too in assonance and alliteration, and
in echoes from earlier poets. His lines abound in echoes, which
come not in the form of direct imitation or pastiche, but like many
of T. S. Eliot's, as half-allusions. Montale also developed
independently Eliot's method of inserting foreign words and
phrases, like the English words *Bank Holiday* in 'Eastbourne'.
What were at first accidental likenesses became later deliberate.
One cannot think of Montale as a pupil of Eliot; there are no
echoes in his poetry of his English exemplar. Yet he learnt some
lessons from him, which had their effect on his third and last
book, *La Bufera e altro* (The Storm and other poems) of 1956.
Here the texture is closer than before; there is a greater unity of
composition, a stronger control of tone. The poetry is more
classical, the emotion more controlled. The poet aims at putting
something between himself and the flux of time:

Splendersi era più facile, morire
al primer batter d'ale, al primo incontro
col nemico, un trastullo. Comincia ora
la via più dura. . . .[2]

---

[1] This is the dream: a vast interminable day that dissolves in splendour between the
almost motionless banks, and at every turn the good work of man, the watched for
morrow that does not inspire horror. And the dream changed once more, but its
reflection, steady on the flowing water, under the nest of the little pendulum aloft and
inaccessible was a very high silence in the constant shout of noon and a longer
morning was evening, the greater ferment was a great repose.

[2] To be consumed was easier, dying at the first flutter of a wing, at the first encounter
with the enemy, a game. Now the harder way begins. . . .

Montale with something of the Metaphysical's ingenuity, has taken the eel as the symbol of man's persistence under hardship. 'L'anguilla' is a poem of great organic consistency; the eel becomes a majestic symbol of courage, the 'spark that says everything begins when everything seems charred, the buried stump, the brief rainbow':

> La scintilla che dice
> tutto comincia quando tutto pare
> incarbonirsi, bronco sepellito,
> l'iride breve. . . .

Montale reaches no positive standpoint. Yet the plus sign of life obtains more widely in these late poems than the minus of death. There are even moments when a miracle seems to be on the point of taking place; loss is turned into gain in the conclusion of 'Per album' (For an album) in an unexpectedly homely chain of imagery:

> Ho proseguito fino a tarde
> senza sapere che tre cassettine
> —SABBIA SODA SAPONE; la piccionaia
> da cui parti il tuo volo: da una cucina,—
> si sarebbero aperte per me solo.
> Cosi sparisti nell'orizonte incerto.
> Non c'è pensiero che imprigiona il fulmine
> ma chi ha veduto la luce non se priva.
> Mi stesi al piede del tuo ciliego, ero
> già troppo ricco per contenerti viva.[1]

Montale's riches are continuously evident; he has, like Valéry, all the wealth of a tradition into which he has infused new life; and he has that private wealth in addition, which makes the creatures and things, as well as the persons in his life, infinitely valuable. The canisters marked Sand, Soda and Soap, the pigeon-house, and the cherry-tree are perhaps familiar objects to him; though the choice of the canisters' contents is dictated by the needs of alliteration. But the lightning, the wavering line of the horizon to the eye dazzled by the flash, the sudden access of

---

[1] I carried on till late without knowing that three containers—SAND, SODA, SOAP, the pigeon house from which you took flight from a kitchen—were to be opened for me alone. So you vanished on the uncertain skyline. There is no thought that can capture lightning, but he who has seen the light will not be robbed of it. I stretched out at the foot of your cherry-tree, I was already far too rich to hold you living.

wealth from loss provide another plane of meaning. Montale's poems thus capture the flux of life itself, which is forever changing levels, capable at one moment of almost grasping a miracle, at another of inhabiting a purgatory of apprehension; and all these levels are illustrated in Montale's poetry.

A parallel progression, though to a position of far greater certainty than Montale's precarious foothold of faith beneath the sign of the 'Great Zero', is marked by T.S. Eliot's development from his 'Prufrock' of 1917 to the *Four Quartets*. Eliot (b. 1888), was confronted at the outset with a problem very different from Montale's. Italian poetic language had been vulgarized by d'Annunzio, but was capable of renewal by a new cross-breeding with the great Classics. The spoken language and the literary were not as far apart as the English of St. Louis, and of London, from the poetic language of the late Romantics and symbolists. Yeats's solution was valid only for a poet with his Irish background and speech-rhythms, and Owen had up to his early death not entirely succeeded in freeing himself from its Romantic hang-over. The situation first became clear to two American expatriates living in London, Eliot and Ezra Pound (b. 1885). They found the contrast all the more striking for their own detachment from all parties. Literary English was to them, as to all Americans of their generation, a dead language, which could be written with perfect accomplishment as a form of pastiche. Joseph Hergesheimer and Willa Cather, contemporary novelists of the second rank, accomplished this task to perfection; James Joyce, from the detached standpoint of an Irishman, was able to parody every form of literary English in the public-house scene of *Ulysses*.

From Eliot's point of view the language appeared to be in decay, yet poetry could only be alive in so far as it reflected this difficult situation. In fact, the contrast between the written and spoken word offered new possibilities in poetic texture. In drawing the portrait of J. Alfred Prufrock, an expatriate teased by half-emotions in a polite world of cliché and 'formulated phrase', Eliot makes the plight of his hero the more pathetic by stressing the distance between his world and one of truer and more dramatic values. But at the same time, in the person of Prufrock, he judges himself as a poet by contrast with Dante and Shakespeare. Not only is Prufrock unable 'to say just what I mean', but Eliot feels himself to be in the same plight, a plight more fully expounded in the lines from *East Coker* quoted at the beginning of Chapter 2. He has not the words, and he has not a belief in his own function as poet.

> No! I am not Prince Hamlet, nor was meant to be;
> Am an attendant lord, one that will do
> To swell a progress, start a scene or two,
> Advise the prince; no doubt, an easy tool,
> Deferential, glad to be of use,
> Full of high sentence, but a bit obtuse;
> At times, indeed, almost ridiculous—
> Almost, at times, the Fool.

But Eliot cast himself neither for the part of Polonius nor of Horatio. In the epigraph to the poem Guido de Montefeltro speaks to Dante as one who will never escape from hell to another whom he supposes to be in the same plight; and Dante does not disabuse 'the sly fox', who on earth was guilty of so much murder and betrayal. The parallel between Guido and Prufrock is an ironic aside, which merely suggests that our sins today are of irresolution rather than of action. What is important is that Eliot had already seen the possibility of making an escape from the disillusioned state of mind in which they shared. Pound has throughout his life sought relief by violence of utterance and opinion, but remained ultimately a bored aesthete, contemptuous of his fellow men. Eliot, on the other hand, entered the limbo of boredom, with Dante's certainty that there is, somewhere, a way out.

Though temperamentally a conservative writer, Eliot had first to break with the tradition of Shakespeare, Milton and Wordsworth, which blocked the free development of English poetry. Ignorant of Hopkins, whose poems were not yet published, he turned to France, the obvious centre for an American expatriate to find a model. He found Jules Laforgue, a poet thirty years dead, whose reputation was overshadowed in his own country by those of Mallarmé and Rimbaud. What drew Eliot to the poet of 'Les Complaintes' was no doubt his technical accomplishment; but it happened that Laforgue had also been an inhabitant of the limbo of boredom. He too had distrusted tradition, parodying the high-sounding Romantic phrase, and

E *

contrasting it with the trivial patter of contemporary speech. He had been conscious of the triviality of his own yearnings, and had contrasted these in his asides and refrains, with some more real and passionate existence in the legendary past. The rhythms of 'Prufrock' are closely related to those of Laforgue's 'Dimanches' (Sundays):

> Bref, j'allais me donner d'un 'Je vous aime'
> Quand je m'avisai non sans peine
> Que d'abord je ne me possédais pas bien moi-même.
>
> (Mon Moi, c'est Galathée aveuglant Pygmalion!
> Impossible de modifier cette situation.)
>
> Ainsi donc, pauvre, pâle et piètre individu
> Qui ne croit à son Moi qu'à ses moments perdus,
> Je vis s'effacer ma fiancée
> Emportée par le cours des choses. . . . [1]

In just this way Prufrock lost the lady to whom he failed to make his declaration. But Laforgue's medium appears to have offered Eliot too little variety. Though it provided the alternative, which no one had yet found, to the dramatic monologue in descent from Robert Browning, who both influenced and exasperated Pound, this new method was as full of echoes— though of French echoes—as the post-Victorian blank-verse line.

Eliot's next endeavour was to adopt the blank-verse line, at the point where it appeared least rigid, that of the Jacobean dramatists, and to return to the couplet before it attained Classical smoothness. Turning away from the French, Eliot seems to have put himself to school with Middleton, Webster and Marvell. 'Gerontion', however, the outstanding poem of his 1920 collection, presents an uneasy mixture of an old and a new style. There are lines which look forward to the 'Waste Land' and even beyond, while others allude in the manner of Pound to mysterious characters whose names mean nothing to the reader; and there are even echoes of Pound's racialist prejudices. But in its best lines, in particular the passage on history, Eliot's poetry strikes very much deeper than ever before:

[1] To be brief I was just about to come out with 'I love you' when I was aware with some distress that in the first place I was not in proper possession of myself.
(My self is Galatea blinding Pygmalion! Impossible to modify that situation.)
So, a poor, pale and wretched individual, who only believes in himself in his odd moments, I saw my fiancée slip away, carried off by the stream of events.

After such knowledge, what forgiveness? Think now
History has many cunning passages, contrived corridors
And issues, deceives with whispering ambitions,
Guides us by vanities. Think now
She gives when our attention is distracted
And what she gives, gives with such subtle confusions
That the giving famishes the craving. Gives too late
What's not believed in, or if still believed,
In memory only, reconsidered passion. Gives too soon
Into weak hands, what's thought can be dispensed with
Till the refusal propagates a fear.

Beyond boredom, beyond even horror, Eliot has come to the point at which he can await only a revelation.

For Blok the revolution, for Owen the final companionship and compassion of the trenches, for Machado the brief sharing in action for the defence of the Republic, provided a way out from the 'cunning passages' and 'contrived corridors' of life in isolation. To Eliot none of these ways was open, and that of aestheticism offered no refuge either. The world is the world of Sweeney, Burbank and Eliot's other symbols of American philistinism, but it is the same world in which Agamemnon was slain, and in which the nightingale still sings even as it did in Greece. Eliot's purpose was to reunite these two worlds, while Pound to the end of his *Cantos* was content to leave them apart, pointing the contrasts.

Musical form is a reconciler of contrasts; it is also free from all time except its own. Telling no story, it presents only sounds in contrast, in combination, in varying mood, and finally in resolution. The thought of using this musical form for poetry was not new at the time of 'The Waste Land'. Many poems have been built of parts contrasting in mood and pace as the movements of a symphony. Tennyson's 'Maud', and Thomson's rather monotonous 'City of Dreadful Night' can be thought of as musical sequences; and Mallarmé's 'Après-midi d'un Faune' is held together rather by its musical pattern than by its intellectual argument. Around the year 1920, however, there appeared Blok's 'Twelve', Valéry's 'Jeune Parque', and 'The Waste Land', in all of which the musical analogy was carried further than ever before; and a little later Rilke concluded his *Elegies*, which can be thought of as so many movements in a gigantic symphony on the subject of transformation.

'The Waste Land' is free both of story-telling and of any temporal sequence of events. Its elements consist of a number of states of mind, symbolized sometimes by characters, sometimes by events, sometimes by quotations, allusions, parodies or references to legend. A sojourn in the *waste land* is a timeless state, shared by the poet and the culture of his epoch. It is a dark night of the mind rather than of the soul, in which all values are confused, yet in which many can be shown to bear negative signs and a few to be marked with a plus, though tentatively only, since all values are in question. The best parallel is with Montale's work of this and later date, though Montale's is a far more private view of the Universe than Eliot's.

The first movement of 'The Waste Land' leads from fear and boredom to horror. Yet in its first lines its reference is to spring, not as in the poetry of Laforgue, or in 'Prufrock' to autumn. Its opening speaks of the pains not of dying but of rebirth:

> April is the cruellest month, breeding
> Lilacs out of the dead land, mixing
> Memory and desire, stirring
> Dull roots with spring rain.
>
> Winter kept us warm, covering
> Earth in forgetful snow, feeding
> A little life with dried tubers.
> Summer surprised us. . . .

Winter is here shown as comfortable; warmth and forgetfulness are contrasted with the cruelty of a month in which memory and desire—the memory of living and the desire to live again—are revived. It is the rebirth of memory that is the principal subject of the poem. But first, variations are played on the themes of boredom, fear and vacuity: the boredom of the girl Marie's life, after her moment of fright; the terror of the Hyacinth girl's lover, who found only silence where he expected ecstasy; the fear of the future in Madame Sosotris's clients; the boredom of the crowds going to work over London Bridge; the horror of the corpse buried in the garden, which is at the same time the only root from which rebirth can spring; the death of the old life.

The second movement is simpler; two scenes of sterile disillusionment, on the barge and in the pub, the first luxurious, the second bare and ugly, are contrasted and united, while the wind

under the door in the first and the barman's insistent HURRY
UP PLEASE IT'S TIME in the second point to the fact that time
is getting short. If the 'stony rubbish' will throw up no shoots, it
will be consumed in the fire of the third movement, which is the
fire of purgation. Here, however, there appear, for the first time
intimations of another kind of life; beauty enters in with the
sound of children's voices singing beneath a dome, and on the
riverside below the scurry of London Bridge we can sometimes
hear

> The pleasant whining of a mandoline
> And a clatter and a chatter from within
> Where fishmen lounge at noon: where the walls
> Of Magnus Martyr hold
> Inexplicable splendour of Ionian white and gold.

But the beauty can come only after the purgation. The lyrical
fourth movement gives a promise of peace outside time and
history, but the fifth brings us back to the mood of the first. We
do not return exactly to the point we have come from, however.
A demand has been made, and is reiterated by the thunder.
Surrender of the will, which has been hinted at in the person of
the girl in the second movement, who forgives her seducer,

> I made no comment. What should I resent?

is demanded once more and more insistently at the poem's
conclusion. A question is asked, but unlike other questions that
are asked earlier in the poem, this one receives an answer:

> what have we to give?
> My friend, blood shaking my heart
> The awful daring of a moment's surrender
> Which an age of prudence can never retract
> By this, and this only, we have existed

The last words of the poem present the only real obscurity; for
a reference to *The Spanish Tragedy* hardly indicates the relevance
of the mad Hieronymo, in whose person Eliot makes his first
actual entry into this poem. The implication, which will only be
clear to a reader of Kyd's play, is that he will not 'ply himself to
fruitless Poesy', whereby he may 'make mad the guilty and appal

the free'. The thunder makes its final demand for surrender and the poem ends.

'The Waste Land' presents considerably more difficulties than Rilke's *Elegies*, or any other poem so far noticed in this book. The poet provides notes, but these merely send the reader to his sources; they do not elucidate the meaning of a difficult line or phrase. Just as the significance of Hieronymo is only plain to someone who knows 'The Spanish Tragedy', so only familiarity with an obscure work of anthropology, Jessie Weston's *From Ritual to Romance*, will explain the references to the Fisher King.

There being no longer any accepted corpus of knowledge that will be common to the poet and his reader, Eliot has chosen his images and quotations somewhat arbitrarily from his own reading and interests. Once the Bible, classical legends and the writers of Greece and Rome would have supplied the necessary illustrations and comparisons. But the modern poet cannot assume that his audience will have read the same books as he. Therefore he draws his imagery from where he will, and offers a few perfunctory clues to anyone persistent enough to follow them.

An understanding of 'The Waste Land' is not, however, entirely dependent on the reading of its source books. The subject of the poem is clear, and the effect of the contrasting music of its various sections and subsections is to move an audience even despite their ignorance of the Gita, the Upanishads, and the lesser Elizabethan dramatists.

Between 'The Waste Land' and the *Four Quartets*, Eliot made some further explorations into the dry territory of boredom and fear; in the Sweeney poems and 'The Hollow Men', and in some others, he dwelt more fully on those remembered moments of surrender 'which an age of prudence can never retract'. Here the musical element is as subtle and pervasive as before, and sometimes leads to the use of quasi-Biblical refrains and repetitions. Emotion begins to edge even further into what had been the domain of intellect. The style is, moreover, less condensed, and less elucidation is needed. The sequence 'Ash Wednesday' draws not only on Dante but on the Bible and the Liturgy; and many of its rhythms are patently liturgical. The poet from a questing agnostic has become a practising Christian. But to many of his readers the new language and imagery is no easier than the old. It is probably true that Eliot's later work cannot have the same

meanings for the outsider as for a communicant member of the
Church of England. The poet says as much in the first of his
quotations from Heraclitus which stand as an epigraph to the
Quartets. 'Although the Word is common to us all', it reads,
'most men live as if each had a private wisdom of his own.' 'The
Waste Land' was written for those of private vision; the *Quartets*
are addressed to those who share his belief. They can, however,
be understood by those who do not, provided they will accept
the possibility of communication between man and God.

The *Four Quartets* form a closer unity than the nearest
corresponding work in modern poetry, Rilke's ten *Elegies*. They
repeat the musical patterning of 'The Waste Land', though in a
somewhat different form. But they make use of quotation in an
entirely different way. Here it is unnecessary to track down
Eliot's sources. 'Burnt Norton' stands for any country garden
where life was once led with grace and dignity; the next, 'East
Coker', is the house from which the poet's ancestors set out for
America; the third, 'The Dry Salvages', are a group of rocks off
the Massachusetts coast associated with the poet's boyhood, and
the fourth, 'Little Gidding', refers to a house where an Anglican
religious community lived in the seventeenth century.

Each *Quartet* too is concerned with one of the four elements,
earth, air, water, fire. That is to say that much of the imagery is
based on that element, and the *Quartets*' essential statement is
that there exists a point at which these four elements are united.
This is the moment of mystical union.

'Burnt Norton', which is more philosophical than theological
in its language, speaks primarily—at the end of its second
movement—of the moment of higher consciousness which
appears to be outside time:

> Time past and time future
> Allow but a little consciousness.
> To be conscious is not to be in time
> But only in time can the moment in the rose-garden,
> The moment in the arbour when the rain beat,
> The moment in the draughty church at smokefall
> Be remembered; involved with past and future.
> Only through time time is conquered.

The first movement is mysterious; what is and what might have
been appear to have become mingled in 'the moment in the rose-

garden', which, when it has passed, points back to the present.
There is a hinted perception of time as a road with many parallel
possibilities; life in this house and the 'door we never opened into
the rose-garden' have been unrealized, yet become real in the
poet's moment of expanded consciousness, which is shown in the
second movement to transcend the contradictions that run
through the whole of his early poetry. The third movement takes
us back to the theme of London Bridge in 'The Waste Land'.
We are taken into the world of boredom, reflected in the faces of
passengers in the London Underground. From this twilight
existence we are shown two escapes: into the light of the rose-
garden, or by the acceptance of a deeper darkness:

> This is the one way, and the other
> Is the same, not in movement
> But abstention from movement; while the world moves
> In appetency, on its metalled ways
> Of time past and time future.

The fourth movement is a brief lyric of expectancy. Again we are
in the garden, and the moment of consciousness may return.
The poem concludes by stressing the difficulties of artistic
expression:

> Words strain,
> Crack and sometimes break, under the burden

and by a reaffirmation of the initial experience. In its last lines
time dissolves once more.

'East Coker' is not founded on a single event, but takes the
form of a meditation on the passage of time. The first movement
shows the life of this village as a recurring sequence of birth,
growth and decay; and the place itself is presented in recognizable
detail, in the heat of a summer afternoon. But in the second
movement the seasons are confused:

> What is the late November doing
> With the disturbance of the spring
> And creatures of the summer heat. . . .

There is war too among the Constellations. But the poet turns
abruptly to a vision of the same disorder in the life of the

individual. Our plight is more desperate he suggests than Dante's
at the opening of the Inferno:

> In the middle, not only in the middle of the way
> But all the way, in a dark wood, in a bramble,
> On the edge of a grimpen, where is no secure foothold,
> And menaced by monsters. . . .

All the wisdom that there can now be is the wisdom of humility.
The third movement is one of darkness, like that of 'Burnt
Norton', and the motif of travelling in the Underground occurs
once more. The ending is upon a paradox:

> To arrive where you are, to get from where you are not,
>   You must go by a way in which there is no ecstasy.
> In order to arrive at what you do not know
>   You must go by a way which is the way of ignorance.

But there is triumph in the darkness, and the lyric that follows
is a poem on the Passion; pain must be accepted and 'to be
restored, our sickness must grow worse'. The conclusion is more
personal than any other movement in the *Quartets*. The poet
tells of his own 'largely wasted' years, of his endeavours, each of
which

> Is a wholly new start, and a different kind of failure.

It ends, however, with a more general and profound exhortation:

> Old men ought to be explorers
> Here or there does not matter
> We must be still and still moving
> Into another intensity.

The last image is that of the sea, towards which man must go,
and with a vision of the sea the third Quartet 'The Dry Salvages',
opens. It presents a triple image of water; it is the river of a man's
life, it is the sea of historical time with its flux and reflux, but
within it also is the ground swell 'that is and was from the beginning'; and of this the bell on the buoy sounds a warning, as
the Angelus summons men to prayer.

The second movement reverts to the theme of the moment in
the rose-garden, and to the recollection of such moments as the

clue to the third way of life announced by the ground-swell of
the first movement:

> but the sudden illumination—
> We had the experience but missed the meaning,
> And approach to the meaning restores the experience
> In a different form, beyond any meaning
> We can assign to happiness.

The measure of psychological progress between the stage of
'Burnt Norton' and that of 'The Dry Salvages' can be gauged by
this transfer of the accent from experience to meaning, from
light through darkness to recollection. In the third movement the
theme of railway travel occurs once more. But the journey is in
the light; the passengers carry their whole lives with them, past,
present and future, and the journey itself is illusory:

> Fare foreward, you who think you are voyaging;
> You are not those who saw the harbour
> Receding, or those who will disembark.
> Here between the hither and the further shore
> While time is withdrawn consider the future
> And the past with an equal mind.

The mood of this poem changes in the middle; from the third
movement onwards it is concerned with hope, 'not the hope that
the future will somehow be different from the past . . . but a
present hope'.

The fourth movement is a prayer to Our Lady for 'all those
who are in ships' on the sea of this world; and the fifth contrasts
two attitudes to the future, that of those who view it with anxiety,
consulting the successors of Madame Sosostris 'whether on the
shores of Asia or in the Edgware Road', and of those who are not
anxious but, like the saints, strive

> to apprehend
> The point of intersection of the timeless
> With time.

or, like the ordinary man, 'with hints and guesses'.

Time is thus redeemed by the intimations we receive of
another order of existence, hinted at by the tolling of the bell,
suggested by the mysterious tossing of the ground-swell, and

revealed in such rare moments as those in the rose-garden, which occurred in time, yet have a timeless existence in the memory.

'Little Gidding', the last of the Quartets, has the deepest stratification of meanings of them all. It is the poem of fire, of the fire of the love of God, revealed in that 'midwinter spring' of the opening, which is a season unexpected and 'not in time's covenant', to Nicholas Ferrar and his friends at a moment in history 'now and in England'. But this is also a moment free from the common laws of time, since the experience is of eternity, 'never and always'. To Little Gidding the poet comes to pray, since here 'prayer has been valid'.

The second movement opens with a lyric of death and decay in which the themes of each of the other Quartets are referred to, by way of quotation. The metre then changes to Dante's terza rima, in which the poet, appearing in his own person, describes a warden's walk through the streets of London at dawn just before the All Clear. The fires that are now raging were kindled by the flying bombs. The poet is joined in his walk by a stranger, in whose features one may find those of several dead poets— Virgil, perhaps, and Dante himself, and Milton. The unknown revenant recalls also that third figure who walks beside the poet in the last section of 'The Waste Land', and therefore suggests the appearance of the Risen Christ at Emmaus. He speaks comfortingly of the poet's mission and of his old-age; two matters that have preoccupied Eliot in the earlier Quartets and before; and here is introduced for the first time the motif of sin, in contrast to the more passive vices of indifference, boredom, and despair. Among the 'gifts reserved for age', the speaker catalogues first 'the cold friction of expiring sense', second that 'conscious impotence of rage at human folly' which exasperated Yeats in his last years, and then, more specifically Christian:

> the rending pain of re-enactment
> Of all that you have done, and been; the shame
> Of motives late revealed, and the awareness
> Of things ill done and done to others' harm
> Which once you took for exercise of virtue,

And the remedy for all these lies only in

> that refining fire
> Where you must move in measure like a dancer.

There seems here once more to be a reference to Yeats, in whose
two Byzantium poems fire and dance are brought together to
symbolize the ascent above the 'mire and blood' of the common
life.

The third movement goes beyond Yeats's metaphysics however, which remain dualistic to the end, and accepts in the words
of Dame Julian of Norwich, the great fourteenth century
visionary, sin itself as part of the divine pattern:

> History may be servitude,
> History may be freedom. See, now they vanish,
> The faces and places, with the self which, as it could, loved them
> To become renewed, transfigured, in another pattern.
> Sin is behovely, but
> All shall be well, and
> All manner of thing shall be well.

The 'old factions' and 'old policies' of the past cannot be revived
or restored.

> These men, and those who opposed them,
> And those whom they opposed
> Accept the constitution of silence
> And are folded in a single party.

From reconciliation and the acceptance of sin, the poem turns
in its fourth movement, to a consideration of two fires, that of
bombs and that of purgation, that of self-love and that of love
of God.

The final movement returns to the moment: the moment in
the chapel at Little Gidding which is the same as the moment in
the rose-garden: life and death are here united.

> The moment of the rose and the moment of the yew-tree
> Are of equal duration.

The beginning and the end are linked together in the dimension
of Eternity, and the quest for the end is shown to lead only to the
rediscovery of the beginning:

> the end of all our exploring
> Will be to arrive where we started
> And know the place for the first time.

The *Quartets* apparently conclude Eliot's work as a poet; his work of late years has been devoted chiefly to the theatre, and though in his plays he has worked out many of the themes from the *Quartets*, he has made no advance beyond them. Perhaps no advance is possible. Several poets among his contemporaries—Yeats, Blok and Rilke in particular—have seen as deeply as he. But their perceptions though often richer—for Eliot has since 'The Waste Land' become very sparing in his imagery—have not been translated into so sustained or so self-consistent a music. Eliot, alone among modern poets, has reached the further border of poetry, known to Blake, to St. John of the Cross, to Vaughan and to Traherne, at which individual language and imagery yield to paradox and to the repetition of other men's words, to the point where originality—or even poetic statement itself—becomes secondary to the conveyance of truth.

The poetry of personal experience leads no further. For in the 'twenties and 'thirties the importance of personal discovery was called into question by two external schemes of thought which invaded the field of poetry, sometimes singly and sometimes in uneasy partnership; the theory of revolution, by which the single man's perceptions were called into question, and the psychological theories of Freud, which questioned the authority of the mind itself.

7

New violence breaks in

THE revolutions of Freud and of Lenin were as one in their
attitude to violence. Psycho-analytical theory accepted it as a
constant factor in man's unconscious thoughts: and communist
practice welcomed it as a necessary means of carrying through
the inevitable world revolution against the forces of oppression.
Both, in their furthest utopian dreams, saw the prospect of a
peaceful and non-violent universe, but only at such time as their
own remedies had taken full effect. Peace would come when the
forces of capitalism had everywhere been defeated, and when the
state had consequently withered away: and at least a greater
measure of peace might follow a deeper understanding of man's
unconscious motives, together with a more informed method of
dealing with them.

The poetry of revolution and the poetry of exploration into
the instinctive life have had therefore so much in common, that
they allowed the introduction of violent imagery into the poem,
and encouraged looser and more rhetorical forms of writing, that
would catch the rhythms of instinctive rather than of intellectual
reasoning. The poetry of Vladimir Mayakovsky, of García Lorca
in his New York period, and of the later Edith Sitwell, all
attempt to present as valid emotion the strong urges of love and
hate, attraction and repulsion, in contrast to the poetry of
Machado, Montale and Eliot, which seeks to combine emotion
and intellect to the exclusion of these instinctive feelings.

The Russian Revolution occurred at a moment when poetry
in Russia was in a state of violent experiment. The Symbolists,
and even Blok, had come to be looked on as a dull and academic
older generation, and at least two new movements called for a
return to poetic realism. Of these the Futurists, who had derived
their original impetus from the Italian manifesto of 1909, were

from the first anti-traditionalist, while the Acmeists combined a demand for subjects from immediate experience with a greater devotion to form.

Vladimir Mayakovsky (1894-1930), the chief of the Futurists, was adopted as the revolution's Laureate, and the Acmeists, who were labelled counter-revolutionaries, were by various means silenced. Mayakovsky had been a party member since 1908, but his excitable and disjointed style was at first unsuitable for the political work that was asked of him. What the Communists required was a poetry suitable for platform recitation, that would be readily understood by illiterate audiences. This Mayakovsky in his later years attempted to provide, at the cost of disciplining his essentially undisciplined talent.

The first manifesto of the Russian Futurists appeared in 1912, under the title *A Slap in the Face of Public Taste*. Its first points aim merely at shocking. 'Throw Pushkin, Dostoevsky, Tolstoy, etc., overboard from the steamer of modernity' and similar remarks, are more extreme than the actual opinions of the signatories. Mayakovsky, in fact, in his Jubilee poem to Pushkin in 1924, though he lifted the great man down from his statue, addressed him as an admirer and a fellow-poet.

> Maybe
>   I'm the only one
>   that's really sorry,
>   Alexander,
>   that you're not here alive with us today'
>   (transl. Herbert Marshall)

he writes, and condoles with the great man on the unhappiness of his life and the misunderstandings he has met with since his death.

What was more important than any heaving of brick-bats at the illustrious great, was the Futurists' demand for the right 'to enlarge the vocabulary with arbitrary and derivative words—neologisms'. This extension of vocabulary to include foul language, dialect expressions and coinages was a prime preoccupation with the other signatories to the manifesto, of whom only Victor Khlebnikov (1885-1922) wrote poetry of any significance. His position was that of a pioneer. Taking the Futurist gospel from Marinetti, he and his friends had rejected the man as a repulsive reactionary. Futurism to Khlebnikov was to be the poetry of a revolution which would lead back to simplicity and link Russian culture once more with old gods who had been destroyed by Christianity. In the manner of Joyce he made experiments with words, sounds and disjointed syllables, and in developing a new and freer style opened the way for a far less consequent experimentalist, Mayakovsky. Like Eliot, and Pound, the two men for a while played the parts of pupil and mentor. Mayakovsky had little reading in the classics; he was a townsman without inherited culture. For him the new style was an elementary need, for which he demanded no theoretical justification. He has indeed so extended the resources of Russian poetry that his successors have so far failed to take advantage of the new capital offered them. Russian poetry has no more caught up with Mayakovsky's originality than American poetry had caught up with Whitman's twenty-five years after his death.

The earlier, pre-revolutionary Mayakovsky overflows with egoism.

> How can you understand
> why I
> calmly,
> laugh at the thunder
> and bear my soul on a platter
> to the feast of the passing years?
> Spouting my useless tears
> down the unshaven cheeks of the squares.
> I am,
> perhaps,
> the last poet.
> (Transl. H. Marshall)

Thus opens the Prologue to the 'Tragedy, Vladimir Mayakovsky' of 1913, in which he himself appeared in the title role, to knock down various aunt sallies, erected to typify the idiocies of the moment. Its successor, Cloud in Trousers, is a far more concentrated and far more terrifying work. It is a self-portrait in the role of absurd, hopeless and rejected lover: one which Mayakovsky did not outgrow to the last, and which finally led him to kill himself. But the poem does not merely tell the story of his own rejection in intimate and self-pitying detail. In the most violent language, it also threatens to bring the whole world toppling down in revenge:

I,
jeered at by tribal contemporaries,
like a lanky
discarded rhyme,
see that which nobody sees,
coming over the mountains of time.

There where man's cut short of vision
by the heads of the hungry that surge,
in the thorny crown of revolution
I see nineteen-sixteen emerge.

And I amongst you—am its prophet.
                    (transl. H. Marshall)

In fact Mayakovsky was a year out in his prophecy.

In his early poetry, Mayakovsky not only saw himself as poet and prophet, but also in the role of martyr and saviour. Rejected in love, he claimed in the poem 'To himself the beloved . . .' that he was too big and powerful to give himself to any woman, even though four women were wooing him.

If I were as small
as the Great
Ocean
I would stand tiptoe on my waves
and caress the moon with my tides.
Where can you find me
a mistress equal to me?
The sky would be too tiny to contain her!

Mayakovsky saw two huge forces at work in the world; his own and the revolution's. The principal endeavour of his later and greater poetry was to reconcile the two. But at the same time he endeavoured on the technical side to expand the resources of his original Futurism. In his early poems the images are isolated; they are thrown in, one after another, like those of the German expressionists, but not developed. His rhythms too are abrupt, his use of rhyme and half-rhyme arbitrary. Up to the time of 'Cloud in Trousers' he is still preoccupied with the task of shooting-up the Symbolists.

Listen!
Moaning and groaning
they preach,
today's screeching-lipped Zarathustras!

We
with faces like slept-on sheets,
with lips suspended like hanging lustres,
we, prisoners of the city lazar-house, grew
where gold and dirt have ulcerated leprosy,—
we are cleaner far than Venetian blue,
washed simultaneously by sun and sea

To hell that in Homeric and Ovidian hymns
there's no one like us,
pitted with sooty pox-holes.
I know—
the very sun would grow dim
seeing the golden scatterings of our souls!
                              (transl. H. Marshall)

The language abounds in rougher juxtapositions than can be
brought over in translation. The rhyme *leprozoria* (lazar-house)
and *lazoria* (azure blue) is poetically *beautiful*, and throws into
sharp relief the comparison of 'our' faces to slept-on sheets, and
to the plebeian *plyevat* (to spit) rendered by the translator *to hell*.

But for the last twelve years of his life the poet of 'Cloud in
Trousers' was no longer in opposition; his task was to give himself to the government and the new culture that he had advocated.
His inflated ego was put into the service of his country.
Mayakovsky wrote poetry for the party, he travelled abroad as
its cultural representative, visiting the Paris in which Apollinaire's
poetry was just becoming fashionable and the New York of the
post-war boom, whose life and bustle fascinated him, but which
he described in terms of the prejudices with which he had arrived.

One building
               is as tall as the stars
others
         tower to the moon.
The Yankee
             idly slaps
                         his heels;
there's a stopping
                   and an express lift.
At seven
           the human tide flows in,
at five
         flows out again.
Machines grind
               clatter and hum.

But in the hum
          the people are dumb.
All that they stop for
             is to chew gum,
and to call out:
       'Make money! What?'

As a poet of social comment Mayakovsky might be compared to
Hood, supposing Hood to have been tied to a party-political line.
But even in his prejudices he was ironically frank. He was no one-
sided critic. Though he did not let himself be carried away by
anything that he saw abroad, he had no time either for the growing bureaucracy at home, with its endless committees, and queues
of applicants. The poem 'In re Conferences' is a fantastic satire
at the expense of these weaknesses. Lenin is said to have re-
marked that he did not know what to think of it as poetry, but
that he had greatly enjoyed it 'from the political and administra-
tive standpoint.' The 'I' of the poem, after being referred from
waiting-room to waiting-room over several days, returns home
foiled and wearied, to dream that he has burst into a conference,
at which only halves of people are sitting. A clerk explains the
reasons:

'They're in two conferences at the very same time.'
'Twenty conferences
  we have to attend to
every day—
  and more to spare.
So we're forced to split ourselves in two!
Here to the waist,
  and the rest—
    over there.'

and the poem ends with the wish:

    Oh for just
        one
            more conference
regarding the eradication of all conferences!
            (transl. H. Marshall)

This poem was written before Mayakovsky began to travel
abroad, as was also his 'Most Extraordinary Adventure', a conversation with the sun itself, which visits him in his country

cottage, where they drink tea and discuss poetry. Mayakovsky's egoism is here transformed into pleasing fantasy.

> And the sun
> says—not to be outdone:
> 'Well, comrade, I declare,
> we are a pair!
> let's go!
> Poet, let's sing,
> and shout to scare
> the drabness of the world.
> I'll pour out light,
> you'll do no worse
> in pouring forth your verse.'
> (transl. Babette Deutsch and Avram Yarmolinsky)

Mayakovsky continued after the revolution to look on himself as, like it, an elemental force. The parallel is pointed in the most serious of the poems of travel, 'Atlantic Ocean', which contains a comparison between the Revolution and the sea. Mayakovsky is travelling on a liner from Spain to America, and watches the sea as it throws up first a watery Revolutionary Committee. Then a spray of guards—the partisans of the deep—rise from further down, tower to the sky and fall back, tearing the marble of the foam to fragments.

These poems were written to be recited at party meetings; the broken lines reproducing the staccato of Mayakovsky's enunciation. Poetry had once more become a public activity. But though the poet had gone so far to meet his audience, he did not lower his standards. In an article on 'How Poetry is Made' he set out the processes of composition that had gone to the making of the opening lines of his poem to Esenin. In its first form it came only as a rhythmical scheme:

> ta-ra-rá/re rá/ ra, ra, ra, rá/ ra rá/
> ra-ra-ri/ra ra ra/ra ra/ra ra ra ra/
> ra-ra-ra/ etc.

Then some of the words presented themselves, the gaps between them remaining mere rhythms. Various phrases were inserted in the gaps, and discarded, before a final choice was made, and during this process of trial and rejection various schemes of rhyme and half-rhyme were tried. But the pattern remained constant, and there was a constant effort throughout the process of composition to achieve greater and greater compression. Mayakovsky admits, however, that this revelation of his method does not exactly correspond to facts.

It was not his intellect, as he admits, but his emotional and rhythmical faculties that chiefly governed this process, which depended chiefly on his ear and on his visualization of the printed page. The essay proves, however, that Mayakovsky did not write poetry easily, and that the apparent informality of some of his lines is deceptive. In fact, he put the whole of himself into his work as poet. To this extent he subordinated himself not only to the Party's requirements but to a very severe creative discipline. His language, though much less arbitrary than of old, still fulfilled the demands of the Futurist manifesto. Mayakovsky retained the right to score off his critics, to take tea, when he would, with the sun, and to sport with the Atlantic Ocean. The discipline of observing a compromise with the Party, however, was useful to him, since it compelled him to avoid his youthful excesses of style.

In his poem to Esenin, which deplored his fellow-poet's suicide, Mayakovsky admitted that life in the present was far from pleasant. The continuous necessity of compromising with ignorant Party bosses, and various personal unhappinesses were reducing the Soviets' laureate to misery.

> Our planet's
> > not well shaped
> > > for happiness.
> We'll have to
> > rip our joy
> > > out of the future.
> In this existence
> > it's not hard
> > > to die.
> To make a life
> > is certainly
> > > much harder.

Thus he replied to Esenin's own despairing last lines before suicide. But he found it increasingly difficult to maintain his buoyancy.

He was again charmingly buoyant, however, in the poem 'What shall I be', which listed the attractions of all the jobs a child might take up—carpenter, doctor, tram-conductor, driver, airman—in the new society. He celebrated the October revolution and his part in it, on its tenth anniversary in his greatest sustained poem 'Very Good'. This is realistic both in its pictures of the street fighting, which are a little reminiscent of Blok's 'Twelve', and of that first fireless winter in Petrograd when 'only poets and robbers' roamed the streets. But the Revolution seemed now to have less need of its poets, and to demand a greater conformity from those who were to survive. The writer's organization RAPP called Mayakovsky to task; for all his socialist enthusiasm the pronoun I continued to proliferate in his poems. The revolution celebrated in 'Very Good' seemed almost to be his revolution.

> My own name
>   in poetical rubric.
> Makes me glad
>   —those are my works
> merging with the work
>   of my Republic.
>   (transl. H. Marshall)

It is scarcely surprising that his last poem, the first section of 'At the Top of My Voice' is in effect a defence of poetry.

> Verses stand
>   heavy as lead
> ready for death
>   and immortal fame

he claimed, and addressing his 'esteemed comrade descendants', claimed that it had been his part to wipe up

>   tubercular spit
> with the rough voice of a poster.

He practised his old verbal violences to the last, but the new Soviet bureaucracy had no use for such things. Once Mayakovsky had captured an audience, but times were rapidly changing. In 1930 he followed Esenin's path. Disappointed in love and unable to conform to the demands of RAPP, whose aim was to turn poets into reporters, he committed suicide.

The second great poet of Communist Russia, Boris Pasternak (b. 1890), made no such determined efforts to please the Party as

Mayakovsky, and has for long periods been unable to publish the poetry he has written. He has thus been able to preserve his integrity and deepen his insights, while earning his living by making new and brilliant translations of Shakespeare and of various German poets. Pasternak was from a boy on the side of the Revolution, which seemed to him, as it had to Mayakovsky, a vast natural force. His long poem *1905* tells of his participation in the events of that year, though with it is mingled a good deal of student autobiography. But in the midst of the revolution he could see it as from above:

> Once we were people. Now we're epochs.
> It struck us—with its train flashed by
> —we're tundra to the panting tender's
> tune, to pistons', sleepers' rending.
> And we'll fly off, break through, and touch,
> we'll whirl round like a gust of crows.
>
> It's past. You'll understand it later.
> So, when the morning wind, one moment
> on the floor, has threshed the straw pile,
> the meeting of the trees is ever
> after talking of him, tossing
> stormily over the shingle roof.

Pasternak belonged to no movement. But he accepted the Futurist demand for a renewal of poetic language, and he also learned from a small and unimportant group of Imagists to concentrate on the striking metaphor. Being an intellectual poet, however, he was prone to work out his images to the length of a whole verse or more.

Pasternak's great period of production lies between 1917 and 1922; the publication of his work and its popularity date from the next year, 1923. His lapse into silence has been complete since 1932, except for two small books of poems published during the war, and a handful of poems that appeared in the last section of his suppressed novel *Doctor Zhivago* (1958), together with a few more that have, like these, circulated abroad in the last few years.

The whole of Pasternak's first important collection, *My Sister Life*, dates from the months between Kerensky's revolution and Lenin's; and its successor, *Themes and Variations*, belongs to the months of the civil war. It might seem that these critical events made little impression on the poet. The poems are princi-

pally devoted to themes of love and nature and to childhood
memories. Yet interwoven with them are everywhere references
to the Revolution as to a natural force of the same order as the
poet's more private experiences. Though he greatly admired
Mayakovsky, Pasternak was not tempted to write any revolutionary poetry. He accepted the revolution as part of the
historical scene, no stranger than the sudden bursting of the ice in
the spring thaw.

Primarily, Pasternak is a nature poet, with a painter's careful
eye for detail, and a musician's talent for combining seemingly
contradictory themes. In youth he received some training in both
the sister arts, as well as in philosophy, which he studied in
Germany; and his central standpoint is philosophical. The events
of the world, in all their vivid and bewildering variety, are for
him reflections of psychological happenings. His 'Definition of
the creative power' puts this case succinctly:

> Gardens, ponds, palings, the creation
> foamed with the whiteness of our tears,
> are only categories of passion
> gathered by the human heart.

Travelling in a train at night, the poet is the fixed point, which
everything else passes. Unlike T. S. Eliot's passenger, he expects
to descend in the morning the same man that boarded the train.
In the title poem of *My Sister Life* the new burst of life in spring
is compared to a night journey to some unspecified place:

> For every time the shrieking brake shakes up
> quiet villagers over their home-made wine,
> they look up from their cushions: 'This my station?'
> and the sun condoles with me as it goes down.
>
> And after its third splash the bell swims off,
> apologizing still: 'Sorry, not here!'
> The night is burning out beneath the blind
> And the plain crumbling between step and star.
>
> Winking and blinking, somewhere folk sleep sweetly,
> and like a mirage my beloved sleeps,
> just as the heart, splashing along the train,
> scatters the carriage doors about the steppe.

The train's destination is, no doubt, on another plane, the new
world that the Revolution will bring. But at each stop the station

master's bell signals it on; for the poet is more interested in
travelling than in arriving. Nature is perpetually exciting to him,
and its variations are often related to the transitions of the human
mind. Those of the human mind moreover are frequently
described in terms of the weather and its changes. Nature takes
on human aspects, and the mind behaves like a natural object.
Many of the images in which these equivalences are worked out
are most surprising. A lover dozing with his girl in a wood finds
himself dropping into another dimension of time, with different
clocks regulated to nature's law:

> It seemed he slumbered to the figures' tick
> while in harsh amber high above his head
> they set in the ether strictly tested clocks
> and regulate them there to suit the heat.
>
> They shift them round about and shake the needles,
> and scatter shadow, swing and bore a place
> for darkness, that's erected like a mast,
> in day's exhaustion, on its blue clock-face.

The theme of love is constant in Pasternak's poems. Love
is for him, as for Mayakovsky, a force as violent and disruptive
as Revolution or poetic creation:

> And the Andean thaw's poured into kisses,
> and morning's on the steppe, beneath the sway
> of stars that fall in dust, as the night stumbles
> about the village, and its bleating fades.

When love comes to the poet,

> Chaos creeps up again into the light
> As in the far-off ages of the fossil.

He may wish to escape with his love into some such retreat as the
wood in which nature lives by her own clocks and men seem only
'to lie in pairs and sleep'. But such exclusiveness at other times
seems stifling. There is always air and light and flowing water in
his poems; stuffiness, restriction, bourgeois self-satisfaction, and
'people with cheap watch-chains' who grumble about conditions,
are his bugbears. But they are referred to objectively, and
glimpsed from a caricaturist's angle. Pasternak's most surprising

F

imagery, however, is reserved for nature herself. A cold walk
home at dawn is unforgettably presented in the poem 'Encounter',
in which he and the March night return together from a meeting:

> Swift came the March night and the author.
> From time to time they threw a glance at
> a ghost that, flashing by, looked real,
> then of a sudden disappeared.
>
> It was the dawn. As in a theatre,
> appearing at the witch's call
> the morrow came to them both, after
> its proclamation on the steps.
>
> Like a framemaker with his moulding,
> it came. Trees, houses, churches, framed
> in that intangible square, seemed
> not of this world but of another.

The light strip in the sky against which trees and buildings stand
out seems to the poet to be framed in a moulding, and the whole
scene to have been conjured up as if by a witch's magic. With
similar and equally striking unexpectedness the heavy drops of
rain falling from the trees in a woodland clearing are compared
to the steps of a surveyor deliberately crossing it with his clerk:

> Lately the rain strolled through the woodland clearing
> like a surveyor with his clerk. The leaves
> of lilies of the valley were weighed down
> with tin bait, and rain stopped the mullein's ears.

The observed detail, of drops lying like tin-bait on the lily-of-
the-valley leaves, and stopping the ears of the tall yellow mullein,
is exact. But Pasternak's is not merely a painter's poetry: with
him landscape corresponds to mood, and the chief mood whose
objective picture he is anxious to capture is that of poetic
creation. This he presents almost light-heartedly as an automatic
process.

> Images fly askew in showers,
> rush into rhyme from hook, from wall,
> and high road, that's blown out the candle,
> and fall in rhythm. I don't stop them.

Yet the poet is haunted by the possibility that the real world may
be 'behind a mask', that the images which fall so freely on his
senses and are so readily transmuted into poetry may not be the

true reality. In one of a group of love-poems published in 1932, which are simpler in their imagery than the work of ten to fifteen years before, he confessed that poetic creation was not as simple a matter as he had once supposed, for

> when the heart dictates the line
> it sends a slave on to the stage
> and there's an end of art and there's
> a breath of earth and destiny.

Pasternak's war poems reveal a certain simplification of his style. His images are no longer so unexpected, and his reasoning is less complicated. All his old joy in nature and the seasons persists, and there is still a youthful freshness of response to the stimulus of the senses. But alongside this is a deep and un-exaggerated sorrow for the devastation of Russia. This con-tinuance of his old style displeased the critics, who attacked the collection on ideological grounds as insufficiently angry and patriotic. Though his feelings about the war were right, they were, it seems, too individual.

There followed a silence broken some twelve years later by the publication in an anthology of some poems belonging to the last section of his novel *Doctor Zhivago*.

Several of the Zhivago poems develop themes from the New Testament—'The Star of Bethlehem', 'Evil Days', 'The Garden of Gethsemane', and two devoted to Mary Magdalene. The blend of his old sharp-sighted imagery with a new reverence combine to produce poems of great and moving beauty, in which the citing of actual phrases from the Gospels creates no discord. Among these twenty-five pieces are love poems, landscapes and descriptions of mood; and throughout the early brilliant Pasternak is present, subdued, wiser and less dazzling, but more profound in his reading of life.

A comparison between the first poem in this series 'Hamlet' and that from which my last quotation was taken, shows a remarkable continuity of thought. In the early poem the poet pictures himself as one with a stage role to play that demands more of the actor than he had expected when first he came on the boards. But it is ironic, almost wryly light-hearted, in its accept-ance of the situation. In the later poem, on the other hand, Pasternak begs to be excused the role. 'I am alone', he pleads, 'and everything is drowned in Pharisaism'. In the words of the Gospel he begs: 'Father, let this cup pass from me'. Pasternak finds the defence of spiritual standards in Russia almost too hard to undertake. Yet, as this poem would suggest, he remains a poet of courage and irreproachable standards, whose mature work has attained great depth.

While the Revolution in the names of Marx and Lenin expressed itself only partially in Mayakovsky's poetry, and entirely failed to deflect Pasternak from his own line of development, that which was simultaneously conducted in the West in the name of Freud had a considerably greater effect. Communism can, on the whole, influence only the content of poetry. But psychoanalytical theory radically altered the poet's choice of form and imagery, and also his attitude to the task of creation. The whole style of the Surrealists and their allies was dictated by this attitude to life.

The break with tradition announced by the Surrealist Manifesto of 1924 was a continuation of the anti-intellectual revolt which was proclaimed by Rimbaud, and continued by a number of minor figures up to the outbreak of the Kaiser's war. Both the German Expressionists and the Italian and Russian Futurists were anti-intellectual in their abandonment of strict form, in their attacks on grammar and syntax, in their revolt against the accepted poetic vocabulary. Even more extreme, because essentially nihilisitic, was the Dadaist group, which was formed in Zurich during the war, to attack all bourgeois aesthetic values.

The poetry of Dada—the name of the movement is taken from the French word for hobby-horse and is said to have been picked at random from Larousse—was little more than a stammering. Aiming to reproduce the confusion both of noises and of values in the contemporary world, it was only expressive when cocking a ribald snook. 'Le docteur Freud ayant mangé les pieds de son père, les resultats s'appellent le psycho-analyse' was a Dadaist aphorism. The movement, however, with its principal theorist, the psychologist André Breton (b. 1896), was destined to be itself eaten by the great doctor. Dadaism was finally dismissed by Tristan Tzara, its principal poet, as an anarchical and unproductive revolt. But Surrealism—the term was invented by Apollinaire—appeared to offer some more positive values. Its intention, as expressed by Breton, who had gone over to the new movement, was to be 'a pure psychic automatism, by which it is proposed to express, either in speech or in writing, or in some quite other way, the true working of thought, in the absence of all control exercised by the reason, and without any aesthetic or moral preoccupation.'

Surrealism was not a literary theory; it proposed rather to inaugurate an entirely new attitude to life, in which the unconscious mind should guide a man's actions and the reason play a subordinate part. The surrealist revolution was proclaimed in the name of liberty and under the joint banners of Rimbaud and Marx, as the psychological and economic prophets respectively of the new freedom. Politically, the movement splintered and wavered, losing in course of time its avowed communists; psychologically, however, its attitude changed very little.

From the beginning great importance was attached to automatism. The free association of ideas, demanded by the psycho-analysts of their patients, seemed to Breton and his friends to open up also the true founts of poetry. For this any device might prove satisfactory, but that of automatic writing and similar trance phenomena seemed the most promising. Despite their many manifestos and the extent of the movement's polemics, it is still not clear what precisely the Surrealists hoped to find in the depths of the unconscious mind. Was their ideal a 'liberating disorder', as Rimbaud had expressed it, or did they hope that the images which arose in this haphazard way would prove to be those archetypal images which Yeats also sought in trance phenomena, but which in his case coincided with the images which he found in books? No answer has been provided.

Surrealism's best poet, Paul Eluard (1895-1952), was less muddled than the rest in his practice. Even when writing in the full Surrealist tradition, he carefully distinguished between dreams and surrealist texts, composed in automatic ways, on the one hand, and poetry, 'the consequence of a well-defined purpose', on the other. There is certainly a well-defined purpose behind several pieces from his collection *La Rose Publique* (the Public Rose) of 1934, which are love-poems with a simplicity all their own.

De tout ce que j'ai dit de moi que reste-t-il
J'ai conservé de faux trésors dans des armoires vides

Un navire inutile joint mon enfance à mon ennui
Mes jeux à la fatigue
Un départ à mes chimères
La tempête à l'arceau des nuits où je suis seul
Une île sans animaux aux animaux que j'aime
Une femme abandonnée à la femme toujours nouvelle
En veine de beauté
La seule femme réelle
Ici ailleurs
Donnant des rêves aux absents
Sa main tendue vers moi
Se reflète dans la mienne
Je dis bonjour en souriant
On ne pense pas à l'ignorance
Et l'ignorance règne
Oui j'ai tout espéré
Et j'ai désespéré de tout
De la vie de l'amour de l'oubli du sommeil
Des forces des faiblesses
On ne me connait plus
Mon nom mon ombre sont des loups[1]

This poem presents far fewer difficulties than its apparent
arbitrariness and its lack of punctuation might suggest. The
images may have arisen in dream or reverie; they have none of
the actuality of Pasternak's—to take one instance—which are so
clearly based on observation expanded by intellectual comment.
Yet Eluard's poem has a shape which only the guiding intellect
could have imposed on it. The final gesture of defiance alone
seems to break the poem's line, deflecting it from the mood of
optimistic tenderness, which is to be found in much of his later
work. This last line is reminiscent of Breton himself, whose poems
have a certain nightmare force, founded on what purports to be
the principle of free association. Yet his images seem often to
resemble those used by the painters of the movement. For
Breton's associations follow very closely those of Max Ernst and
Salvador Dali. The same objects occur repeatedly in his poems as

[1] Of all that I have said about myself what remains? I have preserved faked treasures
in empty cupboards A useless ship joins my childhood to my boredom my games to
my weariness a departure to my illusions the storm to the vault of the nights when I am
alone an island without animals to the animals that I love a forsaken woman to the
woman always fresh (and) gifted with beauty the only real woman here (or) elsewhere
Giving dreams to the absent her hand outstretched towards me is reflected in mine I
greet her with a smile One does not think of ignorance and ignorance reigns Yes I have
had hopes of everything and despaired of everything of life of love of oblivion of sleep
of strength of weakness No one knows me any more My name (and) my shadow are
wolves.

in their pictures. One cannot but suspect that choice of imagery is not entirely free when one reads such lines as these of Breton's:

> Ma femme aux tempes d'ardoise et toit de serre
> Et de buées aux vitres
> Ma femme aux épaules de champagne
> Et de fontaines à têtes de dauphin sous la glace
> Ma femme . . . etc.[1]

The attempt is to build up towards some feeling of universality. Twenty-nine comparisons however fail to establish the wife's reality, and though the last calls in the four elements of antiquity, to describe Mme Breton as possessing 'eyes on the level of water on the level of air of earth and of fire', the conclusion seems to err on the side of intellectuality. The ending is merely contrived for fear that the catalogue of attributes may be endless.

Surrealism in itself had none but negative effects upon the poet. Used as a liberating technique by writers who do not subscribe to the theory, however it has brought back to poetry qualities which had been missing since the Romantic epoch. Prevailing rhythms began to change, and the range of images to be extended to include the physical and tactile. The mood of the poem changed also from that of thought to that of reverie.

The chief poets to sustain the surrealist influence without succumbing to it were not French. In the country of its origin the movement retained too much authority to allow poets to use some of its techniques without subscribing to its theory. Those poets therefore who are to be thought of as having gained most from Surrealism have been either English-speaking or inhabitants of the Spanish language areas. One alone, Jules Supervielle (b. 1884), though born in Uruguay, has spent much of his life in France, and writes in French. Though his short stories are rather French than Spanish in their wit and fantasy, his poetry of essences and absences is more closely related to the poetry of Vicente Aleixandre in Spain, and Ricardo Molinari in Argentina, than to that of the Surrealists proper. Each poem is like a section from an unknown myth of which one guesses the outline without understanding the details, or guessing at the nature of the characters.

[1] My wife with temples of slate and a hot-house roof my wife with moisture on the panes my wife with shoulders of champagne and of fountains with dolphins' heads under the ice my wife . . .

Les femmes se donnaient, en passant, sur des tertres,
Chacune allait toujours vers de nouveaux miroirs,
Même l'homme loyal était sans souvenirs,
Les lettres s'effacaient, seules, au tableau noir,
La mémoire dormait, ivre de rêverie,
Et voulait-on tenir la main de son amie
Que déjà l'on touchait une main étrangère,
Plus douce entre vos mains de ce qu'elle changeait,
Bougeait et devenait mille mains à venir.[1]

The imagery seems to be that of dream, yet the description is
of a sharply rendered state of mind in which the future presses on
the present. Some vaguely apprehended disaster is impending.

Supervielle's poetry appears to have meanings not only on
the personal plane but on the cosmic. When he says that letters
blotted themselves out of their own accord on the blackboard, he
is ascribing not only to the dreamer but to his world a shifting
scale of values. This becomes clear in the handful of poems which
he wrote from abroad at the time of France's conquest by the
Germans. Supervielle's poetry hardly develops. It is always a
poetry of things rather than of people, of things taken in isolation
—stones, houses, trees, which are to him more real than man
with his changing moods. When God thinks of man in one of his
poems, seeing him at the window of a house not yet created, He
thinks of him much as He thinks of a tree in a companion piece,
as an idea conceived by a poet, rather than as something existing
in its own right. Supervielle is delicate in his rhythms, which
began as vers-libre punctuated by half-rhymes, and his poetry has
gradually become more regular both in metre and in rhyme.
What it lacks is concentration. It is always the poetry of reverie,
never of harshly observed fact.

This unfortunate lack of concentration is common to much
of the poetry that makes use of the new licence to dream provided
by the Surrealists. The line becomes long, the images rare and
repetitive, and the sharp impact of observation is usually missing.
The mind has been pushed into second place, but not by strength
of emotion. For despite the surrealist theory, this does not live on
the level of dream but on that of greater consciousness. The

---

[1] Women gave themselves casually on hillocks, each one was always moving towards
new mirrors, even the loyal man had no memories, letters blotted themselves out of
their own accord on blackboards, the memory slept besotted with dreams, and if one
wanted to grasp one's lover's hand, one was already touching a stranger's softer
between your hands because it stirred and became a thousand hands to come.

danger, therefore, to which all these poets are subject, is that of falling into a congested rhetoric which takes the place of poetic concentration.

Hart Crane, for instance (1899-1932), an American poet with a tireless zest for words, attempts to repeat the headlong charge of Rimbaud's 'Le Bateau Ivre', yet without Rimbaud's talent for capturing an exact image. The reader is often at a loss in his ambitious 'Marriage of Faustus and Helen' to know what the references signify; many of the words seem to be used only for their sound, and in order to convey the illusion of profundity:

> Anchises' navel, dripping of the sea,—
> The hands Erasmus dipped in gleaming tides,
> Gathered the voltage of brown blood and vine;
> Delve upward for the new and scattered wine,
> O brother-thief of time, that we recall.

In a similar way, Edith Sitwell, having made an initial statement of some emotional depth, will sometimes attempt to reinforce it by repetitions, much as the drums of a tribal dance prolong and exacerbate the excitement of an African feast. The appeal is, however, to the senses alone, the words cease to convey any mental picture, or to strike with any emotional impact:

> Said the Skeleton lying upon the sands of Time—
> 'The great gold planet that is the mourning heat of the Sun
> Is greater than all gold, more powerful
> Than the tawny body of a lion that fire consumes
> Like all that grows or leaps . . .' so is the heart
> More powerful than all dust.

Here technique has got the better of sense; a single apocalyptic image by Blok, a dead-pan metaphysical statement by Eliot, or a carefully worked out piece of symbolism by Montale, will convey the intuition—for it can be no more—that sun and heart share values that transcend those of time and the skeleton, better than this somewhat over-positive statement, muffled in high-sounding words. Crane and Miss Sitwell are both on a small scale excellent poets; it is when theory and rhetoric inflate their statement, when words take command of sense that their poems fail, much as those of Swinburne failed in the last century. The cause of this failure does not lie with Surrealism itself, with which neither poet has

F *

been in sympathy, but with the new licence granted by the Surrealists to poets in general, to substitute strong physical imagery, unobserved at first hand, for the more disciplined imagery that has been subjected to the reasoning mind. As a short cut to valid emotion, either in the poet or his reader, it disastrously failed.

The strengths and weaknesses of Dylan Thomas (1914-1953) lie along these same lines. A naturally unintellectual poet, he allowed a dream-like association of images, many of them taken from childhood memories, to form the connecting thread on which a poem was to be hung. Mental development is lacking in even the finest poems of *Deaths and Entrances*, which do not lead from a defined beginning to an end but elaborate a subject which has often not been explicitly stated.

Thomas's earliest poems have, however, a concentration much greater than Crane's or Edith Sitwell's. Published when he was only twenty, they take licence for their frequent obscurity from the obscurity of the moods they chronicle. The early Thomas is self-imprisoned; without the philosophical understanding to say so in the manner of Eliot or Pasternak, he is puzzled by the unreality of the events and things outside him, which seem to have reality only as stimuli to his own senses. The early poetry is sensual, because neither thought nor emotion has so far engaged the poet's attention. If the earth is real, it is because he is part of it; if water has a language, it is that of the blood that flows through his own veins. Night and dawn are internal events, to be described only by their physical impact:

> Night in the sockets rounds,
> Like some pitch moon, the limit of the globes;
> Day lights the bone;
> Where no cold is, the skinning gales unpin
> The winter's robe ;
> The film of spring is hanging from the lids.
>
> Light breaks on secret lots,
> On tips of thought where thoughts smell in the rain;
> When logics die,
> The secret of the soil grows through the eye,
> And blood jumps in the sun;
> Above the waste allotments the dawn halts.

The prose statement of these two verses from the fourteenth of Thomas's first *18 Poems*, is no more than that there are inner events, the oncoming of puberty, perhaps, and the beginning of thought, that correspond to outer events, the coming of spring and the budding of plants. The originality lies in the choice of images and the harsh rhythms of the lines. No poet before Thomas would have attempted the alliteration in *l* and *t* of the first three lines of the second verse; none would have dared the repetition of *thought* and *thoughts* or the abrupt double meaning of *tips* which involves a double attitude to thought, as a waste product that is thrown out on a tip, and as something which smells and buds, and perhaps springs from the same tip on which it has been dumped. The end of the poem does not resolve the paradox; since allotments from which thought might spring are now described as waste, and the dawn, whether as an external or an internal event, comes to a halt.

Thomas's second book, *Twenty-Five Poems* took him further in the direction of obscurity. Like Hart Crane, he came to rely on the hypnotic nature of words, lifting from what he read incantatory but half understood phrases, and so compressing his imagery that, though it may be explicable by close analysis, it can never make anything but a dulled impact:

> Black-tongued and tipsy from salvation's bottle,
> Rose my Byzantine Adam in the night;
> For loss of blood I fell on Ishmael's plain,
> Under the milky mushrooms slew my hunger,
> A climbing sea from Asia had me down
> And Jonah's Moby snatched me by the hair

References to the jargon of the Nonconformist chapel both direct (fell on Ishmael's plain) and ironic (tipsy from salvation's bottle) are mingled with personal imagery (under the milky mushrooms) and references to reading (Jonah's Moby, Ishmael's plain) but the whole is ill-coordinated, and at its conclusion the poem borders on nonsense:

> By waste seas where the white bear quoted Virgil
> And sirens singing from our lady's sea-straw.

The white bear quoting Virgil is perhaps a surrealist property— for Thomas had by now heard of the surrealist movement—and our lady's sea-straw is a pun on the common wild-flower, lady's bedstraw. Something is being said about the horror of the Nativity, with sirens as Our Lady's midwives, just as at the opening of the poem something was said about the violence of the Annunciation in which Gabriel's part is played by a cowboy-cardsharper. It is not clear whether Thomas means to assert that the usual picture of these events is a common fake. It is more likely that the extent of his statement is that horror and violence are present everywhere. What binds the poem together is not its sense, which is doubtful and can make a little impact even with analytical reading, but its alliteration, adumbrated in the two *s,s* of the penultimate line, and fully developed in the five *s,s* of the last. This produces the charm of magic.

This highly conscious attention to texture, shared by Thomas and Edith Sitwell, and by Gerard Manley Hopkins before them, replaces concentration on the intellectual argument of a poem. This Thomas generally left to look after itself, as many traditional poets had done with their sounds. But here the sound counts for more than the sense, and undertakes, when the latter is deficient, to carry the poem forward alone.

Under the impact of the war, Thomas wrote several poems of deep feeling, from which the obscurity, nevertheless, was not completely dispelled. In this situation Edith Sitwell too was visited by a sharpness of emotion that compelled her to be brief. Thomas's 'Refusal to Mourn the Death, by Fire, of a Child in London' and her 'Lullaby', together with passages from 'Little Gidding', all alike commemorate the raids on London. Thomas uses his familiar physical imagery for a new purpose:

> Deep with the first death lies London's daughter,
> Robed in the long friends,
> The grains beyond age, the dark veins of her mother
> Secret by the unmourning water
> Of the riding Thames.
> After the first death, there is no other.

The poem is bewildering, but satisfactory in that it expresses the bewilderment of the poet himself. The controlling factor in all human events had hitherto seemed to him to be the body; the strongest energy that of sex. Confronted with a violent death, he could not however see it as purely a return of earth to earth.

The majesty and burning of the child's death now seem to him an event of greater emotional charge than a mere return of the body to

> the round
> Zion of the water bead
> And the synagogue of the ear of corn.

Zion and the synagogue, in fact, represent greater realities than he has yet faced. His refusal to mourn is, therefore, a renunciation of the glib response. He faces mystery. The child has returned to 'her mother', robed in 'the long friends' (perhaps the vegetable kingdom embodied in the cloth of her shroud). Yet something remains over that is unexplained.

It is better explained in the more overtly paradoxical 'Conversation of Prayer', in which both life and death are accepted, life in the person of the child who

> not caring to whom he climbs his prayer
> Shall drown in a grief as deep as his true grave.

and of the man on the stairs 'who climbs to his dying love' but who

> To night shall find no dying but alive and warm
> In the fire of his care his love in the high room.

Thomas's poetry is born of the contradictions between glory and decay, between entrance into the world and death, between flesh and ghost. It is in its final phases a religious poetry, though such an overtly religious poem as 'There was a Saviour' fails, since the attempted simplicity of its statement is contradicted by the involutions of its associative imagery. Its religion lies in its acceptance of the cycle of birth and decay, of creation in the flesh and destruction by fire, in the joy which the poet took in the world, a joy reminiscent of Traherne's or Vaughan's. His is a mysticism of the senses that transcends the sensuality with which he began. It is at its most eloquent when he is remembering his childhood:

And I saw in the turning so clearly a child's
Forgotten mornings when he walked with his mother
   Through the parables
     Of sunlight
And the legends of the green chapels
And the twice told fields of infancy
That his tears burned my cheeks and his heart moved in mine.
These were the woods the river and sea
    Where a boy
   In the listening
Summertime of the dead whispered the truth and joy
To the trees and the stones and the fish in the tide.
   And the mystery
    Sang alive
Still in the water and the singingbirds.

The poetry of Edith Sitwell (b. 1887) is seldom as direct as these verses of Thomas's poem in celebration of his thirtieth birthday. She too has always been preoccupied with the sound of words, attributing density and depth of meaning to particular combinations of syllables, almost regardless of the words to which they belonged. In this she has followed the French theory of *correspondances* already referred to. Her early poetry consists largely of five-finger exercises in the use of sound. Her occasional successes capture the simplicity of nursery-rhyme, and the rest are pleasing rigmaroles. Experimentally she had reached beyond the achievements of Dada. Like Khlebnikov, she had broken the old moulds. What remained was that she or another should play the part of Mayakovsky and use the new style to some purpose. For herself she was immersed in childhood memories, and prone to accept a Russian ballet backcloth as a substitute for reality. Her intention was to recapture the intensity of the early Romantics, but the poems were literary in content, and pseudo-Baroque in decoration. She did not learn from the Baroque its one powerful lesson in the art of concentration. There was behind her work between 'Facade' and 'Gold Coast Customs', a mixture of yearning and protest, but no subject canalized it until she came to London, and wrote this last poem.

'Gold Coast Customs' was inspired by the poverty and unemployment of the Great Slump. The relations of rich and poor are described in terms of certain barbarous African customs, the chief of which was cannibalism. To express this the poet's new rhythms, related as they were to those of negro jazz, were par-

ticularly suitable. The poem was a poem of protest, partly
political but chiefly moral: essentially it was a statement of the
poet's own responsibility:

> Behind the bawdy hovels like hoardings
> Where harridans peer from the grovelling boarding
> House, the lunatic
> Wind still shakes
> My empty rag-body, nothing wakes;
> The wind, like a lunatic in a fouled
> Nightgown, whipped those rags and howled.
>
> Once I saw it come
> Through the canvas slum,
> Rattle and beat what seemed a drum,
> Rattle and beat what seemed a bone.
> O Christ, that bone was dead, alone!

Like Mayakovsky, Edith Sitwell had come to think of poetry in
terms of recitation rather than of reading in the study. 'Gold
Coast Customs', indeed, is clearly designed for a mass audience.
But whereas the Revolution threw up the necessary audience for
Mayakovsky, Edith Sitwell could only rely on audiences that
came to be entertained; and much of their entertainment was
derived rather from the novelty of the work, and the poet's feuds
with her critics, than from the poetry's intrinsic quality.

Edith Sitwell continued to be imprisoned in the cage of
fashion except for those brief movements during the war when
her compassionate horror at the evil unleashed found a form
which owed nothing to fashionable mannerisms:

> There's nothing left but earth's low bed—
> (The Pterodactyl fouls its nest):
> But steel wings fan thee to thy rest,
> And wingless truth and larvae lie
> And eyeless hope and handless fear—
> All these for thee as toys are spread,
> Do—do—

This 'Lullaby' for a child of 1940 comes at the meeting point of
the poet's two styles. Sorrow which amounts almost to despair is
admirably expressed in the mechanical syncopation of the lines;
manner and meaning for once coincide.

Edith Sitwell's later poetry seldom achieves this clarity. She
has evolved a rhetoric which, though a magnificent instrument,

too often takes control. Compassion, social indignation, meta-physical insights, romantic memory and wonder are all presented in the same long and richly orchestrated lines. But these have become insensitive to change of mood and content, and are too frequently studded, in the manner of a Wagner score, with motifs which do not rise to the emotional force of symbols. Such a poem as 'The Shadow of Cain', whose subject is the atomic bomb, moves forward with a tremendous surge. But the quotations from poets and philosophers that are embedded in it, are never entirely welded, like those of 'The Waste Land', to the poem's argument. Although the feeling is genuine, it is overwhelmed by the repetitive clamour of the versification.

The fatal rhetoric of vers-libre has overwhelmed many poets. It has always been a danger to Vicente Aleixandre (b. 1898), a Sevillian poet who has lived most of his life in Madrid. Aleixandre's initial experiments were less violent than Edith Sitwell's, and the distance that separates his early work from his late is smaller. His sense of direction has been consistent from his first collection *Ambito* (Region) of 1928 to his *Historia del corazón* (History of the Heart) of 1954; and the evolution of his technique has gone hand in hand with the general widening and deepening of his compassion. The whole of his poetry might be described as the history of a heart. 'The theme of most of these books,' he wrote in an introduction to a selection from his whole work, 'has been, if the expression does not sound presumptuous, Creation, the whole of nature, or—to put it better—its unity, and man has remained confused with it, an element in that cosmos from which he is not radically differentiated.' Later, considerably later, '*Historia del corazón* reverses the terms, and now man is the immediate protagonist, and nature no more than the background against which the history of man's passage takes place and develops.'

By *La Destrucción o el amor* (Destruction or love) of 1933, Aleixandre's experiments were completed, his influences absorbed, and an individual style evolved. These influences came chiefly from Freud, directly, through his writings, and indirectly, by way of surrealism. They encouraged the poet to use the imagery of dream. Like Thomas in his *18 Poems*, Aleixandre first developed the theme of man's physical unity with nature; like Thomas too he came to think of death and birth as one, speaking of death here, as *Nacimiento ultimo*—the final birth. In a poem to a dead girl, he finds her now more living in his memory of her bodily presence than she had been in her life:

> Tu generoso cuerpo, agua rugiente,
> agua que cae como cascada joven,
> agua que es tan sencillo beber de madrugada
> cuando en los manos vivas se sienten todas las estrellas.[1]

The images are entirely tactile, and the rhythms, with their reinforcement of repetitions and their frequent alliterations, belong to the same order of physical existence. In this first principal book of Aleixandre's there are also poems of greater violence, and images, of blood and of sex, that are more patently Freudian. The poet summons all nature to love. But love is for him a consuming flame, and a flame is the symbol of death, rather than—in the Christian sense—a purging of the old Adam. Destruction and love are not, as he sees it, opposites. The deepest roots of love are only to be reached by destroying oneself and being born afresh in the blood of the beloved. Man cannot be at one with Nature till he has yielded his individuality to it. The poetry is fervent and pantheistic; the poet identifies himself with all that is active and instinctive in the world:

> Soy el caballo que enciende su crin contra el pelada viento,
> soy el león torturado por su propia melena,
> la gacela que teme al río indiferente,
> el avasallador tigre que despuebla la selva.
> el diminuto escarabajo que también brilla en el día.[2]

La Destrucción o el Amor was followed by a book very different in subject. *Sombra del Paraíso* (Shadow of Paradise) of 1944, is dedicated to the theme of childhood remembered, like that of the previous book a principal theme also with Dylan Thomas. The opening vision is of the world without man seen as a child's primal discovery on the seashore at Malaga, Aleixandre's childhood home:

[1] Your noble body, a roaring water, a water that falls like a young cascade, a water that is so simple to drink at dawn, when all the stars can be felt in the living hands.

[2] I am the steed who kindles his mane against the naked wind, I am the lion tortured by his own mane, the gazelle that fears the impassive river, the enslaving tiger that destroys the population of the jungle, the tiny beetle that also shines by day.

La presencia de peces por las orillas, su plata núbil,
el oro no manchado por los dedos de nadie,
la resbalosa escama de la luz, era un brillo en los míos.
No apresé nunca esta forma huidiza de un pez en su hermosura,
la esplendente libertad de los seres,
ni amenacé una vida, porque amé mucho: amaba
sin conocer el amor; sólo vivía. . . .

Paradise is the world of childhood, of immediate apprehensions, of loving without knowing it. It is the dawn of life to which the poet will always strive to return, 'a journey towards a promised land, just glimpsed'. The attitude is of romantic pantheism, but the texture of the poetry is far more subtly organized than that of Edith Sitwell or even of Thomas. Aleixandre's poems often open on a question, couched in uncertain rhythms, which leads to a development both thematical and musical and concludes with a resolution in more certain metres. The effect is of a poem started in perplexity that attains its own shape as it is written. The internal organization of alliteration, repetition, and sustained imagery, the introduction of symbols or *leitmotive*, however, argue a more conscious guidance by the organizing intellect. At first sight, it might appear that Aleixandre has allowed his 'unconscious' mind to dictate the form of his poem. But when any part of *Sombra del Paraíso* is compared with the work of Breton and his disciples, one is aware that whereas the surrealists admit associative imagery, Aleixandre prunes and limits his invention. The organizing mind is conservative, even Baroque, in its influences. A truer comparison than with Breton is with the Eliot of the *Quartets*. What dictates the poem is not dream but a reverie that follows its own logic, which is both musical and intellectual.

Aleixandre's work is far more highly organized than it appears at a first reading. His books are, furthermore, conceived as entities in themselves bound by a common subject and attitude. Only one, *Nacimiento ultimo* of 1953, contains poems unrelated to its main theme, which is still that of the cosmos without man. The entrance of man, and of human love and responsibility occurs in *Historia de corazón* of 1954. Here the poetry descends

---

[1] The presence of fishes on the shores, their nubile silver, the gold discoloured by no one's fingers, the slippery scales of the light, were a brightness in mine. I never grasped this fugitive shape of a fish in its beauty, the resplendent liberty of creatures, nor threatened a life, for I loved greatly; I loved without knowing love; I only lived. . . .

from timelessness into the world of time, abandoning memory and
isolation in favour of participation in the whole of life. 'There are
poets', Aleixandre has said, 'who address themselves to what is
permanent in man. Not to the refinements that distinguish one
from another, but to the essence that unites them all.' The poem
'Coronación del amor' (Love's Coronation) is, like much of this
book, a hymn to that union, as positive in its acceptance as the
last of Rilke's *Elegies*. In it reality is raised to myth. Here are the
primal lovers, majestic as the gods painted by Titian, gods who
have passed through the fires of carnality, who have taken flesh
in which to express their spirit:

> Miradlos ahora dueños de su sangre, vencido
> el tumultuoso ardor que flamígera puso
> su corporal unidad, hecha luz trastornada.
> Los dorados amantes, rubios ya, permanecen
> sobre un lecho de verde novedad que ha nacido
> bajo el fuego. ¡Oh, cuán claros al día!
>
> Helos bajo los aires que los besan
> mientras la mañana crece sobre su tenue molicie,
> sin pesar nunca, con vocación de rapto leve,
> por que la luz quiere como pluma elevarles,
> mientras ellos sonríen a su amor, sosegados,
> coronados del fuego que no quema,
> pasados por las alas altísimas que ellos sienten cual besos
> para sus puros labios que el amor no destruye.[1]

This poem achieves all that D. H. Lawrence failed to achieve
in his confused and violent hymning of the senses. Aleixandre
transcends the physical, yet does not leave it behind. The poetry
arises from the circumstances of the poet's own life, of his
measured advance from physical to spiritual passion, from
reveries of childhood to an acceptance of the whole of life as
'a lightning-flash between two darknesses'. The imagery of this
last book has become more traditional; it is like a new version of
that of the *Song of Songs*. Gone are the dream-symbols, the

[1] Look at them now, masters of their blood, the tumultuous flaming passion that
imposed its corporeal unity, conquered and turned to light of a reverse order. The
gilded lovers, fair now, lie on a bed of fresh green that has been born beneath the fire.
Oh how bright they are in the day!

See them beneath the airs that kiss them while the morning grows over their tenuous
fatigue, never weighing on them, its rapture being light by nature, since the light wishes
to raise them like a feather, whilst they smile at their love, quieted, crowned by a light
that does not burn, born by the highest wings, which they feel like kisses on their pure
lips that are not burned by love.

surrealist juxtapositions of *La Destrucción o el amor*. Aleixandre's
is now no longer a private vision but one of mankind as a whole
advancing towards a destiny that is independent of nature's.

> Y el sol se abre sobre las frentes
> Y en la cumbre, con su grandeza, están todos ya cantando.
> Y es tu voz la que les expresa. Tu voz colectiva y alzada.
> Y un cielo de poderío, completamente existente,
> hace ahora con majestad el eco entero del hombre.[1]

So ends the poem 'El Poeta canta por Todos' (The Poet Sings
for all), with an affirmation that rises from Aleixandre's total
experience. For the stages of his advance have corresponded to
critical events in his country to which he has responded as a poet.
Le Destrucción y el amor was published the year before the outbreak of the civil war, and reflects the growing violence and
isolation of the outward scene. Spain was returning to her dark
and bloody past, out of the comparative light brought by the
liberal and Europeanizing influences at work in the ill-fated
Republic. His second principal book returns in dark days to the
theme of childhood. For the poems were written at the height of
Franco's repressions, when murder was still a legitimate method
of revenge, and the third book, *Historia del corazón*, came when
the indignity and hopelessness had become endemic, and when
only the poets, and the students, saw any future for Spain and her
civilization. In short, Aleixandre's poetry is the expression of a
personal evolution that coincides with a national destiny. In this
it is comparable with Mayakovsky's which, in the same way,
though with less happy results for the poet, accompanied the
forces of history. In contrast that of Dylan Thomas remained
private to the end, while Pasternak's evolution cannot finally be
understood until more of his work of the last twenty-five years is
published.

---

[1] And the sun opens above their foreheads, and on the hilltop, in their greatness, they
are all singing now, and your voice is the one that interprets them. Your raised and
collective voice, and a heaven of power, completely existent, now majestically returns
the full echo of man.

8

The poetry of resistance

THE dangers which threatened poetry in the 'thirties were principally political; it was Fascist dictatorship that destroyed the moribund literature of the Weimar Republic, and that effectually drove Italian writers into exile or hermeticism. It was a Communist dictatorship that destroyed the freedom of Russian writers, which had been granted them in the Leninist phase of the Revolution. Any future talent as undisciplined as Mayakovsky's was not likely to be encouraged by the Party bosses who presided over the state publishing houses, and those who directed cultural policy from even higher eminences. It was similar frightened repressiveness that led to the minor stupidities of the ban on Joyce's *Ulysses* and on Lawrence's *Lady Chatterley's Lover* in this country, where the attack on intellectual freedom did not gain much ground. But in Spain, the scene of a Fascist uprising, with foreign help, against a republic which actually fostered literature, for the first time since the French Revolution a clear cause seemed to be presented to writers, and a choice offered them between a neutrality which might in the end impair their own freedom of expression and an unquestioning advocacy of the Spanish Republic's cause. Most of the important writers of Europe were concerned on behalf of Spain. Indeed the implications for the poet of the Spanish war were clearer even than those of the Second World War that followed.

The generals' conspiracy struck Spain at a moment when poetry had reached a higher level than at any time since the middle of the seventeenth century. In addition to the older poets already noticed—Machado, Jiménez, Guillén and Aleixandre, there was a considerable younger generation, whose principal figures were Federigo García Lorca and Rafael Alberti, but which included half-a-dozen other poets of eminence, none of whom was to remain in Spain after the Republic's defeat. Franco landed in a country with a flowering culture. When he had conquered it, the few writers who remained were forced to be silent; the rest had gone into exile in the United States, Mexico, Argentina or Britain. Some had been murdered, or lay in prison.

The murder of García Lorca (1899-1936) occurred in the first days of the uprising. To what extent it was a political act, and what part private revenge played in it, is still uncertain. It was an event, however, that could only have taken place in Civil War conditions. Lorca was the first poet to be butchered by the forces of reaction, and as such became a symbol. Whatever part political badgering may have played in the suicides of Esenin and Mayakovsky, here for the first time the case was abundantly clear.

Lorca was not a political poet. It is, in fact, impossible to detect in his poems any political standpoint at all. He was however employed by the Spanish government as a producer of plays with a slightly tendentious twist, and a member of his family was at the time of the revolt the Social-Democratic mayor of his native city of Granada. He belongs among the poets of resistance, however, on account of his attitude to mass civilization. The keynote of Lorca's work is a protest against the barrenness that he found in himself and in contemporary society. Only the primitive corner of his native Andalusia seemed to him to be still alive and vital, and amongst Andalusians he found the greatest positive qualities in the gipsies who lived on the edge of society, preserving their own songs and dances, and at perpetual feud with the *almas de charol* (patent-leather souls), of the Civil Guard. When in the 'thirties Lorca made a somewhat unhappy trip to America, he found these same virtues in the Negroes of New York, though in this case the identification was rather one of imaginative sympathy since, lacking English, he had little opportunity of making their acquaintance.

Lorca's poetry grows out of that of Juan Ramón Jiménez, though, coming in a decade when Surrealism had licensed the use of more violent imagery, his metaphors are more surprising than his master's. He had moreover dramatic qualities that were lacking in the poet of Moguer. Not only in the plays but in the poems of the *Romancero gitano*, there appear characters, highly coloured and acting with the arbitrariness of a dream, but characters nevertheless. The most consistently present character, however, in Lorca's early poetry is that of Death, the Lady Death of 'La Luna y la Muerte' (The Moon and Death) of 1921:

> La luna tiene dientes de marfil.
> ¡Qué vieja y triste asoma!
> Están los cauces secos,
> Los campos sin verdores
> Y los árboles mustios
> Sin nidos y sin hojas.
> Doña Muerte arrugada,
> Pasea por sauzales
> Con su absurdo cortejo
> De ilusiones remotas.
> Va vendiendo colores
> De cera y de tormenta
> Como un hada de cuento
> Mala y enredadora. . . .[1]

The fairy-tale quality that persists throughout Lorca's poetry, up to its supreme moment when death sweeps all decorative accessories aside, immediately separates it from the sophisticated poetry of Jiménez. Jiménez could go into exile and continue his poetic development in another continent, Lorca was happy only in his own province, which was, even so, largely the country of a dream.

The poetry that followed his first *Libro de poemas* is based on the songs and dances of the Granada gipsies. The influence is of traditional Spanish folk-poetry, adapted to the particular fantasies which Lorca associated with this primitive community, and for which he found licence in the more sophisticated poetry of his contemporaries, French and Spanish.

Lorca was no deliberate primitive. He was well read in the literature of the seventeenth century and had some knowledge of modern French writing since Baudelaire. He had, however, an unacademic approach to tradition. If he echoed the seventeenth century in some of his images, or owed something to the tradition of Baudelaire, he relied always on the inspiration of his own *duende*, a creature half-fairy half-demon. Poetry came, in his belief, not from a struggle with an angel or a muse, but from this Andalusian creature of whom a local singer had told him; 'The

---

[1] The moon has ivory teeth. How old and sad she looks! The watercourses are dry, the fields have no green, and the trees are withered, with no nests and no leaves. Wrinkled Lady Death passes through the willow plantations with her absurd cortège of far-away illusions. She is selling the colours of wax and storm, like a fairy-tale witch, a wicked busybody. . . .

days I sing with *duende*, no one can do anything with me.' An angel or a muse was a distant being. Lorca claimed to have met his only twice, but a *duende* was an intimate, and peculiarly Spanish. German art was generally the produce of a muse, he said, Italian of an angel, but 'Spain is at all times moved by the *duende*, being a country of age-old music and dances, in which the *duende* expresses lemon-trees at dawn, and being a country of death, a country open to death'.

Lorca's theory of the *duende* was poetic and personal; it represented nevertheless a quality of spontaneous music which he attained in his collection of songs and poems on themes of the *Poema del cante jondo* (The Flamenco poem). These poems are however fragmentary, and depend for their full appreciation on a knowledge of the gipsies' singing and dancing. The *Romancero gitano* (Gipsy Ballad-book), on the other hand, composed between 1924 and 1927, in the metre of the traditional ballads, builds a number of interrelated myths, in which figure gipsies, policemen, dancers and angels; and these have a consistency of their own.

The world of the *Romancero* is one of sensual freedom. All the senses are evoked. The light is harsh, men act with violence, nature and the elements are endowed with feelings and desires as irresistible as man's. Pride, desire, and a sense of having belonged where they do since the beginning of time, are the predominant qualities of these gipsies, who flash their knives in feud with the Guardia Civil, and take their women with equal fierceness. Preciosa the dancer pursued by the wind with a hot sword, after rousing the police, takes refuge with the English consul who offers her a glass of warm milk and a tot of gin. This she refuses, while the foiled wind howls outside.

> El inglés de a la gitana
> un vaso de tibia leche,
> y una copa de ginebra
> que Preciosa no se bebe.
>
> Y menitras cuenta, llorando,
> su aventura a aquella gente,
> en las tejas de pizarra
> el viento, furioso, muerde.[1]

The wind does not catch Preciosa, but in another poem the

The Englishman gives the gipsy a tumbler of luke-warm milk and a glass of gin which Preciosa will not drink. And while she weeps and tells these people of her adventure, the wind in its fury bites the slate roofs.

moon snatches up the blacksmith's boy from his forge for
threatening her that the gipsies will get her. Events in this kingdom of the *duende* to which Lorca gives the name of Andalusia
are arbitrary. All alike, winds, moon, gipsies, lovers, saints and
smugglers, seem to be dancing to traditional steps, known only
to Lorca himself. All are in fancy dress; the saints with swaying
hips wear the lace of gaudy village images that are carried in pro-
cessions; the moon wears a bustle of starched lily-petals.

Many of Lorca's *romances* are in this way decorative, and
contemporary taste has come to reject them. His mingling of
tactile, aural and visual imagery produces a 'confusion of the
senses' different from that advocated by Mallarmé, and now
considered cloying. 'La Casada infiel' (The Unfaithful Wife) is an
example of Lorca's over-rich style with its curious, elliptical
imagery and its deliberate provocations. The girl's body is
described with a contrived sensuality:

> Ni nardos ni caracolas
> tienen el cutis tan fino,
> ni los cristales con luna
> relumbran con ese brillo.
> Sus muslos se me escapaban
> como peces sorprendidos,
> la mitad llenos de lumbre,
> la mitad llenos de frío.[1]

Sight and touch are brought into an unexpected relationship,
as they are in a passage rather earlier in the poem in which the
gipsy rouses the girl's passion:

> En los últimas esquinas
> toqué sus pechos dormidos,
> y se me abrieron de pronto
> como ramos de jacintos.
> El almidón de su enagua
> me sonaba en el oído
> como una pieza de seda
> rasgada por diez cuchillos.[2]

The language is mannered after the style of some minor poets
of the seventeenth century. Yet there is a popular element in this

---

[1] Neither nards nor conches have so fine a skin, nor do mirrors under the moon shine
with that brilliance. Her thighs escaped me like fish surprised, half full of fire, half full
of cold.

[2] At the last street-corner I touched her sleeping breasts, and they opened to me
suddenly like spikes of hyacinths. The starch of her petticoat sounded in my ears like a
piece of silk ripped by ten knives.

poetry, which quickly found Lorca a public. His *romances* were, in fact, recited in the trenches at the time of the civil war. Much of Spain's traditional ballad poetry had circulated in sophisticated versions, and the *Romancero gitano* no doubt reminded unsophisticated readers of these artificial ballads. But another feature of the collection struck even more directly home: the close observation of popular habits and ways of thought. When the lover in 'La Casada infiel' finds that the girl he has slept with was not a virgin, he dismisses her with a trumpery present. His pride has been hurt. Much of the *Romancero* seems to the discriminating reader wilfully picturesque, with exaggerated metaphor taking the place of feeling. But the Andalusian recognizes its truth to his own country.

Lorca's feelings are not truly engaged by the theme of sex, and not entirely by that of pride. What moves him most is always cruelty and death. It is they that give poignancy to the mysterious 'Romance sonámbulo' (Somnambular Ballad), the outstanding poem of the volume. Here a drama of death is worked out. A gipsy is pursued by the Civil Guard and returns home bleeding. He tries to climb up to the verandah of his house so that he may die in holland sheets. But his girl sees him bleed to death, and as he dies he sees her swinging over the water tank like a splinter of the moon. The incident is more than picturesque; it has the magic of fairy-tale.

This preoccupation with death is a feature of the Spanish mind and even more of the Mexican. But in Lorca's case it chimed with a deep personal sadness, and perhaps also with premonitions of his own death and the terrible slaughter in which three million Spaniards, men, women and children, were soon to perish. Lorca's horror of death and of the prospect of dying unfulfilled, informs his next volume, *Poeta en Nueva York* (Poet in New York), which was written in America, where he had gone to escape from some personal distress. In New York his *duende*, certainly a local deity, deserted him. Encouraged by the Surrealist painter Salvador Dali he began to experiment with Surrealist techniques, the violence of which chimed with his own desire for more violent imagery. His poetry, however, with the abandonment of traditional metres, lost form; his images once true to their own system, now became wayward.

The urban American disgusted the poet; only the negro

seemed to him to be still in touch with reality. Where Mayakovsky had been scornful yet admiring of the skyscraper and the milling crowds, Lorca was frightened. Here he seemed to meet death in a new form; ugly words are repeated. It is not a pure death that is present, but death by cancer in a sleepless desert of stone:

> Tu ignorancia es un monte de leones, Stanton.
> El día que el cancer te dío un paliza
> y te escupió en el dormitorio donde murieron los huéspedes en la epidemia
> y abrió su quemada rosa de vidrios secos y manos blandas
> para salpicar de lodo las pupilas de los que navegan
> tu buscaste en la hierba mi agonía. . . . [1]

Lorca returned from his *saison en enfer* in the summer of 1930, travelling back to Spain by way of Cuba. His sole discovery in the year which he spent in the United States was in his own words 'the art of the negro', apart from which he 'believed the country to have nothing to show but machines and automatons'. If any part of the *Poeta en Nueva York* has value it is those poems in which Lorca imitates the negro rhythms, but here he does little more than Vachel Lindsay had done before him, and less than Nicolás Guillén, another negro poet and a native of Cuba, whom he met in Havana, was already doing.

Lorca devoted the latter part of his life chiefly to the drama. On the establishment of the Republic of 1931 his proposal to organize touring companies of students to present classical plays in the villages was accepted, and he himself wrote a series of dramas. They were in prose, though with poetic passages. He was, however, anxious to eliminate all poetic imagery and to produce purely realistic drama, which he finally did. He wrote little poetry in these years, but among this little is his masterpiece, the lament for his friend, the veteran bullfighter Ignacio Sánchez Mejías.

'Spain', he wrote in his lecture on the *duende*, 'is the only country where death is the national spectacle'; and in the bull-fight he found the supreme display of this quality. 'The bull has his orbit,' he wrote, 'and the bullfighter has his' and between

---

[1] Your mindlessness, Stanton, is a mountain of lions. The day that the cancer beat you down and spat on you, in the ward where the hosts of contagion were dying, and opened its burnt rose of parched glass and soft hands to spatter the helmsmen's eyes with mud, you sought my agony in the grass.

orbit and orbit a danger point, which is the culmination of their terrible by-play. At this point Sánchez Mejías was gored:

> Ya luchan la paloma y el leopardo
> *a las cinco de la tarde.*
> Y un muslo con un asta desolada
> *a las cinco de la tarde*
> Comenzaron los sones de bordon
> *a las cinco de la tarde.*[1]

Whereas the poems written in New York were full of undirected horror and of self-pity, here the pity is for the dead man, the horror for the manner of his death. Thus Lorca achieved the quality of compassion which had been absent from his poetry till then. The poet himself stands aside, yet in the last section he praises the dead bullfighter in terms that would apply equally to himself a year later:

> Porque te has muerto para siempre,
> como todos los muertos de la Tierra,
> como todos los muertos que se olvidan
> en un montón de perros apagados.
>
> No te conoce nadie. No. Pero yo te canto
> Yo canto para luego tu perfil y tu gracia.
> La madurez insigne de tu conocimiento.
> Tu apetencia de muerte y el gusto de su boca.
> La tristeza que tuvo tu valiente alegría.
>
> Tardará mucho tiempo en nacer, si es que nace,
> un andaluz tan claro, tan rico de aventura,
> Yo canto su elegancia con palabras que gimen
> y recuerdo una brisa triste por los olivos.[2]

There is in this final characterization of the dead bullfighter more than a partial self-portrait. Lorca himself had 'an appetite for death', and beneath the gaiety of his songs is always a savour

---

[1] Now the dove and the leopard are struggling, *at five in the afternoon*. And a thigh with a desolate horn, *at five in the afternoon*. The sound of the refrain has struck up, *at five in the afternoon*.

[2] Because you have died for ever, like all the Earth's dead, like all the dead who are forgotten in a pile of snuffed-out dogs.
Nobody knows you. No. But I sing of you. I sing for posterity of your profile and your grace, of the signal maturity of your understanding, of your appetite for death and the taste of its mouth, of the sorrow that was in your valiant gaiety.
It will be a long time before there is born, if born there is, an Andalusian so distinguished and rich in adventure. I sing of his elegance in words that moan, and remember a sad breeze among the olive-trees.

of sorrow. For though theoretically a Christian, he thought of
death always as the end, as the moment when a man was finally
confronted with his *duende*, and was inevitably defeated. Though
his whole poetry is a protest against the invasion of the last
corners of Europe by a levelling mass-civilization, it never seems
for a moment that the process can be stayed.

The quality which makes the 'Llanto por Ignacio Sánchez
Mejías' the greatest of Lorca's poems is, in its way, a *depuración*.
Much of the imagery of the *Romancero gitano* is, as has been
said, decorative—a Baroque incrustation on a fabric in itself
slight. In the *Poeta en Nueva York*, Lorca accepted the surrealist
licences and piled up a dream imagery of violence and horror.
There is here some parallel with the second phase in Dylan
Thomas's work—which was actually later in time—and with
Aleixandre's *La Destrucción o el amor*. In Lorca's case, as in
Thomas's, the new imagery had to be mastered, and rhythms
struck that would prevent its gaining complete control. The
decisive factor was the event of the Sánchez Mejías' death, an
objective event outside Lorca's imprisoning dreams. His imagery
is here governed by the details of the bullring and the fight, the
goring and the dead man's character. When he speaks of a fight
between a dove and a leopard, between a thigh and a desolate
horn, he is not resorting to fanciful association. For a moment it
is a heraldic contest, then at the next the horn pierces the thigh,
and 'death laid her eggs in the wound'. The language fits the
situation, and from a single moment of loss springs compassion
for all the dead, who will be forgotten even by the people and
things that were most familiar to them, even by the creature and
the moment that dealt them their death:

> No te conoce el toro ni la higuera,
> ni caballos ni hormigas de tu casa.
> No te conoce el niño ni la tarde
> porque te has muerto para siempre.[1]

Lorca's European fame began at the moment of his murder.
He has ever since been the symbol for the forces of creation
destroyed by violent politicians. Perhaps this symbolic situation
has somewhat affected his valuation as a poet, giving him friends

[1] The bull does not know you nor the fig-tree, nor the horses nor the ants of your
house. The child does not know you nor the afternoon, because you have died forever.

who would not value his poetry and who praise him for ideological reasons. His strongest claim, apart from his dramatic
career, lies in his having written in the *Romancero* some of the
little modern poetry of value that is capable of a wide appeal, and
in the *Llanto* a celebration of death comparable with the great
poetry on this subject of the age of Villon, Dunbar and Lorca's
compatriot Jorge Manrique.

Rafael Alberti (b. 1902), a friend of Lorca and a more intellectual poet who underwent the same influences, is more easily
placed both in relation to tradition and in his political sympathies. His protest is much simpler than Lorca's; it is, in fact,
the age-old protest of Spanish liberalism against the selfishness of
landowners and the obscurantism of churchmen. If he has lived
a *saison en enfer* its causes lie in the outside world, in the destruction of war and the long years of exile from his own corner
of Andalusia, which he loves as dearly as Lorca loved Granada.

A most important event in the development of Spanish poetry
occurred in 1925: the tercentenary of the death of the Luis
Góngora, which had an impact equal to the rediscovery of Donne
and the publication of Gerard Manley Hopkins' manuscripts in
England in the 'twenties.

Góngora's reputation since the reintroduction of 'correct'
taste at the end of the seventeenth century had been of a poet who
after a short early phase in which he used the conceit with modera-
tion, had become a poet of great extravagance and obscurity,
transforming himself, in Lorca's words, from an angel of light
into an angel of darkness. The publication in that year of an
anthology of Góngora and his contemporaries concluded a change
of attitude towards the great poet of Córdoba. This reaction had
in fact been initiated ten years earlier by the Mexican poet
Alfonso Reyes. The re-estimation of Góngora and the publication of the anthology made an immediate effect on the poets of
Lorca's generation. Though neither Lorca nor Aleixandre
resurrected Góngora's forms both were influenced by his use of
elaborate metaphor and figures of speech, by his hyperbole and
his inversions, his substitution of colours for their objects, and
his use of rare mythological allusions.

Rafael Alberti was, as the most intellectual of the group, at
the beginning the most consistent Gongorist. But he was also,
like Lorca, capable of writing poems in the folk-song tradition

almost as unforced as their originals. His subjects were of two
kinds, one drawn from the memory of his own childhood on the
seacoast near Cádiz, and the other modish in its references to such
familiar idols as Charlie Chaplin and Buster Keaton. In 1927,
however, in a book entitled *Sobre los ángeles* (About the angels)
Alberti developed his own mythology. It is no simple matter to
decide what significance these angelic figures had for the poet.
Certainly they are unrelated to the angels of theology, and are not
readily to be associated with Rilke's, yet they too in a sense were
transforming the visible into the invisible. They represent not
qualities of inspiration, but mental or psychological states. At
the outset Alberti speaks of a state of self-confidence and happiness, which has unaccountably disappeared:

> ¿Adónde el Paraíso,
> sombra, tú que has estado?
> Pregunta con silencio.
>
> Ciudades sin respuesta,
> ríos sin habla, cumbres
> sin ecos, mares mudos.
>
> Nadie lo sabe. Hombres
> fijos, de pie, a la orilla
> parada de las tumbas,
>
> me ignoran. . . . [1]

Paradise is lost for the poet, who is condemned to be the guest
of the shades—the phrase is taken, like one or two other key-
phrases in this book, from Gustavo Adolfo Bécquer, whose small
output of poetry was devoted to the loss of a shadowy love. This
perhaps provides the clue to the nature of Alberti's misfortune,
which he describes only figuratively in language that owes
some of its licence, as does some of Lorca's, to surrealism. The
misfortune is briefly referred to in a short poem, 'El mal minuto'
(the Evil Minute).

> Cuando para mí eran los trigos viviendas de astros y de dioses
> y la escarcha los lloros helados de una gacela,
> alguien me enyesó el pecho y la sombra,
> traicionándome.

[1] Which way to Paradise, shadow, you that once existed? Question followed by
silence. Cities without an answer, rivers that cannot speak, peaks with no echo, mute
seas. Nobody knows. Men motionless, standing on the slow edges of graves, do not
know me.

Ese minuto fué el de las balas perdidas,
el del secuestro, por el mar, de los hombros que quisieron ser
      pájaros,
el del telegrama a deshora y el hallazgo de sangre,
el de la muerto del agua que siempre miró al cielo.[1]

Alberti's symbols present none of the difficulties of Breton's
or even of Eluard's; they divide simply into those representing
childish innocence and those which record the shock of betrayal.
Alberti's imagination has some of the freshness of Pasternak's.
But although Alberti too has some skill as a painter, his vision is
far less complex. He is also readier than his Russian contemporary
to see situations in black and white. Intellectual though the
organization of his poetry may be, he has still accepted some
inheritance from the Romantics. Like Aleixandre, he moves from
a private to a social vision. His angels are not only embodiments
of his own moods and states of mind but are also active on the
social plane. 'El ángel avaro' (the Greedy Angel) only faintly
disguises its political comment:

Ese hombre está muerto
y no lo sabe.
Quiere asaltar la banca,
robar nubes, estrellas, cometas de oro,
comprar lo más difícil:
el cielo.
Y ese hombre está muerto.[2]

The greedy angel is on the one hand the poet himself in a
mood of violent desperation, on the other a symbol of the
capitalist world, which, unaware that it is dead, feels that everything could be bought with its money. Alberti realized that a
disaster was approaching, that his own desperation echoed that
of a world riding into crisis; and he welcomed the crisis, willing
that with the loss of his inspiration and the direct vision of childhood from which it derived, the whole earth should perish. Yet
ultimately he believed that there was a solution to be found.

[1] When the wheat, for me, was a dwelling-place of stars and gods and the frost the
frozen tears of a gazelle, someone plastered my heart and my shadow, betraying me.
   That was the minute when the stray shots were fired, when the sea kidnapped the
men who wanted to be birds, of the untimely telegram and the discovery of blood, and
of the death of the water that always gazed at the sky.

[2] This man is dead, and does not know it. He wants to storm the bank, steal clouds,
stars, golden comets, to buy what is most difficult, the sky. And this man is dead.

The moon and the stars might be hostile, yet in himself as a man, without supernatural aid, there lay the possibility of remembering the rules of his own being. This is clear from one of the last poems of the book, *Luna enemiga* (Hostile Moon), in the conclusion of which he invokes that other side of himself which remembers:

Salvadme de los años en estado de nebulosa,
de los espejos que pronuncian trajes y páginas desvanecidos,
de las manos estampadas en los recuerdos que bostezan.
Huíd.
Nos entierran en viento enemigo.

Y es que mi alma ha olvidado las reglas.[1]

In the last poem of the book, it appears that Alberti has learnt the lesson of his disaster, that the living moment with its imperfections is more vivid than a fading vision of the past, that an experience is the more beautiful for the imperfections that threaten at any moment to destroy it. It is with almost biblical certainty that he addresses 'Los ángeles feos' (the Hideous Angels)—who are perhaps the poor—telling them that they are 'only sleeping in the luckless vapours of the marshes so that the most unhappy dawn may revive them in glory of dung'. Here the negative sign changes to positive, for dung is not only excrement but nourishment for a new life. 'You,' he says to these hideous angels, 'have been the cause of this journey', which has brought him through nightmare and horror to a mood in which he can proclaim:

Pero yo os digo:
una rosa es más rosa habitada por las orugas
que sobre la nieve marchita de esta luna de quince anos.[2]

Alberti had survived his crisis. His next important poem was an elegy for the same dead bullfighter whom Lorca celebrated in his better-known poem. Alberti's tribute, written on a visit to Mexico, is in a Gongoristic manner, and consists of sonnets linked by free verse passages and echoes of folk-song. In it his two styles, artificial and surreal, are juxtaposed but insufficiently

---

[1] Save me from the years in the state of nebula, from mirrors which pronounce suits and pages to be out of date, from hands impressed on yawning memories. Flee. They are burying us in hostile wind. And it is because my soul has forgotten the rules.

[2] But I say to you: a rose is more rose when it is the home of caterpillars than on the faded snow of that fifteen year old moon.

blended. The necessary simplification was the product of political partisanship and civil war. Many of Alberti's war-poems are polemical, as are several of the pieces written immediately before them on his visit to Mexico and the West Indies. Like Mayakovsky he travelled in prejudiced certainty of what he would find: exploitation by the rich, and original virtue among the poor. In a few short poems, however, written during the siege of Madrid, Alberti succeeded, under the stress of compassion for the Republican fighters, of whom he was one, in expressing his immediate apprehension of events, in all their simplicity, in a form that derived its tautness from the seventeenth-century masters he had followed in the past. 'Los campesinos', the title of one, are the peasant battalions recruited to defend the legitimate government:

> Se ven marchando duros, color de la corteza
> que la agresión del hacha repele y no inmuta.
> Como los pedernales, sombría la cabeza,
> pero lumbre en su sueño de cáscara de fruta.
>
> Huelen los capotones a corderos mojados,
> que forra un mal sabor a sacos de patatas,
> uncido a los estiércoles y fangales pegados
> en las cansinas botas más rigidas que patas.[1]

Alberti saw these peasant soldiers, ignorant of their cause, yet fired by the hope that they could 'kill death in order to gain life', as men at one with the soil that they were destined soon to feed with their bodies. Spain, he believed, must be dunged with the bodies of her sons, in order that a new life could spring up. The war was lost, no new life sprang up, and the poet himself was driven into exile.

The later poetry of Rafael Alberti is a poetry of exile, written for the most part in Argentina, a country of which he has not made himself part. Always he looks back on the Andalusia of his youth and early manhood. Yet the later poetry has almost none of the bewilderment of *Sobre los ángeles*. The sense of loss is pure and the retrospect unstained by self-pity. Gradually there has come, after the poignancy of the first exile, an emptiness that

---

[1] You see them marching hard, the colour of bark that repels the torch's attack and does not change. Like flints, their heads are dark, but there is fire in their dream as in fruit rind.
Their great capes smell of wet lambs, with linings reeking like potato sacks, greased with the dung and mire that sticks to their worn-out boots which are stiffer than animals' legs.

repeats that of some moods recorded in the Angel poems, but always with greater resolution. Alberti feels the desolation of a great city, Buenos Aires, and the curious rawness of this culturally empty land under the Southern Cross,

> esta desconocido cielo solo,
> sustantado por árboles y montes,
> pampas, mares, y gentes nunca vistos,
> al girar de las horas trastrocadas.[1]

But to this confusion succeeded a deliberate evocation of the civilization left behind and half destroyed by the rebel armies. Alberti began to write first of the painters in the Prado Museum, then of his own boyhood and youth in the south, and finally, on the occasion of the trimillennary of the foundation of the city of Cádiz, of Spain in the long perspective of its history. His poetry has thus gained in breadth and assurance. Few poets since the Symbolists can move with his certainty and deliberation in the address to Menestheus. This was the Homeric hero whom Strabo credits with a voyage past the pillars of Hercules, to touch at that seaboard where Cádiz was afterwards founded:

> Hoy quisiera tu antigua espada homérida,
> tu valor, tu anteniense, clara sabiduría.
> Tronchadas las Columnas de Alcides, presa y rota
> su inexpugnable fortaleza, oh, surge,
> levántate y recorre las arenas. Tus naves,
> todavía arboladas, te esperan junto al rio.

The measure is classical, and the assurance of the line suggests that heroic style demanded by Arnold, but hitherto, on account of the modern poets' uncertainties, absent from modern poetry. *Ora maritima* (Sea shore) of 1953, the volume in which this poem appears, is the only book of Alberti's that is permitted to be sold in Spain. It is strange that the censorship has not noticed this eloquent plea for the reconquest of the country by a Hercules who incarnates the Europeanizing forces defeated in the civil war. The poems of this collection reflect, however, a deep understand-

---

[1] This unknown, solitary sky, sustained by trees and mountains, pampas, trees, and peoples never seen (before), to the revolution of hours turned upside down.

[2] Today I long for your ancient Homeric sword, your valour, your Athenian, clear wisdom. The columns of Alcides (Hercules) are cut down, his impregnable fortress taken and destroyed, oh rise up, raise yourself and run across the sands once more. Your ships, still masted, await you beside the river.

ing of historical processes on the part of a poet who once brashly attached himself to the Communist party. Its predecessor, published a year earlier, *Retornos a lo vivo lejano* (Returns to the living and distant) attempts, in the manner of Browning in his *Parleyings with Certain People*, to view the long succession of the poet's dead selves returning from his far-away European life. Here too he is trying to acquire a sense of history, though on a personal plane. He seems to be searching for some permanent entity in himself, for something behind this succession of past states, like the quality which long ago made him accept the rose as more truly a rose when lived in by caterpillars, which now makes him accept life even as he moves forward into death:

> ¡Ah, no poder de pronto empujar tanta noche,
> tantos compactos años de terror, y rompiéndolos
> arrebatar al fin esa vedada
> luz que sabes que existe,
> que por saber que existe
> hasta contando marchas de verdad a la muerte![1]

The first meaning of this light is no doubt liberty and justice, seen as the powers that will overthrow the present régime in Spain. But there appears to be a secondary application to the poet's own life, a hope that he will emerge from uncertainty and rootlessness, in a country strange both spiritually and physically, where even the seasons are reversed. On the strength of these two volumes it is possible to think of Alberti as a poet still gaining assurance and still exploring new territory. Some light ballads that have appeared recently show no further signs of the poet's eventual direction. But there is throughout much of this late work the promise of spiritual or psychological development. Alberti, having perfected a style over many years, is now with Pasternak and the Chilean Pablo Neruda, one of the few important poets from whom further progress may be expected.

The poetry of resistance in France for a moment found a similar popularity to that of Lorca's poetry in the Spanish civil war. Circulated in clandestine pamphlets during the German occupation, it seemed to promise a new bond of union between writers and the people. The chief resistant poets were former

[1] Oh, not to be able to push away all this night, all these packed years of terror, and by breaking them finally seize the forbidden light that you know exists, and because you know it exists go forward, even singing, actually into death.

surrealists who had simplified their styles under communist influence, and outstanding among them was Paul Eluard.

Paul Eluard's poetry of the 'forties made no radical break with his earlier work. Love had always been his principal theme, and now it was extended from the field of personal relationship to include feeling for his fellows in national humiliation, and for humanity. The transparency, the quick succession of images, and the lack of punctuation mark his poems of this time, despite their publication under pseudonyms, as by the poet of *Capitale de la Douleur*. Even this earlier title was apposite, for Paris was now, far more truly than in the 'thirties, the *Capital of Grief*. Eluard's beliefs were simple. In the new communist world that would follow the defeat of the Germans all wrongs would be punished, all hatred would vanish, and the world would be clean once more. But with this naïvety ran a vein of simple goodness. The poet was capable of love, and he believed the rest of the world to be so too. The past could be buried, he proclaimed in the poem 'Enterrar y callar' (Bury and be Silent) under the full rigour of the occupation, and could then be passed over in silence: here in 1943 he already looked forward to a new dawn:

Frères cette aurore est vôtre
Cette aurore à fleur de terre
Est votre dernière aurore
Vous vous y êtes couchés
Frères cette aurore est nôtre
Sur ce gouffre de douleur

Et par cœur et par courroux
Frères nous tenons à vous
Nous voulons éterniser
Cette aurore qui partage
Votre tombe blanche et noir
L'espoir et le désespoir

La haine sortant de terre
Et combattant pour l'amour
La haine dans la poussière
Ayant satisfait l'amour
L'amour brillant en plein jour
Toujours vit l'espoir sur terre.[1]

[1] Brothers, this dawn is yours, this dawn at earth's level is your last dawn, and you are bedded on it, brothers, this dawn is ours over this gulf of sorrow.
And by our heart and our anger, brothers, we stand by you, we wish to immortalize this dawn which shares your tomb of black and white, hope and despair.
Hate springing from the ground and fighting for love, hate in the dust, having satisfied love, love burning in broad daylight, always sees hope on earth.

The poem commemorates comrades murdered by the
Germans, yet its sorrow is outbalanced by its hope, its hatred
consumed by love. Hatred indeed is described as fighting for love,
and of falling to the dust when it has yielded to love. Many of
Eluard's war-poems contain hideous images, yet they are far
less hideous than those employed by Lorca to describe a peaceful
New York. The nightmare is continuous, but is always relieved by
the promise of an eventual awakening. These lyrics have the
clarity of Blake or John of the Cross, yet without any supernatural overtones. Eluard is the poet of life upon earth as its
purest, of life in which the coarsest scribbling on the wall will be
a poem. He experimented after the war with a *Poesie ininter-
rompue*, which he considered to be his most important work, and
which he wished to be read straight through, like a newspaper.
The first of these continuous works is a love poem which with
repetitions leads from darkness to light, by way of gnomically
ecstatic statements:

Le soleil naît sur la tranche d'un fruit
La lune naît au sommet de mes seins
Le soleil fuit sur la rosée
La lune se limite
La vérité c'est que j'aimais
Et la vérité c'est que j'aime
De jour en jour l'amour me prend première
Pas de regrets j'ignore tout d'hier
Je ne ferai pas de progrès.[1]

Eluard appears to be feeling towards a poetry of the living
minute, in contrast to which he presents the man divided, with
his eyes fixed on the past, 'the man of slow barbarities', the Nazi
torturer who fought for love and did not find it:

L'homme à l'instinct brouillé
A la chair en exil
L'homme aux clartés de serre
Aux yeux fermés l'homme aux éclairs
L'homme mortel et divisé
Au front saignant d'espoir
L'homme en butte au passé [2]

[1] The sun is born on a slice of fruit, the moon is born on the tip of my breasts, the sun
flees on the dew, the moon is confined, the truth is that I loved, and the truth is that I
love, from day to day love take me first, without regrets I know nothing of yesterday,
I shall make no progress.

[2] Man of clouded instinct, of flesh in exile, man like a flashing greenhouse with
closed eyes, man of lightning, man mortal and divided with his forehead bleeding hope,
man exposed to the past.

Eluard failed to create the natural poetry at which he aimed, and two years later in the poem 'La Poésie doit avoir pour but la Vérité pratique' (Poetry must have practical truth as its goal) accused his friends of accepting his personal imagery and private statements, but refusing to draw the necessary political conclusions. It was perhaps only in the last months of his life, and in his very last poems that he divorced himself as conclusively from the future as he had long ago from the past. A poem finished just before the onset of his final illness, *Blason dédoré de mes Rêves* (Tarnished blazon of my dreams), goes so far in its acceptance as to proclaim that truth can exist without its opposite, that

> Il n'est pas une erreur au monde
> Le jour banal et la nuit ordinaire
> Et des attaches pour toujours
> Avec un point fixe la vie
> Ni bonne ni mauvaise.[1]

And beyond this point, Eluard, a poet seemingly without religious belief, could see a life that began rather than ended at death. It is with this affirmation that his last poem ends:

> Non je dors et malgré le pouvoir de la nuit
> J'apprends comme un enfant que je vais m'éveiller
> Mes draps sont le linceul de mes rêves je vis
>
> Et du gouffre je passe à la lumière blonde
> Et je respire comme un amoureux se pâme
> Comme un fleuve se tisse sous une hirondelle
>
> Je sais que je ne suis pas seul ma fièvre augmente
> Je m'élance et je monte et j'affirme mon but
> Je suis enfin sorti de mon sommeil je vis.[2]

Still a master of the compressed image of his surrealist days, still as direct as in the years of the Resistance, Eluard here added another dimension to his poetry, writing, at the last, in praise of

---

[1] It is not an error in the world, commonplace day and ordinary night, and attachments for ever as a fixed point, life neither good nor bad.

[2] No, I am sleeping, and despite the power of the night I am learning like a child, that I am going to wake. My sheets are the shroud of my dreams, I am alive. And from the gulf I pass to the fair light and I breathe as a lover faints, as a river weaves itself beneath a swallow, I know that I am not alone, my fever increases, I throw myself forward and climb and I affirm my goal, I have at last emerged from my dream, I am alive.

a liberty beyond that of surrealism, the liberty to awake from dreams.

A parallel poetry grew up in Italy in the next years, during which the country suffered under allied air-raids, under invasion and conquest, and under the suppression of her occupying ally and the demoralized Fascist party. In this situation, Ungaretti played the part of Eluard, in his ability to see Italy's fate with the wide vision of one whose private sorrow chimed with sorrow for his country. *Il dolore* speaks most profoundly of the 'silent cry of the dead' who suffered in no cause but paid most dearly for Italy's brief spell of false grandeur. Eugenio Montale, on the other hand, was as hermetic in his wartime poems as ever before. His remarkable 'La Primavera Hitleriana' (Hitler's Spring) describes the Führer's parade through Rome 'flashing past amidst the chanting of henchmen', an occasion that Montale thinks of as 'a holiday still if it freezes this death to death.' Here public and private imagery are mixed. Parts of the poem are as mysterious as 'Eastbourne' or 'Barche sulla Marna', but the conclusion is a clear paean of hope that dawn may rise again for everybody over the parched wadis of Africa—where the Italian army was then going down in defeat:

> Forse le sirene, i rintocchi
> che salutano i mostri nella sera
> della loro tregenda si confondono già
> col suono che slegato dal cielo, scende, vince—
> col respiro d'un alba che domani per tutti
> si riaffacci, bianca ma senz' ali
> di riccapriccio, ai greti arsi del sud. . . . [1]

Salvator Quasimodo (b. 1901) is an idyllic poet of the South who has been saved from a pleasing smoothness by a haunting sense that even the Sicily of his childhood happiness was threatened by the cruelty which made him for a brief moment Italy's first poet of the Resistance, and turned him afterwards into a political partisan of the left. His originality is less one of subject than of accent; his achievement is chiefly remarkable for a *depuración*, which has at times made his utterance gnomic. Here,

---

[1] Perhaps the sirens, the tolling bells that greet the monsters on the evening of their witches' Sabbath are already mingling with the sound that, unloosed from heaven, descends, conquered,—with the breathing of a dawn that tomorrow, for everyone, breaks again, white, but without wings of horror, over the scorched wadis of the south. . . .

if the example was Ungaretti's, the manner was Quasimodo's own. He had already perfected it in a few of the poems in his first volume of 1930, *Acque e terre* (Waters and Lands), as for instance in 'Vento a Tindari (Wind at Tindari), in which he addresses his native country from the hostile north:

> A te ignota è la terra
> ove ogni giorno affondo
> e segrete sillabe nutro:
> altra luce ti sfoglia sopra i vetri
> nelle veste notturna,
> e gioia non mia riposa
> sul tuo gremio

> Aspro è l'esilio,
> e la ricerca che chiudevo in te
> d'armonia oggi si muta
> in ansia precoce di morire... [1]

The style was already prepared for the moment when the fear of death seemed no longer premature; for the twenty poems of *Giorno dopo Giorno* (Day after day), written during the worst days of the war and published in 1947. Here devastation is expressed in single images of telling economy:

> Io ti ricordo quel geranio acceso
> su un muro crivellato di mitraglia. [2]

With similar economy he characterized the whole spirit of these war-years, as in the poem 'Uomo del mio Tempo' (Man of my time)

> Hai ucciso ancora,
> come sempre, come uccisero i padri, come uccisero
> gli animali che li videro per la prima volta.
> E questo sangue odora come nel giorno
> quando il fratello disse all' altro fratello:
> 'Andiamo ai campi.' E quell' eco fredda, tenace,
> è giunta fino a te, dentro la tua giornata. [3]

[1] The land is unknown to you where each day I grow deep and feed secret syllables; another light unfolds you above your windows, against night's dress, and joy not mine lies in your lap, Harsh is exile and my search for harmony which ended with you is changed today into a premature feat of death.

[2] I call to your memory that flaming geranium on a wall riddled with machine-gun shot.

[3] You have killed again, as always, as your fathers killed, as they killed the animals that saw them for the first time. And this blood smells as on the day when one brother said to the other brother: 'Let us go to the fields.' And that cold, clinging echo is attached to you within your day.

H

Quasimodo here, like Eluard in his poems of 1943, clothes the essential situation in verse which is modern, yet which reverts to a symbolism that is also dateless. Like Eluard, and in the same political terms, Quasimodo sees the promise of a future that shall be free of fears; it is on this note that his poem continues and concludes:

> Dimenticate, o figli, le nuvole di sangue
> salite dalla terra, dimenticate i padri:
> le loro tombe affondano nella cenere,
> gli uccelli neri, il vento, coprono il loro cuore.[1]

Quasimodo's later poetry has developed this theme of hope, but never so profoundly as in these war-poems. Much of the best among his later work is translated from Greek and Latin. For while Quasimodo owes his unrhetorical style to such moderns as Rimbaud, Campana and Ungaretti, his debt is even greater to those older literatures with which he feels his native Sicily still to be deeply imbued.

The poetry of resistance in England is represented by a group of poets who began to write in the 'thirties, who were more or less deeply influenced by a theoretical Marxism, but who, with the exception of W. H. Auden (b. 1907), did not develop their poetry far beyond its point of origin. C. Day Lewis and Louis MacNeice are pleasing and accomplished writers in a tradition that owes everything to Hardy and Yeats. They were deflected only at the beginning by Auden's verve, his bold experimentalism and his freely voiced scorn for the 'old gang'.

Auden is a traditionalist also, but one who has made a new choice of poetic ancestors. Hardy, Owen and Gerard Manley Hopkins among the moderns, together with ballads, folk-songs and the alliterative poets of the Middle Ages, guided him in the development of a style which was new, but in the poetic doldrums of the early 'thirties appeared even newer than it was. Though in fact Robert Graves had by that time worked himself free both from Victorian grandeur and Georgian smugness, Auden appeared the more original poet of the two on account of his more contemporary choice of images: idle factories, abandoned mines, and rusting railway tracks.

---

[1] Forget, o sons, the clouds of blood risen from the earth, forget your fathers: their tombs sink in the ashes, the black birds, the wind, cover their heart.

Auden stands in the same relationship to the European poets of Resistance as Dylan Thomas to the surrealists. Where Thomas, though no surrealist, produced the English equivalent to the poetry, if not of Breton, at least of Aleixandre, an equivalent parallel can be found in Auden's work to certain characteristics of Alberti, Eluard or Quasimodo, all of whom experienced the cataclysm at first hand that Auden only knew as a sympathetic visitor and in the imagination.

Auden has been from the beginning a poet of uncertain taste, and of divided intention. His rebellion, which coincides with the first ten years of his activity, was two-fold, against the repressions of a dead morality, and against what he considered a corrupt form of social organization. In his first *Poems* there are many passages that promise, like those of Eluard or Quasimodo, a quick dawning of love and a quick wiping away of the blood, which must inevitably be shed. Auden's idea of revolution was, however, never purely political; what he demanded was an individual change of heart magnified to mass proportions. At first his poetry was devoted to an examination of the symptoms of decay around him and a warning of the fate awaiting society:

> It is time for the destruction of error.
> The chairs are being brought in from the garden,
> The summer talk stopped on that savage coast
> Before the storms, after the guests and birds:
> In sanatoriums they laugh less and less,
> Less certain of cure; and the loud madman
> Sinks now into a more terrible calm.

This is a poetry of crisis, deliberately flat in tone, yet rendered more threatening by the everyday nature of its imagery. The background is the Great Slump of 1929, which woke English poets to the reality of politics. But for all that, the menace of revolution is for Auden, even in his communistic phase, only an intellectual figment. His real concern is on the psychological side, with the idea of love as the volcanic destroyer of the stagnant autumn landscape of the poet's mind and of his times. But tempted in part by Rimbaud's example in *Les Illuminations*, in part by a juvenile liking for make-believe, secret societies, and practical jokes, Auden adopted in his second book *The Orators*, a farrago of verse and prose, a language so esoteric and at the same time so trivial as to suggest a serious flaw in his creative faculties.

This flaw existed in the form of an intellectual naïvety, which has always prevented his distinguishing between private symbolism, which can be understood by any attentive reader, and coterie language, which cannot. To read Auden, one must be familiar with the factual details of the writer's life; in his case with the jargon of prep-schoolmastering, psychoanalysis, Marxist theory, and, more recently, of certain brands of religious philosophy. What is so often lacking is sufficient emotion to give it living shape. Even in those poems where a breath of this missing element seems about to make all clear, the esoteric fog of allusion may close down again at any instant, as in the poem addressed to an older man, an uncle perhaps, the ninth in his best volume, *Look Stranger!* of 1936:

> Your portrait hangs before me on the wall
> And there what view I wish for, I shall find,
> The wooded or the stony—though not all
> The painter's gifts can make its flatness round—
>
> Through the blue irises the heaven of failures
> The mirror world where knowledge is reversed,
> Where age becomes the handsome child at last,
> The glass sea parted for the country sailors.
>
> Where move the enormous comics, drawn from life,
> My father as an Airedale and a gardener,
> My mother chasing letters with a knife:
> You are not present as a character.

From a subtle character sketch of an entertaining and childlike failure, allusively drawn, we drop in the first three lines of the third verse quoted into the world of family jokes, almost meaningless to strangers. In Auden's later poetry the learned allusion has come to take the place of the family joke.

A further weakness lies in Auden's apparent uncertainty concerning the poet's function. There are moments, as in his off-hand ballads, when one may wonder whether he takes the creative process at all seriously. Perhaps it seems no more to him then than 'a special illness of the ear', to quote a phrase from his sonnet-biography of Rimbaud. At other times, moreover, he states that integrity is not enough, adopts the gestures of a preacher, and sees himself as the only carrier of truth to 'lying men'.

The cause of this uncertainty of grip seems to lie in a fundamental poverty of experience. In contrast to Pasternak, a poet similarly anxious to relate his private perceptions to their historical setting, Auden remained outside the crisis that was his subject. When Pasternak compared the Russian revolution to a locomotive that tossed everyone like straw in its wake, one was aware that he too, while remaining at a mental distance from events, was also carried along with them. Auden was not. From the beginning he was concerned with the idea of a personal Christian God. Yet God to him was merely a hypothesis compounded of father, doctor and schoolmaster, and the religious language a medium which he felt justified in setting aside for a psychoanalytical jargon, modish when he wrote his first poems but now somewhat curious. His prayer or expostulation in the sonnet 'Sir, no man's enemy' takes the form of a reasoned argument into which semi-religious metaphors enter only in the last lines:

> Prohibit sharply the rehearsed response
> And gradually correct the coward's stance;
> Cover in time with beams those in retreat
> That, spotted, they turn though the reverse was great;
> Publish each healer that in city lives
> Or country houses at the end of drives;
> Harrow the house of the dead; look shining at
> New styles of architecture, a change of heart.

Auden is speaking sincerely enough of the change of heart. But this is a subject difficult to approach directly until the performing troupe of intellectual ideas ceases curveting, and clever thoughts no longer obscure the simple play of the emotions. The burden of the poem is obscured however by the restlessness of the language. Auden is not content with a single set of references, but jumbles up a number of dubious sciences in an argumentation that just keeps above the level of schoolboy patter. In many other poems, however, he drops below that level.

In 'Spain 1937', which belongs to a later volume, Auden comes near to writing a poem of resistance, since the issue of Spain was, as has been said, a simpler one for his generation than the apparently more complicated rights and wrongs of the world war that followed. But even here he moves uneasily between the naïvety of

> Tomorrow the bicycle races
> Through the suburbs on summer evenings; but today the struggle,

and the broader perception of its last lines:

> The stars are dead; the animals will not look:
> We are left alone with our day, and the time is short and History
>   to the defeated
> May say Alas but cannot help or pardon.

In the last passage there is a hint of tragedy, and it is in the contradiction between this pessimistic prognosis and Auden's buoyancy in his advocacy of causes that a further weakness of his poetry lies. Throughout his poetic life, he has been, to use his own metaphor, one who while living in a city has never ceased to 'dream of islands'. Logically, he told himself, the poet's task is rather to 'rebuild our cities' than to dream of an escape world:

> Where every day was dancing in the valleys,
> And all the year trees blossomed on the mountains,
> Where love was innocent, being far from cities.

In actuality he abandoned the Isle of Wight,

> that southern island
> Where the wild Tennyson became a fossil,

and even the British Isles, which had for him in the years of Hitler's rise to power something of the significance that they had had for Shakespeare when he wrote John of Gaunt's dying speech—

> This fortress perched on the edge of the Atlantic scarp,
> The mole between all Europe and the exile-crowded sea,

he called it—for the anonymity of life in the vast city of New York. The reasons for this migration, which had serious effects on Auden's poetry, can be seen in the poetry itself. In his finest single volume, *Look Stranger!* of 1936, the tension is between dream and reality, between the private and the public life, between sterility and a postulated purity of emotion. As an anatomist of sterility, Auden based himself on the theories of the German doctor Grodek, who advanced the view that all illness is caused by psychical maladjustment. This is why he presents his father and mother as 'the doctor and the nurse' in Poem IX of *Look Stranger!* from which the passage on a portrait has already been quoted. Doctor and nurse exist only to put cushions behind the heads of patients who enjoy their suffering, but should rise from their beds and walk. A guilty consciousness of his inability to carry out this drastic measure of self-help colours most of Auden's poetry of this epoch. Lacking emotion, he reproaches himself for his lack. He is, in relation to persons, and by ambiguous overtone, to God,

> Your would-be lover who has never come
> In the great bed at midnight to your arms.

How deep is Auden's fundamental despair appears from the penultimate verse:

> Language of moderation cannot hide;
> My sea is empty and the waves are rough:
> Gone from the map the shore where childhood played
> Tight-fisted as a peasant, eating love;
> Lost in my wake the archipelago,
> Islands of self through which I sailed all day,
> Planting a pirate's flag, a generous boy;
> And lost the way to action and to you.

The 'way to action' had been the subject of Auden's first poems. But by now he has recognized that the way to revolution by political action or by the mass change-of-heart is blocked. The only hope lies in the abandonment of the personal will; once will is abandoned the obstacle will prove 'illusive'. So the poem continues:

> Lost if I steer. Gale of desire may blow
> Sailor and ship past the illusive reef,
> And I yet land to celebrate with you
> Birth of a natural order and of love.

Auden's next book, *Another Time*, contains a couple of love-lyrics, but for the rest is made up of intellectual commentary, of wittily contrived poems largely devoted to people and places. The poet is no longer in search of islands, nor yet of any conceivable continent on which he may land. Having abandoned Britain and his hopes of 'a natural order', he no longer protests, but analyses the plight of earlier victims of this paralysis of the will. On the one hand he had understood what the promptings had been even from the beginning of his life:

> Love was the word they never said aloud,

and on the other he identified himself with Voltaire, haunted by all the evil that he could not prevent, but unable to oppose it except by compulsive orgies of work:

> The night was full of wrong,
> Earthquakes and executions. Soon he would be dead,
> And still over Europe stood the horrible nurses
> Itching to boil their children. Only his verses
> Perhaps could stop them: He must go on working. Overhead
> The uncomplaining stars composed their lucid song.

Voltaire's verses were, of course, ineffective. Most of them, in fact, are now unreadable. By comparing himself to a poet who so conclusively failed, Auden betrays his reason for leaving a society in which he belonged for the life of an unknown person in New York. He had abandoned hope of influencing his surroundings; there remained only personal problems. The curiously tasteless comparison of Europe's rulers to 'Horrible nurses itching to boil their children' reveals detached exasperation. Some of the jazz-lyrics in this same volume are equally off-hand in their descriptions of illness and disaster. The hopes of the 'thirties were over, and the poet could hardly believe any more even in the efficacy of pity.

The note of resistance is muted, therefore, to that of mere protest in the poem which states his feelings sitting 'in one of the dives on Fifty-Second Street' on the outbreak of war. 'September 1, 1939' makes a tremendous statement, yet admits the poet's impotence to implement the truth which he has discovered:

> All I have is a voice
> To undo the folded lie,
> The romantic lie in the brain
> Of the sensual man-in-the-street
> And the lie of Authority

Whose buildings grope the sky:
There is no such thing as the State
And no one exists alone;
Hunger allows no choice
To the citizen or the police;
We must love one another or die.

The poet has since disowned this poem, dropping the tell-tale
anarchy of the last lines quoted from his list of permissible
responses. The protest is over. His next poem, *New Year Letter*,
is a prolonged meditation, which contains a few lyrical passages
of great beauty amidst a waste of digressive doggerel. But what
the subject of Auden's meditation is, and what are his findings:
this is not revealed. He is said to have adopted a Christian
philosophy. Evidence for this rests on private statements; the
poetry is to this day muddled in its statements, clever in its
acrobatic off-beat rhythms, and ultimately defeatist. The poet has
taken refuge on an island of intellectualism from which he
fervently proclaims in the most intellectual of language that
intellectualism is a barren pursuit.

Poetry of resistance has died in most European countries
since there is no longer any belief in the purity of causes, or in the
likelihood that rebelling against the present will lead to anything
better by way of a future. In Spain alone, the seat of a brainless
dictatorship, which exercises a random censorship in the combined names of Church, Army and Party, a poetic literature has
arisen which protests not in the name of any political ideal, but
for bare liberty and on behalf of the dignity of man.

H *

Virgin soil

THE problem of the American poet differs from that of the European in two important ways. He is more uncertain of his public, which will not only be limited but will generally be judging him by foreign standards. For the cultures of the New World are still so insecurely based that they are affected by every new fashion from Europe. He is also less certain of his linguistic resources, and swings between extremes of literary language, far from the spoken idiom of his surroundings, and extremes of colloquialism, from which he hopes a new literary language will one day be born. For the American of New York and Chicago, the Argentinian of Buenos Aires and the Mexican of the Federal Capital, are neither new languages nor old. Rhythmically and in their pronunciation, as well as in their vocabulary, they differ so widely from the parent tongue that a common literary inheritance counts for very little. To read Wallace Stevens and Ezra Pound in the accents of Southern England, or Ricardo Molinari, Pablo Neruda and Octavio Paz in correct Castilian is to lose their rhythms and assonances, and to miss their native quality as badly as the reader of Catullus and Virgil misses the lost sound of classical Latin.

Moreover neither the poet himself nor his reader is necessarily of English or Spanish descent. The parent branch of the poet's idiom may be to him almost a foreign tongue. It is for this reason, as much as for reasons of nationalism, that French poetry and fashions have since the middle of the nineteenth century exerted a more profound effect in the Americas than Spanish or English; and the situation has developed so far in the last twenty years that there is no literature of which a Spanish American is so ignorant as of that of contemporary Spain, while in North America quite minor European reputations count for much more than they do in Britain. It is true that new cultures are being born, but the birth is extremely slow. Hardly anything as yet has been produced in North America that has not its roots in Europe. Whitman's independence has been an isolated phenomenon; Pound, Stevens, and the younger men of today are all engaged in a dance of attraction and repulsion around the totems of European culture.

In South America, on the other hand, though one figure of Whitmanlike proportions, Pablo Neruda, has arisen in contemporary Chile, the only movement that promises something new is that of contemporary Mexico, where Aztec and pre-Aztec art and culture are now being blended with the inheritance of the conquerors and their descendants. The United States had nothing in its Indian past that could modify its European inheritance. Till the time of Edgar Allan Poe American literature was a provincial variant of English. Longfellow takes an Indian subject for his famous 'Hiawatha', but the poem is no more Indian than Southey's epics were Aztec or Arabic. Whitman's break-away was not exploited by his successors. His American rhythms and his free-verse, based to some extent on the language of the Bible, were a suitable medium only for a poet who wished to make broad statements. As a medium for lyrical poetry, it was less effective than the French varieties of vers-libre adopted by the chief twentieth-century poets in both continents. Poe, though his romanticism descends from Shelley's, came nearer to modernism in his use of such symbols as the Raven than Whitman in his striving for a new form. Both alike exercised considerable influence abroad, being the first American poets to do so. But the effect of Europe upon America has remained, almost to the present day, far greater than the contrary influence started by these two nineteenth-century figures. The two most important American poets of the modernist movement, Ezra Pound (b. 1885) and Wallace Stevens (1879-1955) are completely European in their derivations, though Pound, in particular, has endeavoured to develop a variety of voices, colloquial, allusive, multi-lingual, European and American, that shall speak for twentieth-century man.

In its beginnings Pound's poetry was extremely literary, and much influenced by Robert Browning's. He was capable of many kinds of pastiche and free translation, and was not afraid, despite

his origins in Idaho, to imitate even the Northumbrian of the
Border ballads. His Provençal settings, soon to be succeeded by
Chinese, are picturesque trappings. The overall impression of his
poetry from 1908 to 1914 is of an aestheticism sustained by great
mastery of technique. It was Pound who first experimented with
the broken monologue of Laforgue, which was used by Eliot with
greater effect in 'Prufrock'. Pound's preparatory sketch for
Eliot's poem is entitled 'Villanelle: the Psychological Hour:'

> I had over-prepared the event,
>   that much was ominous.
> With middle-aging care
>   I had laid out just the right books,
> I had almost turned down the pages.

Half-way between Browning and Eliot, Pound inhabited a series
of dream countries, and succeeded in convincing himself that
they were real. He achieved his most beautiful effects, however,
when as an imagist, he was content to abandon his facile allusiveness and concentrate on a single picture and a single sentiment,
as in his treatment of the legend of Daphne transformed into a
laurel, *The Girl*. This is light poetry, and it is as a light poet that
Pound's competence lay. In an introductory quatrain to the
translation of some verses by Heine, he praised the German for
his power of demolishing 'at such polished ease Philistia's pomps
and Art's pomposities'. Of this he was himself capable. But he
longed at the same time to create beauty, to catch the essence of
those age-old civilizations from which as an American he was a
stranger.

>   And in the quietest space
> They probe old scandals, say de Born is dead;
> And we've the gossip (skipped six hundred years).
> Richard shall die tomorrow—leave him there
> talking of *trobar clus* with Daniel.

This is not the dramatic monologue of Robert Browning; it
is, for all its nostalgia for the past, always half-ironic. The early
Pound is in the same position as Eliot before the 'Waste Land' of
having no belief, and not actively searching for any. In his short
sequence 'Hugh Selwyn Mauberley', he does not advance far in
any new direction. What he delicately satirizes in the first is the

old civilization, the new American's yearning to absorb it, and the effeteness of the New American himself. 'H. S. Mauberley' is a poem concerned with the dilemma so often stated by Henry James. But it differs from a James story in finding no hope either in the old or the new. The poem ends in the same mood as it has opened, with an elegy for its subject, apparently killed in the war. Pound here dismisses the past (or rather the cult of the past), and also dismisses idealism:

> Died some, pro patria,
>   non 'dulce' non 'et decor' . . .
> walked eye-deep in hell
> believing in old men's lies, then unbelieving
> came home, home to a lie.

and he dismisses all hope of making an art for the present:

> The 'age demanded' chiefly a mould in plaster,
> Made with no loss of time,
> A prose kinema, not, not assuredly, alabaster
> Or the 'sculpture' of rhyme.

What Pound had actually to offer was an ironic preoccupation with the past; his poems are, like Eliot's, a patchwork of references; his voice, like Joyce's in the public-house scene of *Ulysses*, takes a variety of accents all freely imitated from the masters.

'Homage to Sextus Propertius', Pound's most important poem before the *Cantos*, is a free rendering of passages from the Latin poet to whom it is addressed. Developing the manner of 'H. S. Mauberley', it has moments of beauty, which depend on perfect and isolated images, a delicate cadence or the timely placing of an echo from Propertius himself. It is, however, interspersed with banalities, which set out to cheapen the Latin past, bringing it down to the level of the ugly American present.

> Though you make a hash of Antimachus,
> You think you are going to do Homer,

he says to Propertius's friend Lynceus, and then, parodying the Propertian note of sensual irony, attacks the faithless and feather-brained young ladies, who are the real subject of his poem:

Of all these young women
    not one has enquired the cause of the world
Nor the modus of lunar eclipses
    Nor whether there be any patch left of us
After we cross the infernal ripples,

'There is a strange discrepancy', wrote Edmund Wilson in reviewing a volume of Pound which contained most of his early poetry, 'between Pound's ideals and his ability to incorporate them in his work. It is as if his conception of style had matured while his taste had remained immature. Everything in life seems to remind him of something in literature.'

The *Cantos*, of which Pound has written almost a hundred in the last thirty-five years are, to quote Wilson once more, full of fine passages . . . that, standing by themselves might lead us to believe them mere ornaments from a masterpiece on the great scale.' Yet the whole work is 'a mosaic which fails to reveal a pattern, a monument, in its lack of cohesion, its lack of driving force or a centre, to a kind of poetic bankruptcy.' Pound who could give lessons to Eliot, and even to Yeats, in poetic technique, who knew better than most of his contemporaries in what the highest poetry consists, has composed only a patchwork, from which could be selected a hundred little poems, few more than a dozen lines long, to form an Imagist anthology. Between Greek phrase and Greek phrase printed in the original will come a lyrical passage rich with the sight and sound and history of the Mediterranean:

The small lamps drift in the bay
And the sea's claw gathers them.
Neptunus drinks after neap-tide.
Tamuz! Tamuz!
The red flame going seaward
    By this gate art thou measured.
From the long boats they have set lights in the water,
The sea's claw gathers them outward.

This evocation of the sea would not suffer from a comparison with some of Eliot's descriptive passages in 'The Waste Land' or the *Quartets*. Yet Neptunus, Tamuz, Scilla recall only a museum of antiquities. Unlike Eliot, Pound makes no statement that will reconcile past and present in a single myth. He remains the provincial American, fascinated by the art and history of Europe,

contemptuous of his fellow-Americans who do not accept these
values, and equally contemptuous of the degenerate European
culture which fails to live up to them. The *Cantos*, in so far as they
contain any reasoned argument, are the record of Pound's search
for a cause of this degeneracy, and of his own failure to strike
roots either in the Old World or the New. Nowhere in his poetry
does he look inward. The plight of Ezra Pound 'born in a half
savage country out of date', like that of his opposite, Mr. Styrax
who 'does not believe in aesthetics', had only one cause. In the
poet's view the world was governed by 'Usura'—a wrong money
policy—which dates back to the Renaissance:

> With usura hath no man a house of good stone
> each block cut smooth and well fitting
> that design might cover their face.
> with usura
> hath no man a painted paradise on his church wall
> *harpes et luthes.*

From this curious centre radiates the whole web of Pound's
allusions and opinions. Hence arises his anti-Semitism, his
admiration of Mussolini, his concern with the American civil
war, in which he sees the wrong side winning, his social and
monetary theories, his anger against financiers, profiteers and
munition makers, and against 'Governments full of their gun-
swine, bankbuzzards, poppinjays'. But the weaver of this web
remains the sensitive and clever young man from Idaho who
accepts himself without reservations and believes that perhaps in
the heyday of Confucianism or in Greece or Florence there might
have been a place of honour for one of such learning and accomplishment as himself. Most of the beautiful passages in the
Cantos evoke one or another of these paradises. Yet hardly a
Canto is free from perverse vituperations. Even the impressionist
evocation of a long-ago China in XLIX, inspired, no doubt, by
some painting upon silk, is marred by an angry reference to
Pound's obsessive theme.

While Pound's poetry is marred by an excess of undigested
opinion, by emotion that is never tranquil, the fault of Wallace
Stevens is a too great tranquillity, a failure indeed to state any
belief stronger than the wish to live by aestheticism if only
aestheticism were a viable attitude. His richness of verbal resources might suggest a corresponding richness of feeling, but this

is absent. A poem or two by Wallace Stevens pleases, but the collected volume fails.

Stevens, while conscious of the need to find an American poetic language, nevertheless accepts the European literary heritage with less criticism than Pound. He is, at the outset, like Eliot, and like Pound himself, a disciple of Jules Laforgue, the master of the off-hand phrase, of the literary allusion and the sudden reminiscence of a music-hall refrain. He strives for a grand style and comes perilously close to writing pastiche.

> In the high west there burns a furious star.
> It is for fiery boys the star was set
> And for sweet-smelling virgins close to them.
> The measure of the intensity of love
> Is measure, also, of the verve of earth.
> For me, the firefly's quick, electric stroke
> Ticks tediously the time of one more year.
> And you? Remember how the crickets came
> Out of their mother grass, like little kin,
> In the pale nights, when your first imagery
> Found inklings of your bond to all that dust.

The opening lines score a success by the use of emotive adjectives. The poem recalls no actual poem of the past, yet it invokes the whole gamut of poetry from the Elizabethans to the Victorians. 'High west', 'a furious star', 'sweet-smelling virgins': the language calls up a nostalgia for the past. The comparison of the firefly's glimmer to the second's tick on some clock of nature's is, however, metaphysical; and the two manners, in uneasy juxtaposition, achieve the ironic purpose of casting doubt on both thought and feeling. Stevens is primarily an intellectual poet. Sometimes, however, words will guide him into a pleasing jingle like one of Edith Sitwell's in her *Façade* period. 'The Virgin carrying a Lantern' is a little piece of this kind:

> There are no bears among the roses,
> Only a negress who supposes
> Things false and wrong.
>
> About the lantern of the beauty
> Who walks there, as a farewell duty,
> Walks long and long.
>
> The pity that her pious egress
> Should fill the vigil of a negress
> With heat so strong!

'Fictive things wink as they will,' says the poem 'A High-toned old Christian Woman', and 'Poetry is the supreme fiction' is the thought with which it begins. Stevens would like to find a truth deeper than poetry, an attitude more fundamental than a disillusioned aestheticism. In the name of 'the Emperor of Icecream', the sovereign ruler of his age, he calls for the recognition of reality.

> Let be be finale of seem

But his beliefs are off-hand, and literary. Nature can only be described in terms of the artificial; the weather or the scene can best be compared to a waiter or a sweetmeat:

> It had to be right: nougats. It was a shift
> Of realities, that, in which it could be wrong.
> The weather was like a waiter with a tray.
> One had to come early to a crisp café.

The world is for Stevens a place of questions answerable only by an ironic comment, or a second and even more baffling question. Purity of experience or response is absent:

> One goes on asking questions. That, then, is one
> Of the categories. So said, this placid space
>
> Is changed. It is not so blue as we thought. To be blue,
> There must be no questions

Like Laforgue's, this is the poetry of a baffled metaphysician. Stevens could find no such easy answers to his questions as Pound. As president of a large insurance company, he was the servant of that very Usura on which Pound threw the blame for the plight of modern man. Stevens looked for reality, but was confronted always with 'seem'. There seemed to be cultural values; but they had very little to do with reality. Valéry and Yeats looked for reality where they supposed it to lie, with the early Greek philosophers or the Theosophists. Stevens sought it in the arguments of his own brain and, not finding it, shrugged his failure off. Perhaps neither he nor his problems mattered overmuch, he concluded, thus striking a self-depreciatory attitude, which was not uncommon among the American poets of his generation. The cause for this lay in a sense of inferiority in face of a European culture which they could neither absorb nor reject, neither imitate nor rival.

The position of the Spanish American writer differs radically from this in that, although he too is deeply influenced by European, and particularly by French fashions, he has no sense of inferiority. It was indeed from Spanish America that Rubén Darío came to revive Spanish poetry in the 'nineties. *Modernismo* was, in fact, a predominantly American movement, and though Spanish America had no poets to compare with the metropolitan generation of the 'twenties, since the outbreak of the civil war her poetry has been more important than Spain's.

Spanish America has, moreover, a literary tradition with deeper roots than anything that the North can show. Mexico can point to her own poets of the seventeenth century, and recently has come to appreciate a body of indigenous poetry that was already old at the time of the Conquest. Peru too has an ancient tradition, which has as yet, however, exercised little influence on its writing in Spanish; and Argentina and Uruguay possess the 'gaucho' or cowboy epics, narrative poems in dialect that go back to the early nineteenth century. The poetry of Spanish America, nevertheless, until the years of the Mexican revolution, was predominantly European in influence.

The beginnings of the new era in Spanish America fall about the year 1920, by which time Mexico had fought her civil war and had moved into an epoch of radical democracy. This was reflected by similar movements in other republics, most of which were to be checked by the military or landowning reaction in the years that followed. Mexico alone carried through a large scale political change, which gave importance to a cultured middle class. It is consequently the Mexican poets who have developed most promisingly in the last thirty years, although in that time Peru, Chile and Argentina have each produced at least one major talent. The peak of this movement was reached, moreover, at the time of the mother-country's deepest humiliation. Up to the Spanish civil war some links continued to hold between Spain and the Spanish speaking New World. At the moment of the generals' rebellion, two of the chief Spanish-American poets, Pablo Neruda and Octavio Paz occupied diplomatic posts in Spain, and were contributing to Spanish periodicals. The technical similarities between Neruda's and Aleixandre's work were at that time strong. But from the moment of the Republic's overthrow all communications were broken. The poets of America, thrown on their own resources, and finding nothing new in the rest of Europe, began to develop a poetry of their own which, while continuing to owe something to the violences of surrealism, found real imagery quite as violent in the empty and dramatic land-scapes of their own countries.

The four principal Spanish American poets of the last thirty years stand each alone in their own countries, no others approach-ing them in stature. Except Mexico, the home of Octavio Paz, no one of these countries has yet achieved anything that can be thought of as a national literature. Certainly there existed no Peruvian tradition to nourish César Vallejo (1895-1937), a man of mixed Spanish and Indian blood from a small Andean village, to which his poems continually revert. Here he witnessed the early deaths of several members of his family, and here he some-times returned as a young man from the city of Trujillo, to which he had moved in search of a career and where he was put in prison on a political charge.

His earliest poetry, influenced by conventional South American models, was written before he left home. From the first he was obsessed with the prospects of pain and death. The *Heraldos negros* (Black heralds) which give the title to his first book of 1918, are the heralds of death, with which his Indians, like those of Mexico, live on familiar terms. Death's premonitory knocking, which he was to hear so many times in his short life, first sounded for Vallejo in the cracking of newly baked bread that burns the hands as it is taken out of the oven: 'There are blows in life so strong,' he writes, 'that they seem to come from God's hatred:'

> Son las caídas hondas de los Cristos del alma
> de alguno fe adorable que el Destino blasfema.
> Estos golpes sangrientos son las crepitaciones
> de algún pan que en la puerta del horno nos quema.[1]

Another metaphor by which the young poet expresses his inborn despair is equally local. It is drawn from the native game of dice:

[1]They are the great fallings of the Christ of the soul from some blessed faith blasphemed by destiny. Those bloody blows are the cracklings of loaves that burn us at the oven door.

       la Tierra
es un dado roído y ya redondo
a la fuerza de rodar a la aventura,
que no puede parar si no en un hueco
en el hueco de la inmensa sepultura.[1]

Perhaps the image of the worn dice is extended too far; the
hollow of the bone and the hollow of the tomb, though related,
are out of scale. Vallejo, a little like D. H. Lawrence, gives the
impression of often writing while his feelings are too hot. It was
after the failure of this book that he made his final move away
from the Andes. Yet to the last his heart remained there, and in
his exile he longed to hear the clatter of the morning dishes, to
see the copper-faced Romeos, of whom as a boy he had been one.

Vallejo's second book, *Trilce* of 1922, contains poems that
have been subject to many influences—dadaist, surrealist, and
futurist. Yet the best of his poems still refer to his childhood, to
visits to his old home, to the pealing of church bells and the
smell of bakeries, to rain and casual love-affairs. They are full of
a tender directness, rich with the love of things seen and sounds
heard. Here beside poems bitter with memories of his cell, and
hatred of the magistrates who imprisoned him, Vallejo writes of
a proposed journey home:

Madre voy mañana a Santiago,
a mojarme en tu bendición y en tu llanto.
Acomodando estoy mis desengaños y el rosado
de llaga de mis falsos trajines.

Me esperará tu arco de asombro,
las tonsuradas columnas de tus ansias
que se acaban la vida. Me esperará el patio,
el corredor de abajo con sus tondos y repulgos
de fiesta. Me esperará mi sillón ayo,
aquel buen quijarudo, trasto de dinástico
cuero, que pára no más rezongando a las nalgas
tatarietas, de correa a correhuela.[2]

This is a new poetry of America, written in a vocabulary and

---

[1] Earth is a worn dice, and round now from so much random rolling, so that it
cannot stop except in a hollow, in the hollow of the vast tomb.

[2] Mother, I shall go tomorrow to Santiago to wet myself in your blessing and your
tears. I am reconciling myself to my disappointments and to the red sore of my useless
errands. The arch of your fear will await me, and the tonsured columns of your griefs
that put an end to life. The courtyard will await me, and the downstairs passage with its
festival decorations and trimmings. My guardian chair will await me, that good, large-
jawed piece of dynastic leather, which only fits protestingly the great-grandchild's
buttocks, with its great and its small straps (*or* by pulling its straps tight).

with turns of expression local to Vallejo's own land, even to his own province. Its connection with the Spanish tradition is extremely tenuous: its influences are solely those of the French fashions that have licensed Vallejo to abandon the language of literature, and use the words—often prosaic words—that have been his since childhood.

Political indignation following on his imprisonment drove Vallejo to Europe, where he arrived in 1923, speedily to be absorbed in Left-wing politics. For thirteen years he wrote little or no poetry. But under the impact of the Spanish civil war and his own impending death from tuberculosis, he began about 1937 to compose poems less finished than those of his two early books. They are full of a nostalgia for Peru, of foreboding, and of simple political faith. Vallejo faced death without religion, and with mingled fear, defiance and self-pity, and his *Poemas humanos* are a moving diary of his moods. As poetry, the violent and declamatory *España, aparta de mí esta cáliz* (Spain, let this cup pass from me) of 1938 is on a higher level. Here Vallejo hymns the heroes of the Republic, celebrates the bravery of the common militiaman and pours savage scorn on Franco's mercenaries. But the sound of an individual voice is no longer heard; only in their preoccupation with the physical presence of death does the dying poet's mark seem to be upon them; otherwise they reproduce the common idiom of their time.

There are few points in common between Vallejo, the angry and despairing exile in Europe, and Ricardo Molinari (b. 1898), the resigned exile in the midst of his native Argentina. Yet both illustrate aspects of their own continent, and of its poetry as a plant that is at least establishing roots in a hostile or indifferent soil. Where Vallejo reproduces the detail of a full landscape and a life abounding in emotion and events, Molinari reflects a different facet of this continent that has not yet been called to life: its emptiness, its wide skies and its slow-moving muddy rivers. Molinari's Argentina is for the most part an unpopulated country, haunted only by memories or by premonitions of an intense life one day to be born. His is not a pessimistic poetry, but rather, like Aleixandre's in Spain, with which it has some technical kinship, the history of a heart that feels itself at one with the great processes of nature. His principal collection of 1943, made up of selections from a number of small books published over sixteen years, is entitled *Mundos de la madrugada* (Worlds of the Dawn). In it there can be traced the influence and the abandonment of a number of passing styles, and the final adoption of a long and finely cadenced vers-libre, alternating with fixed forms based on the seventeenth-century sonnet and the traditional poetry of the Spanish song-books. These two modes of writing have gradually been pulled together to build up sequences of varying mood, similar, though on a smaller scale, to T. S. Eliot's in his *Four Quartets*.

It is not until the Odes in the last sections of *Mundos de la madrugada* that Molinari's poetry reached its maturity. Here the two themes of landscape and memory coalesce:

> En el Sur tormentoso estoy viviendo; donde el polvo cubre hasta la
> hez la hoja
> y la sal muerde la raíz desesperada;
> donde los ríos llevan al mar una tierra áspera
> que ya no empujan las hierbas y sólo mecen
> los vientos. ¡El Sur perdido! (Donde nadie ha de quitarme ya la
> perfume de una boca,
> que llevo pegado
> en los labios.)[1]

Molinari's rhythms are melancholy. Sometimes these poems touch on moments of horror. A lost love, a despairing search for an absent God, and the haunting emptiness of the plains and rivers of Argentina combine to form a single theme. But in his sonnets Molinari calls up a mystical hope. The images are, as in his longer poems, few, but the rhythms are more buoyant, and in the symbol of the rose in love with the winds the poet expresses a positive and trusting attitude to reality. If the outer world is for him empty, he knows that in emptiness alone can a true voice speak. Molinari's is in fact a religious poetry of *the dark night of the senses:*

> Qué busca el viento cuando sale solo.
> Dímelo corazón de hielo, aurora
> de nube, a qué destierro dulce o polo
> ansioso va su luna tañedora.[2]

---

[1] I am living on in the stormy south; where the dust entirely covers the leaves, and salt bites the hopeless root; where the rivers bear to the sea a rough earth through which the grasses no longer push up, and only the winds sway. The abandoned South! (Where no one can take from me the perfume of a mouth that I bear adhering to my lips).

[2] What does the wind seek when it goes out alone. Tell me that, heart of ice, clouded dawn, to what sweet exile or uneasy pole does its moon go, beating her tambourine.

The single point of colour, the image of the moon playing her tambourine, with its half-reminiscence of Lorca and of Molinari's favourite poets of the seventeenth century behind it, has as full an effect as an extended metaphor or an accumulation of detail in a more full-bodied poetry. Even the symbol with which the sonnet ends is only indicated in the most essential outline. The single positive value, half born in the poet's morning sleeplessness, is:

¡Rosa extrema, del viento enamorada![1]

It is this rose that the wind is seeking. But something else calls to Molinari from the past, the continent of Europe which he has visited only once, in 1933, and where he met the poets of Spain and of Portugal. The loss of a love, and isolation from monuments of art and the company of poets—Lorca and Aleixandre among them—which he had once enjoyed cause Molinari to look back even as he looks forward:

Feliz, sin olvidarme, y con apuro
llega en la noche del alma impaciente
a recrear mi cabeza, el continente.
El prado de los días, ¡ay! obscuro.[2]

In his loss and regret there is a sense of religious expectation: an attitude of love for something that has been lost, but that nevertheless still exists. For these poems are free of time; in the emptiness of space there is an absence of all boundaries. The seasons return, the winds blow and the rivers descend in a cycle of recurrence that bears no relation to the one-way stream of time which flows through inhabited places. Here on the pampa, there is an awareness of the presence of angels, and it is they who have inspired this exceptionally limpid poetry.

The Chilean poet Pablo Neruda (b. 1904) covers in his far greater output and more varied evolution experiences similar to those of Vallejo and Molinari. In his *Canto general*, his greatest achievement and the first book of Spanish American poetry to have freed itself almost entirely from the European tradition, he conveys a sense of the poor man's life like that of Vallejo's

---

[1] The highest rose, enamoured of the winds.

[2] Happy, without forgetting me, and with difficulty there reaches me in the night of the impatient soul, to build my mind afresh, the continent. The meadow of the days, now alas dark.

Heraldos negros, a political indignation comparable to Vallejo's in his last phase, and a sense of the newness and emptiness of the South American continent like that of Molinari, though with no religious overtones. If any angels fly over the Andes in Neruda's imagination, they will be found to be carrying red banners.

Neruda is a major writer, indeed almost the only poet writing today for whom the whole material world, from mineral to man, and from his native Chile to Communist China is a subject and an inspiration. He is at the same time, however, so politically committed that many of his poems are no better than crude polemics. In assessing his collected volume of 1,200 pages, one must dismiss quite a third of its contents as monotonous rant.

Fortunately, even among the political poems, there are many in which Neruda raises his sights, to see himself and mankind in a wide conspectus of history, or against a background of living nature. There are others in which he gazes with humorous affection on such familiar things as a plum, a chestnut on the ground—'delicia intacta y rosa comestible' (untouched delight and edible rose), an artichoke, an onion, or the calloused life of an old laundress, or views the winter, a storm, a cloudburst, or an expanse of sea with the simple eyes of childhood. Then, by rejecting all metaphysical implications, he succeeds in presenting a picture crisply outlined, as against a flat white background. He is, in fact, almost the only example of a materialist poet of stature, and this only because in the best of his poems he gazes so intently upon his material as to catch something of its essence, as well as its simple materiality.

Neruda's poetry seems, at a first reading, to be positive in its attitudes. In fact, it is permeated throughout with a sense of unease. The early work, which has sustained an undeserved popularity in face of the far greater depth and accomplishment of the later, tells of an attempt to escape from an oppressive solitude by way of crude sexual passion. The imagery of *Veinte poemas de amor y una canción desesperada* (20 Love Poems and One Song of Despair) of 1927 is brutally and ecstatically physical. Sexual conquest was a necessity to the twenty-three year old poet who had worked his way to the Chilean capital by way of scholarships from a backward Southern town in which his widowed father made an uncertain living. The struggle to survive, expressed in language drawn in general from the second-rate writers he had read, gives this early poetry a certain tasteless force. A Spanish poet might have echoed the psychologically acute and delicately cadenced love-poetry of Bécquer. An American poet born in an area where there was a native culture would have been more original in his imagery. Neruda, however, had a compensating strength that most of his countrymen lacked.

A quick success followed by an appointment to his country's diplomatic service, sent Neruda first to Burma, and then to the Madrid of the fertile years immediately before the civil war. Here, like his friend and contemporary Aleixandre, he turned to surrealism, not as a release from discipline but as a licence to use the violent imagery that his poetry required. But from an obsession with sex, he now plunged into an even more consuming obsession with death. The poet, his official duties, his loves and his possessions were all alike overshadowed by the hideous certainty that physical corruption awaited all things.

Now the hard outline of the world disappeared, and the landscape became cluttered with Surrealist stage-properties. Giant watches ticked with the sound of empty stomachs; lavatory seats stared upwards with their single wooden eyes like half-blind doves. Neruda's method was to find an external scene that recalled his own desolation, to draw it, to discard it, and to search for another that more nearly expressed his impalpable unease. A poem was thus made up of a series of approximations. 'Melancolía en las familias' (Melancholy in Family Life), one of the most striking poems in the second series of his *Residencias en la tierra* (Sojourns upon earth) begins with a confused picture of night and wind and vastness, narrows to the vision of a single deserted dining-room—no doubt a childhood memory—dissolves into vagueness, then picks out the dining-room in greater detail, only to extend the comparison, and thus return to the poet's forlorn state:

> Es sólo un comedor abandonado,
> y alrededor hay extensiones,
> fábricas sumergidas, maderas
> que sólo yo conozco,
> porque estoy triste y viajo,
> y conozco la tierra, y estoy triste.[1]

[1] It is only a deserted dining-room, and around it are extensions, factories under water, timbers that only I know, because I am sad and am travelling, and know the earth, and am sad.

Frequent repetitions, like those of the last lines quoted, serve throughout the *Residencias*, to reinforce a note of melancholy, which is only absent when the poet is writing of some dead material, like timber. For here, perversely, he finds a secret life that is absent from man and the objects that he has made. The poem 'Entrada a la madera' (Entry into timber) is almost a love-poem:

> Dulce materia, oh rosa de alas secas,
> en mi hundimiento tus pétalos subo
> con pies pesados de roja fatiga,
> y en tu catedral dura me arrodillo
> golpeándome los labios con un ángel.[1]

In wood the poet found refuge, as he could no longer in physical love, to which he devoted a large, disorderly poem, 'Las furias y las penas' (Rages and punishments), one of the last that he wrote in the Surrealist vein.

'The world has changed,' he noted on publishing this last poem, 'and my poetry with it.' The generals' rebellion, the murder of García Lorca, and the destruction of Spain before his eyes by civil war, gave Neruda external objects on which to fasten his fears and loathings. He underwent a kind of religious conversion; his feelings turned for the first time towards his fellow-men; he became a political poet, and quite soon a Communist.

Escaping from a despair from which there might have seemed to be no escape within the framework of materialism, Neruda became even more deeply committed to the materialist view of the world. Most of his poems of the Spanish war—and their successors of the Second World War, which celebrated only events on the Russian front—are emptily angry and declamatory. Only when he treats of *things* in his 'Canto sobre unas ruinas' (Song about some ruins), a poem of besieged Madrid, did he succeed in expressing the compassion which he undoubtedly felt for the dead. But he could speak of them only in terms of their shattered and sordid possessions:

> Todo ha ido y caído
> brutalmente marchito.

---

[1] Sweet material, oh rose with dry wings, in my collapse I climb your petals, my feet heavy with red fatigue, and in your hard cathedral I kneel, striking my lips on an angel,

Utensilios heridos, telas
nocturnas, espuma sucia, orines justamente
vertidos, mejillas, vidrio, lana,
alcanfor, circulos, de hilo y cuero, todo,
todo por una rueda vuelto al polvo. . . . [1]

This is an elegy for man driven from the earth, and for the
return of all familiar beauty to its primal nothingness. As war
poetry, it lacks the tenderness, however, of the best of Alberti's,
and the single-minded indignation of Vallejo. Neruda was still
using stage-properties borrowed from the Surrealist painters.
Vision and reality had not yet coalesced for him as they did for
Eluard in German-occupied Paris.

It was not until Neruda returned to Chile, and recovered
contact with its woods and mountains, its rain and its rivers, that
his vision broadened and his poetry gained true depth. Now he
ceased to be a Surrealist poet. The finest sections of his *Canto
general*, indeed, which are those devoted to the history and landscape of his native country, are unsurpassed among his writings.
He is here the poet of America—the continent's first major poet
since Whitman—of its rivers, its mountains, and its rugged
desolation before the coming of man:

Antes de la peluca y la casaca
fueron los ríos, ríos arteriales:
fueron las cordilleras, en cuya onda raída
el cóndor o la nieve parecían inmóviles:
fué la humedad y la espesura, el trueno
sin nombre todavía, las pampas planetarias. [2]

Then, in Neruda's great vision of the past, come vegetation,
beasts, birds, metals, and finally man in all his savagery: the
Aztecs, the Mayas, the Incas, and the inhabitants of the pre-
Incan Andean fastness of Macchu Picchu, which represents for
Neruda the prehistoric counterpart of his own remote birthplace
in the south of Chile. It is in his Macchu Picchu sequence that he
is most persistent in his search for the life principle, that he comes
nearest to a glimpse of the soul. The direction of his gaze as a

---

[1] Everything has perished and fallen, brutally withered. Damaged utensils, night
cloths, dirty foam, urine just spilt, cheeks, glass, wool, camphor, rounds of thread and
leather, all, all ground by a wheel to dust.

[2] Before the wig and the cassock were the rivers, arterial rivers, were the mountains
on whose striped undulations the condor or the snow appeared motionless; there was
dampness and thicket, thunder which had not yet a name, and the planet-wide pampas .

poet is back towards the primitive and the inchoate. In the future he sees a new political state, in which man will dwell in peace with man. But backwards lies a mystery, of which he reads hints in those rare moments of solitude which once aroused his deepest fears:

> Cuántas veces en las calles de invierno de una ciudad o en
> un autobús o un barco en el crepúsculo, o en la soledad
> más espesa, la de la noche de fiesta, bajo el sonido
> de sombras y campanas, en la misma gruta del placer humano,
> me quise detener a buscar la eterna veta insondable
> que antes toqué en la piedra o en el relámpago que el beso
>   desprendía.[1]

Somewhere even earlier, before man became differentiated from the elements of which his body is composed, lies for Neruda the golden age. Already by the time of Macchu Picchu death had entered the world.

If man had fallen from paradise by the time of the first temple-builders, he fell yet further in the epoch of the Conquistadores. Some, like Balboa and the later Spanish captain Ercilla, who defended the Araucanians of Chile against his fellow conquerors, and wrote an epic of which they were the heroes, are applauded by Neruda, but the conquest is for him little more than a gathering of the crows. In that hard country, however, man and nature were at one in their resistance; the woods and mountains hid the fugitive Araucanian warriors; and the rivers held the invaders back. Nature is the heroine of the dozen or two outstanding poems of the *Canto general;* and in them Neruda, in his desire to restore the earth to its earliest inhabitants and to its primitive simplicity, is once more on the side of death. Politically he proclaims the perfectibility of life on earth, but poetically his standpoint has not changed from the beginning. His language is at its solemnest and most plangent as he proclaims the victory of the encroaching forest over the noble invader Ercilla:

> Invaden su armadura con gigantesco liquen.
> Atropellan su espada las sombras del helecho.

---

[1] How often in the winter streets of a city or in a bus or in a ship in the half-light, or in the deepest solitude, the solitude of a festival night, to the sound of shadows and bells, in the very crypt of human pleasure, I have longed to stop and seek the eternal, unfathomable vein that I once touched in stone, or in the lightning released by a kiss.

La yedra original pone manos azules
en el recién llegado silencio del planeta.
Hombre, Ercilla sonoro, oigo el pulso del agua
de tu primer amenecer, un frenesí de pájaros
y un trueno en el follaje.[1]

All returns to silence. But in the end the conquerors triumph; and a system of exploitation is set up which can only end with the universal rule of Marxist communism. The later part of the *Canto general* contains much political comment and indignation. The standards of the poems here are not the standards of poetry, but fortunately poetry persistently breaks in, particularly in the last section devoted to the present-day republic of Chile. Here Neruda remembers the friends of his childhood, the rain falling in a deluge on a solitary horseman, perhaps himself as a youth, and the river Mapocho, which flowed down from the Andes past his own home-town:

Vuelve, vuelve a tu copa de nieve, río amargo,
vuelve, vuelve a tu copa de espaciosas escarchas,
sumerge tu plateada raíz en tu secreto origen
o despéñate y rómpete en otro mar sin lágrimas![2]

Thus he invokes the river of his childhood to flow back to its pristine snows, or to fall into a different sea, that is not a sea of tears.

The final sections of the *Canto general* tell of the poet's flight from his country, whose reactionary leaders were seeking to arrest him; and its sequel *Las uvas y el viento* (The Grapes and the Wind) records his long wandering through countries on both sides of the Iron Curtain. Its poetic level is low, and even its reporting unreliable.

With the *Odas elementales* (Elemental Odes) of 1954, the poet returns to the subject of *things*, to the tastes and smells and textures of familiar objects, for which he feels the same love as in the days before his political conversion. Now when he sees man, it is almost as an inanimate object, a prickly cactus that will one

[1] They invade his armour with gigantic lichen. The shadows of fern tread down his sword. The primeval ivy puts its blue hands on the newly descended silence of the planet. Man, resounding Ercilla, I hear the pulse of the water at your first dawn, a frenzy of birds, and a thunder in the foliage.

[2] Return, return to your snow peak, bitter river, return, return to your peak of vast frosts, drown your silvered root in your secret source or throw yourself down and break in another, tearless sea.

day burst into flower. He has adopted a short line, and his technical complexity is far less than in the *Residencias* or the *Canto general.* Possibly he now feels that it is possible to write for a wide public. Certainly his new buoyancy, and the light that suffuses these last poems, which seem at last to be on the side of life, could make a broad appeal. For the first time a poet of stature seems to have transcended complexity, and to be speaking simply with an authentic voice. But even at their best the poems of the *Odas elementales* are shorn of all metaphysical implications. They are light, because their range is thus limited; bold and charming in a manner practised by only one other modern poet Vladimir Mayakovsky, in his bantering conversation with the sun. Neruda too writes an ode to the sun:

> Oh sol,
> cristal paterno,
> horario,
> y poderío,
> progenitor planeta,
> gigante
> rosa rubia
> siempre
> hirviendo de fuego,
> siempre
> consumiéndote
> encendido,
> cocina
> cenital,
> párpado
> puro,
> colérico y tranquilo,
> fogón y fogonero,
> sol,
> yo quiero
> mirarte
> con los viejos
> ojos de America.[1]

The Odes are as original, though not on as great a scale as the *Canto general.* They are the work of a poet of stature who has invented a new form, and few new forms have been invented in the last twenty-five years. Unfortunately, however, Neruda has

---

[1] Oh sun, paternal glass, timepiece and power, planet progenitor, giant golden rose, always seething with fire, always consuming yourself in your flames, kitchen of the zenith, pure eyelid, choleric and quiet, furnace and stoker, sun, I would gaze on you with the old eyes of America.

overworked his medium, which in his third book of Odes of 1957
has become loosely mechanical. That his Ode is suitable for
something more than surface description is clear from one of his
earlier pieces in this convention, which is addressed to a washer-
woman at night (Oda a una lavendera nocturna). This is a human
poem, with political implications which, however, do not deflect
it from its course:

> va y viene
> el movimiento,
> cayendo y levantándose
> con precisión celeste,
> van y vienen
> las manos sumergidas,
> las manos, viejas manos
> que lavan en la noche,
> hasta tarde, en la noche,
> que lavan
> ropa ajena,
> que sacan en el agua
> la huella
> del trabajo.[1]

Neruda writes of the history of his continent, but not of its
culture. Vallejo, although a citizen of a country with an ancient
cultural tradition, does not refer to the Incas, but only to the half-
Christianized life of the half-breeds from whom he drew his
descent. Molinari describes a country hardly a hundred and fifty
years old. That there existed an Inca, a Maya, and an Aztec—or
rather pre-Aztec—literature is a fact that failed to influence the
poets until the publication in 1940 of Monseñor Garibay's
collection of translations from poems in the Náhuatl language of
Mexico, which had been collected by missionary friars shortly
after the Conquest. This poetry had remained in its ancient
language, though written in the Spanish alphabet, from that
time, occasionally referred to or partially translated by scholars,
but never viewed as a literature that might have lessons for
modern Mexico. It had indeed never been dissociated from the
decadent culture of the Aztecs through whom it had been
transmitted from a people of far higher civilization who had

[1] The movement goes backwards and forwards, falling and rising with celestial
precision, the submerged hands go backwards and forwards, the hands, old hands that
wash in the night, till late in the night, that wash other people's clothes, that rid them in
the water of the trace of work.

inhabited Central Mexico before them. Garibay's *Poesía indígena* has the technical mastery of Arthur Waley's translations from the Chinese. What it offered modern poets was a new symbolism and mythology, and the sudden discovery that they were at one in their metaphysical preoccupations with this early culture that had flourished in their land.

The first poet to draw together the Spanish and the Náhuatl strands of Mexican poetry has been Octavio Paz (b. 1914) who has come to his task by way of a persistent questioning of all reality. 'Paz seems to have set out in search of the most desperate experience in order to emerge from it with at least a grain of hope,' wrote the critic Ramón Xirau. Certainly Paz's early poetry is of violence and disbelief. Technically the influences upon him were both social and surrealist; he witnessed the defeat of the Spanish Republic, and shared with Aleixandre and Neruda the emotional rediscovery of man's physical kinship with nature. But unlike them he came through to no positive values. Paz's early poetry is so negative that it questions both the poet's own existence and the validity of the poetic act. But the solitude that he finds at the heart of every activity rouses in him a glimmer of expectation. Paz's search is in essence religious. In one of his few purely social poems, his 'Elegy for a friend killed in the Civil war,' he states that we stand at the opening of a new epoch in the world:

> Has muerto, camarada,
> en el ardiente amanecer del mundo.
> Has muerto cuando apenas
> tu mundo, nuestro mundo, amanecía.[1]

This is partially a political statement; Paz has always supposed that a new political organization was a necessary prelude to the spiritual change that has been the true subject of his poetry. Like Neruda, he was, in his early writing, necessarily on the side of death, but all the time in search of some power with which to counterbalance it. He moved towards participation, but was driven back into solitude by lack of belief in his own existence:

> In tenté salir a la noche
> y al alba comulgar con los que sufren
> mas como el rayo al caminante solitario

[1] You died, comrade, at the burning dawn of the world. You died when your world and ours was scarcely dawning.

sobrecogió a mi espíritu una lívida certidumbre:
había muerto el sol y una eterna noche amenecía.[1]

Against this despair only one force could be set, the moment
of experience outside time, which is the subject of Eliot's *Four
Quartets*. But Paz's escape from his Waste Land was far from
complete. Theoretically he had accepted a religious attitude:
expectation began to outweigh despair. Yet the experience itself
never took clear shape; or rather many experiences masqueraded
as the true one; vision and hallucination remained indistinguishable, and Freud, the Marquis de Sade, Rimbaud, André Breton
and the Masters of Zen Buddhism were all accepted on a par as
prophets of the new certainty that could be born out of utter
negation. In the poem 'La poesía' (Poetry) the dilemma is stated:

Nublan mis ojos imágenes opuestas,
y a las mismas imágenes
otras, más profundas, las niegan,
tal un ardiente balbuceo,
aguas que anega un agua más oculta y densa.[2]

The poet is describing the processes prior to the composition of
his poem. This is a situation in which he finds himself unreal;
only the poem, rising from a depth at which

quietud y movimiento son lo mismo.[3]

triumphs over all contradictions and by its existence proves to
the poet that he too exists:

Insiste, vencedora,
porque tan sólo existo porque existes,
y mi boca y mi lengua se formaron
para decir tan sólo tu existencia
y tus secretas sílabas, palabra
impalpable y despótica,
substancia de mi alma.[4]

[1] I attempted to go out into the night and communicate at dawn with those who
suffer, but as the lightning strikes the solitary traveller, a livid certainty seized my
spirit: the sun had died and eternal night was setting in.

[2] Opposing images cloud my eyes, and other images from a greater depth deny these,
like a burning babble, waters that a more secret and heavier water drowns.

[3] Tranquillity and movement are the same.

[4] Persist, conqueror, since I exist only by your existence, and my lips and soul were
formed only to proclaim your existence and your secret words, the impalpable and
despotic word, the substance of my soul.

I

Yet in the next verse, the poem too is described as a dream, a dream in which there is both violence and movement. Paz is in fact most in love with the world at the moment when it seems about to slip away into abstraction. The moment of creation is for him a moment of intense living. The parallel is with the harsh imagery of Aleixandre's early poetry. But where Aleixandre moves in a direct line from solitude to participation, Paz, in three most important poems, sets out to reconcile the two opposites, solitude and utterance. The first is the principal piece in the book *Libertad bajo palabra*, (Liberty behind the Words), a vision set in 1948, and entitled 'Himno entre ruinas' (Hymn among the ruins). Here there is an alternation between stanzas of vision and stanzas of comment. The vision is at first abstract, of colour, sea and stone, but it is succeeded by an evocation of contemporary Mexico. Boys are smoking marihuana on top of an Aztec pyramid. Then in the third verse, the vision becomes more sensual; eyes and hands confirm and expand the message of the inner eye. But actuality again breaks in with a 'Waste Land' picture of Europe in ruins, and the rich consuming the poor. At the same time the vision grows in intensity; all the senses are drawn in:

> Ver, tocar formas hermosas, diarias.
> Zumba la luz, dardos y alas.
> Huele a sangre la mancha de vino en el mantel.
> Como el coral sus ramas en el agua
> extiendo mis sentidos en la hora viva:
> el instante se cumple en una concordancia amarilla,
> ¡oh mediodía, espiga henchida de minutos,
> copa de eternidad![1]

The poet's thoughts divide, start again and lose motion. 'Must everything end in a spatter of stagnant water?' he asks. But the last stanza triumphantly proclaims that the poem begins where thinking stops; the solitary broodings of the early work are transcended; the minute becomes rich as the commenting mind sinks into peace:

> La inteligencia al fin encarna en formas,
> se reconcilian los dos mitades enemigas

[1] To see, to touch each day's lovely forms. The light throbs, all darts and wings. The wine-stain on the table-cloth smells of blood, As the coral extends its branches in the water, I stretch my senses in this living hour: the moment fulfils itself in a yellow harmony. Oh moon, wheat-ear heavy with minutes, eternity's brimming cup!

y la conciencia-espejo se licúa,
vuelve a ser fuente, manantial de fábulas:
Hombre, árbol de imágenes,
palabras que son flores que son frutos que son actos.[1]

The title poem of a small collection of lyrics *Semillas para
un himno* (Seeds for a hymn) which he published five years later,
returns to the theme of the moment overflowing with all time in
a manner somewhat reminiscent of Eliot:

Infrecuentes (pero también inmericidas)
Instantáneas (pero es verdad que el tiempo no se mide
Hay instantes que estallan y son astros
Otros son ese mismo río detenido y unos árboles fijos
Otros son ese mismo río arrasando los mismos árboles)[2]

These infrequent moments come, unearned,

Cuando el mundo entreabre sus puertas y el ángel cabecea
a la entrada del jardín.[3]

and it is then that light 'penetrates the sleeping body of water and
for a moment names are inhabited.'

This second poem is, as its name implies, rather a series of
indications than a statement. Its successor *Piedra de sol* (Sunstone),
the outstanding poem in his last volume, *La estación violenta*
(The season of violence) of 1958, is the most sustained piece that
Paz has so far attempted. It is a hymn to the planet Venus in her
two aspects as morning and evening star and, by Náhuatl
symbolism, as sun and water. It is at the same time a hymn to
sexual love as the supreme form of communion between creatures
who are otherwise no more than shadows with no true experience
of their own lives:

el monumento somos de una vida
ajena y no vivida, apenas nuestra,

—¿la vida, cuándo fue de veras nuestra?,
¿cuándo somos de veras lo que somos?,

[1] Intellect finally incarnates in forms, the two hostile halves are reconciled, and the
conscience-mirror liquefies, becomes once more a fountain, a tree of images, words that
are flowers, that are fruit, that are deeds.

[2] Infrequent (but also undeserved) momentary (but it is true that time cannot be
measured there are moments that burst and are stars others that are like a dammed
river and some like motionless trees others are this same river obliterating these same
trees).

[3] When the world sets its doors ajar, and an angel nods at the entrance to the garden

bien mirado no somos, nunca somos
a solas sino vértigo y vacío,
muecas en el espejo, horror y vómito,
nunca la vida es nuestra, es de los otros,
la vida no es de nadie, todos somos
la vida—pan de sol para los otros,
los otros todos que nosotros somos—,[1]

With the exception of T. S. Eliot, Octavio Paz is the only contemporary poet capable of feeling his metaphysics, and calling them to life. *Piedra de sol* is a closely organized poem, composed of precisely one line for each of the 584 days of the revolution of Venus. It is woven of two strands, that of memory and that of vision. For Paz calls up scenes of the past in which love has made life real—in particular a moment during the siege of Madrid in which two lovers embrace to 'defend their portion of eternity, their ration of time and paradise' in face of the Fascist bombardment. The conclusion of the poem, though philosophically more completely worked out, is similar in feeling to the conclusion of 'Himno entre ruinas', an affirmation of birth and light in contrast to the perpetual presence of death and shadow. In time all is dark, out of time lies the moment of communion, the sudden striking of the sun's light on the waters, Eliot's 'still point of the turning world'. One is carried back to the primal imagery of the first chapter of *Genesis*.

abre la mano,
señora de semillas que son días,
el día es immortal, asciende, crece,
acaba de nacer, y nunca acaba,
cada día es nacer, un nacimiento
es cada amanecer y yo amanezco,
amanecemos todos, amanece
el sol cara de sol, Juan amanece
con su cara de Juan cara de todos,

puerta del ser, despiértame, amanece,
dejame ver el rostro de este día. . . . [2]

[1] We are the monument of an alien, unlived life that is scarcely ours. When was life truly ours? When are we really what we are? Truly we do not exist, alone we are only giddy and empty, grimaces in the mirror, horror and vomit, life is never ours, it belongs to others, life belongs to no one, we are all life—solar bread for others, all those others who are ourselves.

[2] Open your hand, lady of seeds that are days, the day is immortal, it ascends, grows, ends by being born and never ends, each day is a birth, a birth is every dawn and I am rising, we all rise, the sun rises with its sun face, John rises with his John face, with his everyone's face.
Gateway to being, awake me, dawn and let me see the countenance of this day.

The male principle celebrates the female principle, night hymns day, and the poet performs his magical act in calling up shapes from the inchoate, light out of darkness. This poem of 1957, the last important poem to be published in the Western World, perhaps marks no more than a stage in the development of a major poet who is still in his forties.

Molinari, Neruda and Paz are the chief living poets of Spanish America. Around them, and sometimes in reaction against them, are many others in the various Republics, where much poetry of a high level of accomplishment is written, though there is little audience for it. Among the younger men, however, there is as yet none who seems likely to attain their stature. But whereas in North America poetry has on the whole taken refuge in the college campus and become an academic exercise, in the south and particularly in Mexico, it is a living pursuit, and the expression of a civilization which is clearly establishing its independence. Perhaps in the next years a literature will evolve less closely connected with European movements than that of today.

10

Where we stand now

THE present position of poetry though still uncertain, is perhaps very slowly clarifying. Of the writers so far considered, none is under the age of forty and few are younger than fifty. Yet it would be difficult to name with confidence even half a dozen younger men who are likely to be their successors. Twenty-five years ago, when Auden, Thomas, Neruda and Paz were publishing their early books, they were already marked out, and widely accepted, as men of great promise, even of some achievement. But the years since the war have been more remarkable for the quick emergence and disappearance of half-developed talents than for any steady advance towards maturity on the part of individual poets. The history of the 'forties and 'fifties is one of rapid changes of style. Reversals which once occurred only once in a century now appear to take place in each decade, leaving the promising poet of 1940 hopelessly wedded ten years later to an out-of-date manner which he can neither develop nor abandon. Yet the rapid shift from the romantic and declamatory to the poem of ironic comment, and the return to Romanticism a few years later only betrays the anxiety of a culture caught in a trap. Seemingly unable to reconcile his mind and his feelings, the contemporary poet gives way almost exclusively to one or to the other. His work is either emotionally turgid and intellectually undeveloped, or highly organized but devoid of emotional insight.

This judgement applies particularly to Britain, where the war-years witnessed the rapid growth of a neo-Romantic movement, represented at its best by Vernon Watkins, George Barker and W. S. Graham, which gave way in the first years of the peace to a new flat intellectualism of limited statements, which finds its best expression in the anthology, *New Lines*, of 1956. But even

238

in the three years since its publication, the poets of yet another anthology, *Mavericks*, appear to be exploiting the legacy of Romanticism once more. How complete these reversals of taste have been can be seen from the history of Auden's reputation; reviled in the 'forties, he has provided models for many poets of the 'fifties, and can expect to be neglected, if not reviled once more, by the emergent poets of the 'sixties. The fate of Dylan Thomas's reputation with practising poets has been exactly the reverse.

Similar reversals of style and judgement have taken place in France and the United States, but at the moment these countries appear to be more fixed in their attitudes than we. The British poet might in fact be described as pulled in rival directions by his colleagues to East and West, by the French towards a bold and sonorous formlessness, and by the Americans in the direction of close and hermetic intellectual organization.

French poetry remains under the influence of Surrealism. There is no living French poet who has not at some time submitted to its disorderly disciplines, none who has yet succeeded in making clear and unambiguous statements. René Char (b. 1907), for example, the most important of them, took some secondary part in André Breton's movement before the war, and even when writing of his own first-hand experience of the Resistance has been unable to separate dream from reality. For the rest a music-hall frivolity, implicit also in surrealist theory—for are not the plots of most dreams absurd?—alternate with grandiose myths and rhetoric reminiscent of the later poetry of Victor Hugo, which has latterly returned to favour.

In the United States, on the other hand, poetry has tended in the last few years to become an academic practice, fostered by Writers' courses in university term and vacation. Many of the best poets are teachers and critics. Technically, American poetry is therefore highly accomplished, and draws on vast resources of cultural allusion. Its closest parallel is the late seventeenth-century poetry of Spain, in which the wit or conceit entirely controlled the line, and no essential statement was made. The poem, in fact, is a kind of problem enunciated in the opening lines, revealed in its several facets as the poem develops, and resolved or half-resolved in its conclusion. The poet's complete resources of thought and reading are assembled to comment on an insight or a memory that has from the outset very little emotional force.

The American poet thus stands in complete contrast to the French, with whom inchoate emotion sparks off a poem that is never sufficiently shapely or organized to be lucid. The language of the French poet is seldom abstruse; it is his failure of precision that defeats the reader. The American, on the other hand, makes use of vast linguistic resources. Learned jargon and ephemeral colloquialism are uneasily combined in lines whose loose speech rhythms confer no real unity of style. Though he claims to be exploiting the riches of common American speech, he is in fact writing in an essentially literary convention which has very little currency outside the Arts faculties of the Universities. Attempting to call up an American tradition to free him from the attractions of the Old World, he devotes many of his poems to the task, which has fascinated every American writer since Hawthorne, of playing one off against the other. He has consequently no greater audience than the post-surrealist poets of France.

Between the French and American extremes, English poetry of the 'fifties irresolutely wavers, attracted first by one, then by the other. For English poets of the neo-Baroque tendency are, like their American colleagues, for the most part, teachers and critics; and latterly some of our own red-brick universities have even adopted the American habit of inviting practising poets to stimulate the creative work of their students. But here the two groups, and the many poets whose positions are in various ways intermediate, are united in their fundamental principles. The prevailing desire is to connect once more with tradition. Revolutionary change, whether political or poetic, seems to most of them neither attractive nor viable. The age of experiment is over, and with it the poet's hopes of cutting an important figure in society. Accepting his position as a minor craftsman, his first care is to preserve himself from falling too irremediably under the influence of the half-dozen masters whose control of the poetic scene is as strong today as it was twenty-five years ago. For there is no doubt that Donne, Marvell, Hopkins, Yeats, Eliot and Graves occupy positions of the same importance with the reader and writer of 1959 that they held with his father in 1934. Foreign influences have come and gone. For the contemporary English poet is less at home in other languages than were those of Auden's generation. He is sometimes, indeed, resolutely insular, priding himself on an acquaintance with foreign works only in the form of translations.

The rapid changes of fashion of the last twenty years have done little to change the poet's essential attitudes. Ever since Matthew Arnold, there have been advocates of a return to classical conventions. Some have even assumed that once the Romantic movement had spent its force, a new classicism would automatically follow it. But the laws of poetic evolution have not proved so automatic. A new classical period would only be possible in the context of a changed attitude to society. Only the revival of some past ideal of empire, or some rebirth of religious belief could give literature the power completely to reverse its valuations, as it did in the age of Malherbe and Dryden. Any classicism would require a limitation of interests. A strict frontier would have to be drawn between things susceptible of clear definition, and the vast area of confusion and dream, into which the modern poet has made so many incursions. Man would have to resume his place in the centre of the Universe, or at least to see himself as capable of a self-development denied to the rest of nature. But ever since Baudelaire he has increasingly dwelt on the limitations of his own ego, and the relative nature of his ideas, ideals and aspirations. A new classicism would require a fresh access of self-confidence, of which there are as yet no signs.

In many countries the situation is even less lively than in Britain and the United States. The Germans are still making up the ground lost during the enforced isolation of the Nazi epoch. Their poets are now absorbing the lessons of Eliot and Eluard, of Mayakovsky and Neruda, of whom they had heard little before the end of the war. Rilke and Trakl too struck them with a fresh impact at the moment when reading and writing again became free.

No such freedoms have yet come to Russia where, despite occasional relaxations of the literary dictatorship, isolation from current influences is almost complete. Little work of true originality has been produced since the 'twenties, and the authors of that little have speedily been compelled to 'reform their styles' in the interests of the revolutionary ideology and achievement. The Communist wish to bring poetry back to common themes and common language has, however, not yet been fulfilled. The

I*

prescribed themes and language have been developed in a thousand poems, chiefly remarkable for the absence of all poetic authenticity. The few poets of the pre-war generation who have continued to write in an individual way have been hampered by directives and, despite the spate of licensed poetic writing during the war itself, no new talents have emerged. The one possibility of new growth, the revival of the popular verse story, has not yet, however, been fully explored. Should progress be made beyond the graphic but somewhat jog-trot work that is at present popular in the Soviet Union, something really interesting might result.

In Spain alone, owing to the survival of conditions loosely parallel to those of the 'thirties on the other side of the Pyrenees, a poetry of resistance has arisen in the last decade, in many ways similar to that written in other countries twenty years earlier. For in Spain the issues are simple; poverty in the midst of comparative plenty, and the petty restrictions of a half-traditional dictatorship, give the poet themes within his competence about which he is capable of having uncomplicated feelings. The vigour of a group of writers too young to have taken any great part in the Civil War, has been stimulated by the struggle for free speech, which has been to some degree successful. Poetry like that of Blas de Otero (b. 1916), with its wide and uncomplicated human sympathies and its impassioned cry for liberty of thought and expression, could not have been published in any other dictatorship country. The Spanish censorship, in other ways strict, has—perhaps out of carelessness, perhaps out of contempt for its tiny circulation—let through a small amount of this new poetry, which, unlike that of Lorca's generation, is explicitly addressed to 'the great majority'. But for the low level of literacy in Spain, and the lack of public libraries, the work of Otero and half-a-dozen others would be understood and appreciated by far wider circles than any other modern poetry in Europe or America.

The outstanding figure in this Spanish 'resistance' is on the whole the least 'committed'. Despite his acquaintance with Franco's prisons at an age when his contemporaries in Britain and America were at school and university, José Hierro (b. 1922) makes no statement that can be construed as political. He is the defender of human dignity under all circumstances, the poet of the private rather than of public life; and his restrained and conversational line, devoid of all embellishment or extravagance, is the most independent and the most assured in contemporary Spain. Though Otero and others may seem equally deserving of detailed attention, a single poem of Hierro's, his longest and best sustained, must be allowed to stand as representative of this new Spanish poetry, since it not only exemplifies qualities that exist in the writing of others in the group, but can be related also to the work of some poets completely unknown to him in England and the United States.

Hierro does not set out to write major poetry. He sees his work as no more than a documentary expression of his time and situation which will lose its value when the issues and problems of today have ceased to be urgent. He is resolutely anti-aesthetic, and outspokenly hostile to the 'pure' poetry of Guillén, also to much of Lorcá's. A poem seems to him hollow and pretentious if it is remote from the interests and perceptions of the common man. The simplicity of his line is for this reason comparable to that of Neruda in his *Odas elementales*. But Hierro's greater appreciation of human weakness and loneliness cause him to write more tenderly and more subtly than the great Chilean. His music is frequently in the minor key. What he proclaims most fervently is the sacredness of private relationships, a theme developed in his outstanding early poem 'Reportaje' (Reportage), which speaks of the poet's isolation in terms of his prison experience. Hierro is the poet of intimacy, always conscious of those shades of meaning which it is almost impossible to convey except in a poem's overtones, for it will evade even the most elaborate net of contrived ambiguities.

> Escucha. Sólo
>
> para ti podrían decirse
> estas palabras. Sólo tú
> las podrás entender.[1]

he says in a love-poem, which sets out to transmit, like 'the note for an agenda' to which his love will have the key, the shared experience of a bright day in the winter of 1953 to some future day, when that experience would otherwise be forgotten.

The weakness of such poetry is that, being united by no

---

[1] Listen. Only for you could these words be said. Only you will be able to understand them.

structure of myth or metaphor, it may easily disintegrate into a
series of such agenda notes. Hierro's most important poem,
'Estatuas yacentes' (Recumbent Effigies), however, avoids this
danger. It develops the poet's favourite theme that human
relationship is the sole means of transcending an otherwise un-
bearable spiritual isolation, but this time objectively, in terms of
two imagined lives in the distant past. This device holds the poem
together, and prevents the poet's voice from dropping into a
whisper of disjointed confidences.

Two recumbent figures on a tomb in Salamanca cathedral,
whose conventional epitaph records only their rank and dignity,
come to life across the centuries. He is a soldier, strong only in
his actions, but at heart a lost being incapable of yielding to his
feelings. Never living in the present or even dwelling in his
memories, he is always striding forward into an imagined future,
preoccupied only with the vision of his eternal glory:

> En la estatua del caballero
> fructifica la dignidad
> de una existencia coronada
> gloriosamente.
>
> Un español
> de cuando el sol no se ponía
> jamás en tierras españolas
> Una piedra ejemplar, un símbolo
> —gracias te sean dadas, Dios—
> duerme en la falda de la muerte.[1]

And she, whom he cherished rather as a daughter than as a wife,
but in whose lap he longed to find repose, was in her life a being
unknown to him:

> Pero era río de ternura:
> pulía la piedra que fuiste
> la hacía rodar por su cauce,
> redondeaba sus aristas.
> Tan transparente era, que nunca
> supiste que estabas sumido
> en su corriente maternal.[2]

[1] On the knight's effigy the dignity of a life crowned with glory bears its fruit. A
Spaniard of the age when the sun never sets on Spanish lands. A pattern in stone, a
symbol—praise be to God—sleeps in the lap of death.

[2] But she was a river of tenderness; she polished the stone that you were, and rolled
it in the bed of her stream, smoothing its edges. She was so transparent that you never
knew you were sunk in her maternal river.

Thus a human relationship is presented: two lives are shown both thwarted by a failure to communicate, and a question is asked with great simplicity: Of what avail is a life if it does not serve other lives?

> Mas de qué sirven nuestras vidas,
> si no enriquecen otras vidas.
> Como de un bosque que se incendia,
> quedarían sólo los troncos.
> Muertas y ocultas las raíces,
> que casan la piedra y la tierra.
> Las hojas, hechas humo, dándoles
> blancura a las nubes de estío.
> Invisible el mágico fuego,
> bajo la ceniza de palabras,
> Sólo palabras quedarían,
> despiadados y muertos signos
> de flaqueza y de pesadumbre.
> Lamento, renuncia y reproche,
> cuando ya no había remedio.[1]

Statements and questions are unembellished, and there is no development of metaphor, no elaboration of rhyme or even of assonance, only a strictly rhythmical and subtly musical monotone, as of a voice talking in deepest intimacy. But what stands out most prominently in Hierro's poetry is its simplicity. There are no doubts, reservations or ambiguities. There is no attempt to speak dramatically or to claim a greater knowledge and insight than the poet possesses. His sole wish is to convey something of that 'magic fire' that is 'invisible beneath the ash of words'. Intellectualism is absent and so is all patent debt to the past. Hierro has a deep sympathy for traditional poetry, in particular for folk-song and ballad, but he never reproduces its tones. He has little knowledge of foreign literature, but a deep feeling for the great European composers. Several of his poems are addressed to them—to Palestrina, Handel and Beethoven—but speak not of the men themselves but of the moods of their music. Hierro's methods of building a poem are, indeed, often musical.

'Estatuas yacentes' comes to a musical, rather than a logical

---

[1] Of what use are our lives if they do not enrich other lives? As if a wood caught fire only the trunks would remain, Dead and hidden the roots that wed the earth to the stone. The leaves turned to smoke give whiteness to the summer clouds. The magic fire is invisible beneath the ash of words. Only words would remain, pitiless and dead signs of weakness and sorrow. Lamentation, renunciations and reproaches when the time for remedies was past.

resolution. The poet can promise the knight and his lady no immortality; he is too uncertain of man's reality during his life to speak of survival after death. There they lie, side by side on their tomb, awaiting the resurrection of the flesh, about which the poet can say nothing, and meanwhile dreaming their lives over again. In that dream, Hierro suggests, which is for them lit by the light of eternity, each may come to see the other more truly:

> En un punto exacto,
> fuera del tiempo, con los mismos
> cuerpos y almas que fueron vuestros,
> volveréis a encontraros. Obra
> de tu mano, hijo de tu obra.
> Volveréis a soñar la vida.
> Pero la luz será más pura.[1]

Then she will be his creation, and he will be hers. This promise, like a musical resolution, speaks directly to the feelings, by-passing the logical mind. Hierro has glimpsed some possibility of a recurrence of lives on this earth, that cannot be translated into a metaphysical statement. For his poetry is centred on the earthly life; he can imagine no existence of the soul without the body:

> La vida
> es el alma y la carne juntas:
> ojos que admiran y que lloran,
> labios que besan y sonríen
> oídos que oyen algo más
> que la muda, celeste música.[2]

This poem of 1955 not only achieves its own perfection, but seems also to be advancing along new lines, which are developed even further in Hierro's last collection, *Cuanto sé de mí* (So much as I know of myself) of 1957. In it, as in 'Estatuas yacentes', intimacy and modesty take the place of mental ingenuity and generalized statement. The poet no longer claims exceptional status, but speaks of himself, in Hierro's own words, as 'a man among other men'.

---

[1] At an exact moment outside time, with the same bodies and souls that were yours, you will meet once more. Work of your hand, child of your work. You will dream life over again. But the light will be purer.

[2] Life is the body and soul together; eyes that wonder and weep, lips that kiss and smile, ears that hear something more than the silent music of the heavens.

Similar tendencies are revealed by the work of two or three English and American poets who stand a little aside from the movements of the day, by Philip Larkin (b. 1922) who shares some characteristics with the *New Lines* group, by R. S. Thomas (b. 1914), a Welshman concerned chiefly with the life of his own region, and by Theodore Roethke (b. 1908), an American academic, whose writing is more personal, lyrical and spontaneous than that of his fellow teachers of literature.

By a remarkable coincidence one of Larkin's best poems treats the same subject as Hierro's 'Estatuas yacentes' and arrives at not very different conclusions. The twin effigies of 'An Arundel Tomb' are seen by Larkin with something of the obliquity favoured by Graves's generation. Unlike Hierro, the English poet cannot refrain from a little ironic comment, which to some degree lessens his implication with his characters:

> Side by side, their faces blurred,
> The earl and countess lie in stone,
> Their proper habits vaguely shown
> As jointed armour, stiffened pleat,
> And that faint hint of the absurd—
> The little dogs under their feet.

Here with the double ambiguity of *proper habits*—correct dress, personal characteristics, or formal behaviour—and the absurdity of the dogs at their feet, Larkin is relegating the knight and his lady to their own century. Whereas the effigies in Salamanca cathedral have preserved their individuality through the years and are still immersed in the circumstances of their lives, the Arundel pair have lost almost all reality with the passage of the seasons and under the eyes of innumerable gazers:

> Snow fell, undated. Light
> Each summer thronged the glass. A bright
> Litter of birdcalls strewed the same
> Bone-riddled ground. And up the paths
> The endless altered people came,
> Washing at their identity.

Larkin's manner of presentation is throughout much more mannered than Hierro's. He is still attracted by such tricks of modernism as the confusion of the senses; birdcalls for him *litter* the grass, and the statues' survival through the centuries is wittily described elsewhere in the poem as 'their supine stationary voyage' through time. Yet in this poem Larkin seems to be moving forward from seventeenth-century conceit towards a greater simplicity. In its last lines, indeed, he is able to reach a firm conclusion that is, like Hierro's, poetic rather than metaphysical. For his final affirmation is both modest and authentic, the poem and its characters have alike progressed by way of artifice to the rediscovery of something very simple:

> Time has transfigured them into
> Untruth. The stone fidelity
> They hardly meant has come to be
> Their final blazon, and to prove
> What will survive of us is love.

The clasping of their hands, which at the moment of their entombment had been no more than a demonstration of 'faithfulness in effigy', has now become the only surviving reality possessed by this long dead couple. Larkin, like Hierro, seems to value only those lives that have enriched the lives of others. Both are poets of compassion.

R. S. Thomas too is inspired by compassion for the living or for the recently dead among his parishioners, for he is a parson in a Welsh village; and he too relates the past and the present in his poetry by presenting his characters in the conspectus of his country's history. Men like his 'Labourer' have existed as long as the world:

> He has been here since life began, a vague
> Movement among the roots of the young grass.
> Bend down and peer beneath the twigs of hair,
> And look into the hard eyes flecked with care.
> What do you see? Notice the twitching hands,
> Veined like a leaf, and tough bark of the limbs
> Wrinkled and gnarled, and tell me what you think
> A wild tree still, whose seasons are not yours,
> The slow heart beating to the hidden pulse
> Of the strong sap, the feet firm in the soil?
> No, no, a man like you, but blind with tears
> Of sweat to the bright star that draws you on.

Thomas's message parallels that of Hierro and Larkin, in that he perceives, transcending differences of circumstance, the essential

similarity between himself and the old peasant whom he draws.
His manner is almost entirely unaffected by modernism. Though
he shows signs of having read Yeats and his namesake Dylan
Thomas, he develops a single metaphor—the comparison of his
labourer to a tree—without metaphysical overtones, and without
conceits or associative images. But finally the metaphor is rejected; the man is not like a tree, he is 'a man like you'. Thomas's
concluding statement is as simple as Larkin's, and almost repeats
the words of Hierro's self-description. Moreover when he goes
further, and sets a decaying Welsh village in its context of world
and universe, he implicitly refuses to make a metaphysical statement. By his rhythm and reference to Plato he evokes the memory
of Yeats, only to claim for the life of this remote place a significance as great as that of any philosopher's speculation:

> Stay, then, village, for round you spins
> On slow axis a world as vast
> And meaningful as any poised
> By great Plato's solitary mind.

Thomas's hope is that of Christian dogma. Like Yeats,
George and Blok he sees around him decay, disbelief and crime,
but unlike them he trusts that all will be purged in a new spring:

> Lost in the world's wood
> You cannot stanch the bright menstrual blood.
> The earth sickens; under naked boughs
> The frost comes to barb your broken vows
>
> Is there blessing? Light's peculiar grace
> In cold splendour robes this tortured place
> For strange marriage. Voices in the wind
> Weave a garland where a mortal sinned.
> Winter rots you; who is there to blame?
> The new grass shall purge you in its flame.

Here is no promise of a Second Coming, no call for revolution,
but a modest restatement of old truths in new language.

Poetry of similar tone, though somewhat harder to discover,
is being written in the United States also, where a tradition of
unemphatic writing has been revived by the great New England
poet Robert Frost. Frost's work is strictly regional, and his
loyalties are to a district as firmly rooted in its own past as
Thomas's Wales. Theodore Roethke (b. 1908), on the other hand,

is, on the evidence of his own poetry, the son of German immi-
grants and a teacher of English, conditions which might have
inclined him to the rootless, intellectual style. Indeed one can
find echoes of conventional conceits in some of his early poems,
but Roethke is driven forward by a pulsing lyricism that refuses
to pause at a single image. He is a poet of intuitions who despises
reason:

> Reason? That dreary shed, that hutch for grubby schoolboys!
> The hedgewren's song says something else.

He is most alive in his memories of childhood, and his sympathy
with creatures, insects, roots and grasses. For in them he finds an
affirmation that is absent from the world of men:

> The lost have their own pace.
> The stalks ask something else.
> What the grave says,
> The nest denies.

Roethke describes a world of childhood fears, and the escape
from it into sensuality. He records the intoxication of the senses,
feeling and seeing as if for the first time:

> A fish jumps, shaking out flakes of moonlight.
> A single wave starts lightly and easily shoreward,
> Wrinkling between reeds in shallower water,
> Lifting a few twigs and floating leaves,
> Then washing up over small stones.
> The shine on the face of the lake
> Tilts, backward and forward.
> The water recedes slowly,
> Gently rocking.
> Who untied that tree? I remember now.
> We met in a nest. Before I lived.
> The dark hair sighed.
> We never enter
> Alone.

An awakening to sex and to nature are here seen to synchronize.
Indeed the chief theme of Roethke's poetry is that of awakening;
the awakening of the senses and with them of a little emotion,
even of some vision of life's significance. The temptation of such
a lyrical talent is to neglect form. The lines just quoted are, like

José Hierro's, held together chiefly by their rhythm, but also by an occasional alliteration. A rough pattern of five-line and three-line stanzas in alternation was, however, insufficient to give unity to Roethke's somewhat untidy early sequences. His remedy was to borrow from 'a man named Yeats' certain cadences and imagery. Roethke's dance poems addressed to the Elizabethan poet of the dance, Sir John Davies, echo Yeats in many details. Their more regular lines, and their pattern of rhymes and half-rhymes lend a weight to their statement that was absent from Roethke's earlier and seemingly more spontaneous writing. Reason is no longer dismissed in favour of bird-song, and even when the influence of Yeats is thrown off the discipline remains.

In the last poem of a later sequence dedicated to the memory of his Irish master, Roethke shows himself to be reaching out even further towards a deeper understanding of the Universe than can be derived solely from sensual experience:

> I've the lark's word for it, who sings alone:
> What's seen recedes; Forever's what we know!—
> Eternity defined, and strewn with straw,
> The fury of the slug beneath the stone.
> The vision moves, and yet remains the same.
> In heaven's praise, I dread the thing I am.
>
> The edges of the summit still appal
> When we brood on the dead or the beloved;
> Nor can imagination do it all
> In this last place of light: he dares to live
> Who stops being a bird, yet beats his wings
> Against the immense immeasurable emptiness of things.

Roethke ends on a paradox. Under Yeats's guidance he has advanced from a dualism by which nature was invoked to combat fear, to a vision of unity in which fear is accepted, and eternity is seen to be man's natural condition. The poetry is one less of philosophical statement, however, than of a personal, groping discovery. In this it is a little like Traherne's. But at the same time it also raises an off-beat echo, in its last line, of a stanza ending from Shelley's 'Ode to a Skylark'. Of the four poets I have chosen to exemplify the new tendencies in the mid-century's poetry, Roethke is perhaps the least independent of influences. But he is one with the other three in inventing no myths, and making no attempt to argue beyond his personal insights. In this he *is* independent of his models. With Hierro, Larkin and Thomas, he is content to be a minor poet, and to speak only for himself.

On the evidence of these four poets alone, who are certainly some of the most interesting among the younger men, it would seem that a great renunciation is being made. The role of prophet, legislator and mythmaker is in process of being abandoned. Poetry no longer aims at making major pronouncements about the nature or fate of the world, but is becoming content again to speak of private experience. The attraction of the *frisson nouveau* is diminishing; only honest statement now seems valid.

This incipient change marks a return to an earlier convention and to an earlier conception of the poet's place in society. Blake and Wordsworth, to choose two great examples, were both poets whose primary material was that of the private life. Both were, however, capable of moments of making political state-ments. A fairer comparison, therefore, is with poets of more restricted vision, with Emily Dickinson or William Barnes, who ventured on no generalizations, and were content to remain within the confines of their own limited but poignant experience.

The cause of this retreat from prophecy to personal statement would seem to lie in the condition of the world. It is possible for poets in retarded Spain to cry for freedom, for Paz to elaborate a new myth of Mexico, or for Neruda at a great distance from European realities to advocate an ideal Communism. But it has been impossible since the outbreak of the second World War, and certainly from the time of Hiroshima, for any poet living near the centre of the crisis to make secular pronouncements concern-ing the world and its fate, or concerning man's place in the Universe. Events have dwarfed all possible comment. Menaced with destruction by weapons for whose power he can find no words, and ruled by governments patently unable to control the situations that they appear to have evoked, the poet cannot view himself as important in any but his own close surroundings. All that he can hope to rescue from an ever-imminent disaster will be a moment of love or insight or a clear perception of truth, which, having once been, can never be destroyed. Unable to place any such experience in a broader context, he will yet record it and return to it, communicating it in the simplest form he can find, since all complication seems pretentious at such a moment in the world's history.

This new simplicity, under the menace of a major human disaster, offers a great hope for poetry once the menace has passed. For with the abandonment of his claim to prophetic insight and a place outside or above society, and with a return to simplicity of form and language, the poet may gain his public again, and the very rare insights which are his may once more be communicated to the great majority of men and women whose essential preoccupations with love, nature, death and survival, with the earth, the stars and the timeless absolute, in no way differ from his own.

BIBLIOGRAPHY AND ACKNOWLEDGEMENTS

In offering a selected bibliography for those who wish to read some of the poets treated in this book, I have taken care to list the most readily available editions, few of which, I hope, will prove to be temporarily out of print when asked for. Most of the books listed should be obtainable through the public library service. I begin with a few anthologies of wide coverage, some of which contain poems in translation, or in both languages side by side. But in the second section will be found the original editions, among which I have starred those which, on the whole, contain the best poems. Permission to quote is usually to acknowledged English publishers only, but I should like to extend my thanks also to publishers abroad whose editions I have used just as freely, without notifying them.

Penguin Book of French Verse 4: *The Twentieth Century*, introduced and edited by Anthony Hartley, which contains selections from all the French poets mentioned and some others, in the original with prose translations.

Mid-Century French Poets, selections, translations and critical notices by Wallace Fowlie (Grove Press, New York) contains poems by Breton, Eluard, Supervielle and others.

An Anthology of Modern French Poetry by C. A. Hackett (Blackwells), a selection from many poets since Baudelaire, with copious notes but without translations.

Penguin Book of Spanish Verse, introduced and edited by J. M. Cohen, contains in its final section a few poems by each of the poets mentioned.

Contemporary Spanish Poetry (Johns Hopkins Press) contains selections from ten poets of Lorca's generation, with translations by Eleanor Turnbull.

Poesía Española, selección de Gerardo Diego (Editorial Signo, Madrid), famous anthology of the Lorca generation.

Laurel (Editorial Seneca, Mexico), an anthology compiled by

254

Octavio Paz and three other poets which gives a splendid panorama of poetry in Spanish, both Peninsular and American, between 1910 and 1940.

Antologia de la nueva poesía española, by José Luis Cano (Gredos) represents all the best poets since the civil war.

Penguin Book of Italian Verse, introduced and edited by George Kay, gives very adequate selections from the four poets dealt with.

Antologia della poesa italiana, 1909-1949, by G. Spagnoletti 3a edizione aumentata, 1954 (Ugo Guanda, Parma), gives full representation to the poets dealt with and many others.

Penguin Book of German Verse, introduced and edited by Leonard Forster, contains poems from all the German poets noticed.

Menschheitsdämmerung, herausgegeben von Kurt Pinthus (Rowohlt, Berlin), an expressionist anthology of 1920, which adequately represents that group.

A Book of Russian Verse and *A Second Book of Russian Verse,* translated by various hands and edited by C. M. Bowra (Macmillan). These two books give fair representation to the modern poets, and I am grateful to Sir Maurice Bowra and the publishers for permission to quote two extracts from poems by Blok in his translation.

Poems from the Russian, by Frances Cornford and E. Polianowsky Salaman (Faber and Faber), contains a few pieces by Blok, one of which Mrs. Cornford has kindly allowed me to quote.

II

RAFAEL ALBERTI

Selected poems, translated by Lloyd Mallan (New Directions, New York).

*Antologia which gives a very fair selection from the poet's early books.

Retornos de lo vivo lejano

Ora Maritima

All published by Losada, Buenos Aires. The first two are unobtainable in Spain.

VICENTE ALEIXANDRE

*Mis mejores poemas, a very adequate selection published by Gredos, Madrid.

GUILLAUME APOLLINAIRE

*Oeuvres poétiques, a definitive edition published by Gallimard in the 'Bibliothèque de la Pléiade'.
A cheap selection is included in the 'Poètes d'aujourd'hui' series (Seghers).

W. H. AUDEN

*Collected Shorter Poems
Nones
The Shield of Achilles
All published by Faber and Faber Ltd. to whom acknowledgements are due. A few important poems have been altered since the original publication, in particular 'September 1, 1939' which appears in the form quoted in Another Time

GOTTFRIED BENN

*Gesammelte Gedichte, Limes Verlag, Wiesbaden

ALEXANDER BLOK

Some translations from Blok appear in the two Books of Russian Verse and in Frances Cornford's anthology already listed. A good and inexpensive one-volume edition of the poetry exists in the series 'Sovietskiy Pisatel'.

DINO CAMPANA

*Canti Orfici ed altri Scritti (Vallecchi, Florence).

T. S. ELIOT

*Collected poems 1909-1935
*Four Quartets
Both published by Faber and Faber, to whom acknowledgements for permission to quote are due.

PAUL ELUARD

Choix de Poèmes 1951 (Gallimard)

STEFAN GEORGE

Poems, translated by C. N. Valhope and E. Morwitz (Panther Books), a selection which also prints the original German. Editions of *Das Jahr der Seele, Der Teppich des Lebens, Der Siebente Ring, Der Stern des Bundes* and *Das Neue Reich* are published by Helmut Küpper, Düsseldorf.

ROBERT GRAVES

Collected Poems 1959 published by Cassell & Co. Ltd. to whom acknowledgements are due, also to the author, contains all those poems which in the poet's opinion pass muster. Many fine pieces that have been discarded must be sought in Mr. Graves's earlier collections, in particular in the Collected Poems 1926 (Heinemann).

JORGE GUILLEN

Cántico (Editorial sudamericana, Buenos Aires) contains all the poet's work up to 1950.

Maremágnum, by the same publisher, includes poems more political in tone.

A small and cheap selection entitled *Viviendo y otros poemas* appears in the 'Biblioteca breve' (Seix Barral, Barcelona).

THOMAS HARDY

Collected Poems, published by Macmillan & Co. Ltd. to whom acknowledgements are due, and to the trustees of the Hardy estate.

GEORGE HEYM

Gesammelte Gedichte (Verlag der Arche, Zurich)

JOSE HIERRO

Antología poetica (Cantalapiedra) contains a good selection from his early work.

Cuanto sé de mí (Agora, Madrid)

The poem 'Estatuas yacentes' has only been printed privately.

HUGO VON HOFMANNSTHAL

Die Gesammelten Gedichte (Insel Verlag, Wiesbaden)

JUAN RAMON JIMENEZ

Tercera antología poética (Editorial Biblioteca nueva, Madrid) contains a large selection from the poet's many books published and unpublished, chosen by his friend Eugenio Florit. A smaller selection, *Pájinas escojidas* (Verso), published by Gredos, Madrid, forms an adequate introduction.

Fifty Spanish Poems, text and translation by J. B. Trend (Dolphin)

PHILIP LARKIN

The Less Deceived (Marvell Press, Hull), 'An Arundel Tomb' is printed in *New Poems 1957*, a P.E.N. anthology, and is quoted by the author's permission.

FEDERIGO GARCIA LORCA

Obras completas (Aguilar, Madrid), in one inconvenient volume contains the best text. Losada of Buenos Aires publish their complete edition in 8 volumes, also cheap editions in the 'Biblioteca contemporánea' of the separate volumes of poetry.

Poems from Lorca by Stephen Spender and J. L. Gili (Hogarth Press) has long been out of print. A selection with translations by J. L. Gili is announced by Penguin Books.

Poet in New York, the original with translations by Ben Belitt (Thames & Hudson).

ANTONIO MACHADO

Poesías completas, 'Biblioteca contemporánea' (Losada, Buenos Aires).

VLADIMIR MAYAKOVSKY

Mayakovsky and his Poetry, edited by Herbert Marshall (Current Book House, Bombay), contains good translations by the editor and others, to whom permission to quote is gratefully acknowledged. A complete edition in many volumes is at present in process of publication. There is a cheap selection published by Moskovskiy Rabochiy.

RICARDO MOLINARI

Mundos de la madrugada (Losada, Buenos Aires), a large selection from the poet's early work.

EUGENIO MONTALE

Ossi de Seppia
La Casa dei Doganeiri
Le Occasioni
all published by Mondadori, Milan.
La Bufera e altro (Neri Pozza, Venice)

EDWIN MUIR

Collected Poems
One Foot In Eden both published by Faber and Faber Ltd. to whom acknowledgements are due.

PABLO NERUDA

Obras Completas (Losada, Buenos Aires), a large and expensive volume. His principal work 'Canto general' makes up two volumes of the 'Biblioteca contemporánea'.
For political reasons, his books cannot be obtained in Spain.
Let the Rail Splitter Awake, translations of a handful of poems by A. L. Lloyd and others (Collet's Holdings, London).

BLAS DE OTERO

Ancia (A. P. Editor, Barcelona), two early volumes with additional poems fused into one.
Con la inmensa mayoria, a fusion of two later volumes, the first of which originally appeared in Spain, but both of which are now forbidden there. (Losada, Buenos Aires).

WILFRED OWEN

Poems, published by Chatto and Windus, to whom acknowledgements are due.

BORIS PASTERNAK

Prose and Poems, published by Ernest Benn Ltd., contains some fifty poems in translation. Acknowledgements are due to them

for permission to quote from their versions, made by myself and
originally published by Lindsay Drummond. Other versions are
included in the second of Sir Maurice Bowra's anthologies. The
last collected edition in Russian dates from 1936. Since then one
small volume only has been published, *Na rannikh poezdakh*
(On early trains), which was republished with additions as *Zemnoy
Prostor* (The expanse of earth). In addition the poems in the final
section of 'Doctor Zhivago' have been printed in English at the
end of that novel.

OCTAVIO PAZ

A la orilla del mundo, collection of early poems (Poesía
hispanoamericana, Mexico).
Libertad bajo palabra (Tezontle, Mexico)
La estación violenta (Fondo de cultura economica, Mexico)

EZRA POUND

Personae: Collected shorter poems
The Cantos
Both published by Faber and Faber Ltd. to whom acknowledge-
ments are due.

SALVATORE QUASIMODO

Ed è subito sera contains most of his early poetry.
Giorno dopo giorno
La vita non è sogno (all published by Mondadori, Milan).

RAINER MARIA RILKE

The Duineser Elegien and *Die Sonette an Orpheus* are both published in bilingual editions by The Hogarth Press, the translations being by J. B. Leishman, in the former case in collabora-
tion with Stephen Spender. Other volumes of translations by
Leishman are published by the same house without the German
originals. The excellent translations of Ruth Speirs have, owing
to difficulties of copyrights, never appeared in book form. The
complete poetry of Rilke is published in four volumes by Insel
Verlag, Wiesbaden, who also publish various selections.

THEODORE ROETHKE

Words for the Wind, published by Secker and Warburg, to whom acknowledgements are due.

EDITH SITWELL

The Canticle of the Rose, published by Macmillan and Co., to whom acknowledgements are due. This includes a selection from the poetry written between 1920 and 1947.
Gardeners and Astronomers (Macmillan), a collection of later poems.

WALLACE STEVENS

Collected Poems, published by Faber and Faber, to whom acknowledgements are due.
Selected Poems issued by the same publisher perhaps offers a sufficient introduction to Stevens's work.

AUGUST STRAMM

A number of his poems appear in the anthology *Menschheits-dämmerung* and in *The Penguin Book of German Verse*. I know of no collected edition.

JULES SUPERVIELIE

Choix de Poèmes (Gallimard)

DYLAN THOMAS

Collected Poems, published by J. M. Dent and Sons Ltd., to whom acknowledgements are due.

R. S. THOMAS

Song at the Year's Turning
Poetry for Supper both published by Rupert Hart Davis Ltd., to whom acknowledgements are due.

GEORG TRAKL

Die Dichtungen (Otto Müller, Salzburg)

MIGUEL DE UNAMUNO
*Antología Poetica

*El Cristo de Velázquez, both in the cheap 'Austral' Edition (Espasa-Calpe, Buenos Aires).

GIUSEPPE UNGARETTI
*L'allegria

*Il dolore

*Sentimento del Tempo

These three volumes published by Mondadori contain almost the complete poetry written between 1916 and 1946.

PAUL VALERY
*Poésies (Gallimard)

CESAR VALLEJO
*Poesías completas (Losada, Buenos Aires)

W. B. YEATS
*Collected Poems of W. B. Yeats, published by Macmillan and Co. Ltd., to whom acknowledgements are due and to Mrs. Yeats.